The Problem Plays of Shakespeare Double Vision in Character and Action

The Problem Plays of Shakespeare Double Vision in Character and Action

DR. SEEMA RAIZADA

1994
Sharada Publishing House
DELHI-110052

First Published 1994

ISBN : 81-85616-18-3

Published by
B.L. Bansal
for SHARADA PUBLISHING HOUSE
(Publishers on India's Past and Present)
E-239, Shastri Nagar, Delhi-110052
Phone : 7516539

Laser Typesetting by
Akriti Computers
B-5/98, Paschim Vihar, New Delhi - 110063
Phone : 5587403, 5584110

Printed at
Garg Offset Work
B 76, Naraina Industrial Area, Delhi

Contents

Preface

Shakespeare's plays have always been not only a rich source of entertainment and pleasure but also a wide field for the student and the critic to explore further in whatever part they wish. Apparently, all parts of the field bear the marks of the toil of critics and, upto a certain point, the whole of Shakespeare has been explained and significances brought out. Different schools of Shakespeare criticism have laboured according to their lights to interpret all his plays. But it is as good as a lark can soar up to the sun. It is taking wing and the upward flight that invariably results in a new perspective. It is also true that one's insights may reveal an altogether new way of discerning what lies yet beyond and forge an instrument to make it intelligible.

In other words, it is the analytical method adopted by a critic which would determine his net gains, particularly in tackling the hitherto recognized "problems" in Shakespeare's plays. The most interesting and complex problems which defy the ingenuity of critics lie in the so called problem plays which originally covered the three 'dark' comedies and *Hamlet* according to the classification by F.S. Boas who first applied the epithet to describe these plays. W.W.Lawrence limited them to three and dropped *Hamlet* but Tillyard restored the classification of Boas. Ernest Schanzer included *Julius Caesar* and *Antony and Cleopatra* dropping *Hamlet, Troilus and Cressida* and *All's Well*.

It appeared relevant to include all the plays which for some cogent reason, were labelled as problem plays. The three recognized members of the group, known as dark comedies exhibit inconsistencies and paradoxes which have not yet been satisfactorily solved. *Hamlet* has long defied all attempts of critics to resolve its problems. *Julius Caesar* and *Antony and Cleopatra*, though generally classed as tragedies, have greater problematic features than *Othello, King Lear* and *Macbeth* which do not evince any insoluble problems or contradictions. Excepting the three tragedies just mentioned, all the plays written during the period 1599 to 1607, incorporate certain traits which justifiy their being put together. There is a general air of questioning and scepticism, disillusionment and disgust at the growth of sin and evil. The plays incorporate vices pitched against virtues, faith against doubt, negation against affirmation often without any conclusive outcome. An excess of intellectual activity seems to inhibit spontaneous development. Values are confounded, wrong choices are made, conflicts are aggravated without ending in tragedy. There are contradictions, ambiguities and ambivalences in character and action, so that the same character or action appears to be good or evil according as we view it from different angles. Yet very often, there is an effect of great immediacy and intensity and a drift to resolution. The final play which stands at the end of this period-*Antony and Cleopatra* -is a play of supreme resolution.

A more considered view would reveal that most of these impressions of an inner disorder, contradiction and ambivalences are superficial and the plays belong to a genre which presents richness and complexity as an end in itself and in this process poses problems which, in the very manner or presentation, are the stuff of the plays. While both the creative imagination and the intellect were functioning at the pitch of their power, a proper fusion was effected only in the great tragedies which were written during the same period, while *Hamlet* in spite of its being one of them, remains in a class apart due to its lack of synthesis. Of these plays, it is only *Antony and Cleopatra* which synthesizes the contrary elements but remains problematic due to the very excess of these elements in character and action which has gone to its making.

Thus the duality in characters and the contraries like appearance and reality, the secular and the spiritual, moral seriousness and low life, justice and mercy, providence and will, revenge and forgiveness, folk-lore and realism, virtue and sin and even life and death-all characteristically emerge as problems as we read these plays and critics have treated them as the distinguishing features of these plays and let them stand as they are without pushing the inquiry further as to why should each opposite appear in a heightened form.

It is the contention of this book that the duality of the problem plays and the accentuation of the contrary elements in character and action are due to the working of Shakespeare's double vision which was most active during the period these plays were written. The negative and the positive visions projected the contrary elements establishing powerful polarities which co-exist in situations and characters and are manifested in their make up and their actions. Sometimes, the dividing lines fade and almost disappear creating insoluble complexities and dilemmas. I have tried to illustrate this with referernce to each play under consideration.

I have also traced the origin of the problem play to *Antigone* of Sophocles, particularly of the type of problem play Shakespeare has developed. I have not presumed any direct acquaintance. But there is a strong conjecture that Shakespeare was influenced by Euripides in translation and I have referred to Anne Barton's conclusions. The weighing of scales on both sides of the problem which we find in Shakespeare's problem plays has a close resemblance with *Antigone* while the duality, scepticism, disillusionment and 'debunking' have a strong resemblance with Euripide's *Ion, Helen* and *Orestes.* In my opinion, the understanding and interpretation of Shakespeare's problem plays will be far greater if we place them side by side with those of Sophocles and Euripides. The typical qualities of Shakespeare's problem plays—transmutation and transvaluation—have emerged as a result of the inquiry and have been discussed and illustrated.

So far as I am aware, the problem plays of Shakespeare have never been tackled from these points of view and if this study contributes to the enhancement of critical awareness in this direction, the purpose of this book will have been served.

I cannot adequately thank my husband Dr. Ajit Raizada for his constant encouragement and inspiration to complete this work. I also thank my father Dr. R.R.Khare for several useful suggestions.

Dr. SEEMA RAIZADA

them equal as they are without considering the motive [illegible] as to why should each of [illegible] appear in [illegible].

It is the contention of [illegible] book that [illegible] problem plays and the [illegible] that the [illegible] characters [illegible] double vision which [illegible] plays were written. The [illegible] and the [illegible] project the contrary elements [illegible] ties which co-exist in situations and characters [illegible] manifested in their make up and their actions. Sometimes [illegible] [illegible] and [illegible] creating [illegible] complexities and dilemmas. I have tried to [illegible] the [illegible] reference to each play [illegible].

I have also traced the [illegible] of the problem [illegible] Antigone of Sophocles, particularly of the type of [illegible] play [illegible] I have no [illegible] direct [illegible] acquaintance. But there is a strong [illegible] that Shakespeare was influenced by [illegible] I have referred to [illegible] of scales on both sides of the problem which [illegible] Shakespeare's problem play has a [illegible] resemblance with Antigone [illegible] [illegible] have a strong [illegible] [illegible] and [illegible]. In my opinion, the [illegible] interpretation of Shakespeare's problem [illegible] [illegible] and [illegible] the [illegible] [illegible] and [illegible].

[illegible] I [illegible] to [illegible] [illegible] [illegible] [illegible] [illegible] to [illegible] [illegible] this [illegible].

I [illegible] thank [illegible] for [illegible] and [illegible] to complete this work [illegible] suggestions.

[illegible]

CHAPTER I

Introduction

The problem play is not a new dramatic form. Its origin goes back to the origin of drama. The essence of drama consists in conflict and the eternal opposition of good and evil is actually a representation of this essence. Since its beginnings in Greek drama when actors (to a maximum of three) were added to the chorus, one of them invariably represented evil and the protagonist who often stood for good, was confronted with the problem of battling with it. The anthropomorphic gods also took an active part in guiding the action and as in Aeschylus' *Oresteia* or Sophocles' *Oedipus Tyrannus*, the evil was manifested as a curse on the house which descended as a result of some 'impious deed'. "Some past impiety, some grey old crime/Breeds the young curse, that wantons in our ill."[1]

The problem of the *Oresteia* was to end the curse and from the larger viewpoint of the dramatist it was to be done by evolving a solution for the old practice of exacting 'blood for blood' which was a relic of the Cthonic gods. This was resolved by Aeschylus by presenting the new method of solving the problem of blood-feuds through justice which was the way of the new Olympian gods. The evil committed by Atreus is seen at work in *The Agamemnon* resulting in the murder of Agamemnon, a further chain of which is seen in the *Choephoroe* in the murder of Clytemnestra and Aegisthus, and *the Eumenides* presents the solution in the conversion of the Furies and the acquittal of Orestes through justice. However unsatisfactory in the upshot, the trilogy aimed at solving the problem of evil. In *Prometheus Bound* the evil is committed by Zeus in punishing Prometheus for his service to humanity but Prometheus is also guilty of hybris. The problem is tackled in the revelation of the future which would eventually bring his release.

In the Theban plays of Sophocles, the problem of evil which began with the curse on Laius shows the ruin of Oedipus in *Oedipus Tyrannus* but is seen to reach a resolution when Oedipus, purged of his sin, meets his end in a state very much like regeneration in *Oedipus at Colonus*. But the play which really lays the clear pattern of the problem play is *Antigone* which can be considered an archetypal play in the modern sense. It presents two sides of a question, develops the conflict and suggests a resolution and yet does not explicitly state it. The case is presented as a moral dilemma which has continued through the ages—the problem of choice between duty and love or between two concepts of duty.

When Antigone is faced with the choice between obeying the order of the state and burying Polyneices, she decides to bury her brother because she loves him but more because she considers it her spiritual duty to bury him. The secular duty to obey the order of the king is considered by her to claim the second place. On the other hand, Sophocles gives an equally fair chance to the sense of duty to the state from the standpoint of Creon who holds the view, "There is no more deadly peril than disobedience".[2] When Haemon puts the viewpoint of Antigone against that of his father, the two views in themselves are so weighty that the chorus says: "There is something to be said, my lord, for his point of view, And for yours as well; there is much to be said on both sides".[3]

Similarly, the opposition of the secular and the spiritual can be seen in *Antony and Cleopatra* and in the twentieth century in 'problem plays' like *Strife* in the opposition of Anthony and Roberts or in 'poetic plays' like *The Cocktail Party* in the difference between the way of life represented by Edward and Lavinia and that by Celia and their respective choices.

In the plays of Euripides the sceptical, questioning spirit is carried further and in plays like *Ion, Helen, The Trojan Women, Medea* and *Bacchae*, he has posed baffling moral problems. It is in Euripides that the quality of the iconoclast which is associated with the problem playwright is first found. He exposed the shallowness of established beliefs and values and paves the way for more rational thought. Another quality of realism which belongs to a problem play also appears for the first time in Euripides. All these make for the drama of disillusionment which we find in this category of plays from Shakespeare to Shaw. *Ion* exposes the hollowness of the belief that the gods are infallible, that they do not tell lies or trick and cheat like human beings. Ion realizes that Apollo's oracles are lies at least in his case and the gods 'put pleasure first and wisdom after' - a far cry from Aeschylus who says, 'Tis Zeus alone who shows the perfect way/Of knowledge.'[4]

Helen shows how infinite suffering and devastation were wrought for a phantom and not as the Greeks thought for honour. As the messenger puts it, "What? All our sweat and blood-spent for a ghost?"[5]

The whole basis which men adopt for similar wars is demolished at a stroke. It is not far different from Thersites' ridicule of the Trojan war, or Falstaff's of the Battle at Shrewsbury or Bluntshli's of the Serbian war.

The Trojan Women presents a similar spectacle of futility superadded with infinite cruelty and horror, and at the same time makes us peer into the chasm between secular and spiritual values represented by the blood-thirsty Greeks and the passive, infinitely suffering Trojan women like Hecuba and Andromache.

Even *Medea* can be considered a problem play which poses the crucial question of the disaster which follows if the values of the heart are ignored along with the question of freedom which women should have as much as men. A distant relationship with *The Doll's House* can be discerned here.

The Bacchae is yet another enigmatic play presenting the case for acknowledging the power of a god who is ruthless and revengeful. The implicit question is whether such a god deserves worship, while apparently, all the statements seem to argue for such a worship. The ironic contradiction at the heart of the tragedy points to the extreme subtlety with which the problem of belief is dealt.

Thus the problem play as a dramatic form has a lineage as old as Greek drama and the subject matter it presents is realistic and embodies experience which has an intensity and immediacy compelling the attention of the audience on some vital question or aspect of the human condition. For example, *Antigone* of Sophocles communicates the experience of sacrifice for one's spiritual duty and of love as few plays can. The play enlarges one's awareness of the power of such love. It would not so profoundly impress us but for the formidable power pitched on the other side just as the love of Antony and Cleopatra impresses powerfully due to the opposition of an equally mighty opponent on the secular plane, in Caesar.

It is true to say that the problem play in its very inception is a dynamic form because its object is invariably to lead to a heightened awareness of some wrong, some incongruity or of a 'dire dilemma' out of which a way must be found in order to survive or to set right some 'spite'. It is also a heightened awareness of the inner worth of some ideal with a vividness lent by contrast, for example, of the spiritual quality of the Trojans seen beside the secular policy of the Greeks in *Troilus and Cressida*. The virtue of Isabella stands out by contrast with the bestial hypocrisy of Angelo and by a kind of transvaluation, the same appears merely priggish against the naive innocence and love of life of Claudio. This three-dimensional picture of life could be given only by Shakespeare in his problem plays.

Another feature of the problem play closely associated with its realism, is the down-to-earth concreteness of the presentation of the social environment which is invariably connected with the situation and the characters. We often get a better picture of the society of the time in the problem plays than in the tragedies which are more imaginative. The problem play is also serious in tone and may often have tragic elements which arise from the evil which is at the root of the problem. Not being strictly a tragedy, and yet having a serious message to convey, the play has an element of humour and comedy to offset the seriousness (and sometimes the sordidness of its realistic presentation) and to make the criticism palatable to the audience. That is why most problem plays are tragi-comedies. There may be light comedy as in Shaw, where the serious element is much subdued. *Arms and the Man* and *The Apple Cart* are instances to the point. But there may be a deepening of both tragedy and comedy as in *Measure for Measure* and the other two of Shakespeare's problem plays. Even *Antigone* has a comic character in the sentinel to offset the seriousness whereas there is none in *Oedipus Tyrannus*. It shows that the design of that play is more in the direction of the problem play. *Ion* and *Helen* have a lightness of tone and the former has some comic touch in the pranks of the old slave when he tries to poison Ion. *Helen* has a positively farcical element in the reporting of the messenger about the disappearance of the phantom of Helen from the cave and later on in the reporting of the flight of Helen and Menelaus to Theoclymenus.

The critical spirit which is at the heart of the problem play does not allow it to leave the secular and temporal bounds and that is why most plays dealing with problems do not attain the quality of a pure tragedy except those which preoccupy themselves with normal or religious problems like *Antigone* and *Hamlet*. There is a very thin dividing line between the moral and spiritual conflict of a tragedy and that of a problem play. When the problems are more rooted in society, more topical and connected with a transient phase of growth and change, their nature becomes more materialistic and the tragic element is restricted and is not of a timeless quality. This is seen in Galsworthy's *Strife* and *Justice*. It may become almost non-existent as in most plays of Shaw except *Saint Joan* where it is of a timeless quality and enhances the play to the status of a tragedy. On the whole, the critical spirit detracts from the tragic quality as seen in Hamlet but no problem play can exist without it. That is why it also exists as drama of ideas where two opposite ideas are elaborated and characters standing for each are pitched against each other as in *The Apple Cart*. Even *Antigone* reveals the conflict of ideas in this manner.

In the battle of ideas, established ideals are flouted and stripped to reveal their hollowness and the stupidity of those who believe in them. *Arms and the Man* and *Troilus and Cressida* are replete with such iconoclasm.

Thus it can be seen how variously the problem play contributes to a growth of understanding of the true nature of things revealing the truth to the core and in a Socratic manner, letting the audience see for themselves what is wrong rather than baldly stating it as a tractarian would do. So it can also be called an artistic exploration of truth. The dramatist's apprehension of such truths about the human condition is so brought out as to compel our attention to the question as to what is wrong with life and society in general. It may lead to reform in its twentieth century manner or just to serious thought in its Jacobian way but it will succeed and be entitled to be called a problem play in the true sense as long as it pursues its task artistically. To accomplish this, it explicates its theme in terms of character and action assimilating the theme so imperceptibly into them so as to appear unobtrusive and to constitute the only possible stuff which could motivate them not only on the material but on the spiritual plane as well. In other words, the material as well as the spiritual veins of the plot must circulate the essence of this theme which incorporates the problem and the problem itself must seem to grow organically from the actions, thought and behaviour of the characters.

The vision of the dramatist shapes the subject-matter into this organic unity. In Sophocles and Euripides, the plays which display two diverging points of view, also reveal that the play (like *Antigone or Ion*) is a single organic whole and the two opposed points of view are integral to the plot. They are identified with a single theme which is the propriety of the burial of Polyneices in the one and the true parentage of Ion and Apollo's plan to bestow him on Xuthus and Creusa as their son in the other. The main issue incorporates the side issue and the unity is not disturbed. When it comes to these side issues, the dramatist's vision is projected in two ways: positively, to present an argument or idea with a sense of affirmation and to imply a sense of moral good behind it and negatively, with the implication that either evil is directly behind it or may ensue if the view is accepted. This operation of a double vision is not so marked in Sophocles as in Euripides who is more critical and skeptical and whose intention was actually to highlight the paradox of belief in the Olympian Gods whereas that of Sophocles was only to underline a moral dilemma. The double vision is seen to operate more perceptibly in the problem plays of Shakespeare where two opposing points of view are clearly represented without in any way indicating the opinion of the dramatist.

As we shall see the two visions so project themselves with reference to the same character or situation as to create the effect of moral ambivalence which is a peculiar mark of the Shakespearean problem play. This quality is lost in the problem plays of modern dramatists like Shaw and Galsworthy in which it is quite clear where the dramatist's preference lies. Accordingly, with a greater emphasis on this preference, the characters lose their originality and are reduced to mere mouthpieces of the dramatist and the problem play becomes only a play of argument. This is how the true artistic quality which was provided by a subtly balanced projection of the double vision in Shakespeare was lost in the plays of Shaw and Galsworthy. Characterisation became less complex and the action was also reduced to a minimum to make room for verbal exchanges where the dominating tone was that of a mouthpiece of the dramatist.

Thus we see three phases in the evolution of the problem play as an art-form. In the first, the type can be seen in its inception in the works of the Greek dramatists: subsequently, the form was developed by Shakespeare to a point of artistic perfection which bore the mark of his own peculiar genius and finally, in the later nineteenth and early twentieth century, when it frankly assumed the form of a weapon of social criticism but lost the artistic depth and fascination it had in Greek dramatists and Shakespeare. We shall now examine in greater detail the peculiar quality of Shakespeare's problem plays which makes them as enigmatic and meaningful as Mona Lisa to readers and critics alike.

Shakespeare has excelled as an artist as much in his problem plays as in his tragedies and comedies. It is partly because they combine his genius for comedy as well as tragedy. The unique stamp of his genius in both kinds of drama is present along with that peculiar quality which makes them co-exist without a strict dividing line or with a feeling that the two are antithetical to each other. Even in his tragedies he blends the comic elements so naturally that they appear true to life and even the neo-classical critics like Dryden and Johnson defended this practice. The idea of regarding them as belated comedies which got mixed up with tragic elements due to Shakespeare's disillusioned state of mind during 1600-1605 has become out-dated. Nor are they considered as plain examples of what is called tragi-comedy as a genre. The last plays are also tragi-comedies but the two groups are poles apart in spirit. What makes the three plays- *Troilus and Cressida, All's Well* and *Measure for Measure* significant works of art is their own unique blend of contrary elements and the Janus-like quality of their creator which makes them provoking and fascinating. In no case can they be called abortive or still-born products of his mind, whatever their inadequacies. The peculiar quality of presenting two sides of a question with equal justice and sympathy makes Shakespeare's problem plays more engaging than those of the moderns. This more than anything else accounts for the conflicting and even contradictory impressions created by the same character or the same situation. There are uncertain and divided responses on the part of the audience and the dramatist's own view of the matter seems to be so elusive that it puts even a rough conjecture on unsure ground. The impression is very much like the changing colour of shot-silk with a slight change in the angle of vision. It "teases us out of thought", to borrow a phrase of Keats.

It is interesting to note that Shakespeare's problem plays were regarded as serious comedies or at most as dark comedies but nothing problematic was seen in them just as nothing peculiar was seen in *Hamlet* as a tragedy. It was the advent of the problem play with the influence of Ibsen at the end of the Nineteenth Century which prompted critics like F.S. Boas to notice the same qualities with some difference in these comedies of Shakespeare. As Allardyce Nicoll puts it: "It was only after 1890 that Ibsen's influence came to be deeply felt, and...it is evident that from 1890 onward a new spirit and a new enthusiasm have the dramatists in their grip".[6]

Of the influence of Ibsen, Nicoll says: "...as we watch the progress of tragedy from Aeschylus to Shakespeare, from Shakespeare to the writers of the present day, we can witness increasing efforts on the part of the playwrights to subordinate action to thought. Ibsen, representative in his own age of this movement, showed to his contemporaries many methods of securing this inwardness".[7]

Of the dramatists like A.W. Pinero and H.A. Jones who

were influenced by Ibsen, Nicoll adds, "All of these are alike in dealing with problems of social life in a manner tragic or approaching the tragic".[8] Commenting that Pinero "deals with the stuff of tragedy, but rarely in a tragic manner", he compares his plays to the 'drame' which he calls, "a serious problem play where the emotions never rise to tragic height. 'Drame' and tragedy can rarely, if ever, be mingled. The emotions of tragedy are those primarily of terror and awe, allied to a feeling of pre-eminent majesty."[9]

The diagnosis of Nicoll, though strictly with reference to Pinero, goes to lay bare the nature of serious drama akin to the problem plays of Shakespeare which were, of course, not intended to be tragedies but where the tragic element of the kind found in the 'drame' is conspicuous. The difference is that the serious effects of the twentieth century problem dramatists fell short of the drame, while Shakespeare remained up to it and did not rise to tragic height because he so designed them. The comedy which is fused with it is down-to-the earth type, very concrete and realistic, not shunning the limits of conventional morality, yet quite capable of higher spiritual potentialities. Thus fused out of these apparently antithetical elements, these comedies were bound to appear problematic and taking his cue from such contemporary fusion, Boas categorized them in a group as Shakespeare's problem plays. A view of critical opinion from 1896, the year of publication of Boas' book, onward may be illuminating in these changing evaluations of Shakespeare's problem plays and in the grouping under this category.

Boas was keen enough to fix his attention to the issues raised in each of the three plays and found that they "preclude a completely satisfactory outcome".[10] To these he added *Hamlet* as well. The moral issues in *All's Well* and *Measure for Measure* are left unresolved. The psychological issue involved in Hamlet baffles our attention to the very end. In *Troilus and Cressida* the relation between the war-plot and the love story is disjoined-the two plots stand apart. He perceived a general atmosphere of obscurity in all these plays and compared this to "a valley swathed in folds of mist".[11] Thus he concluded that these plays are different from the other plays of Shakespeare and styled them as problem plays in the sense that without presenting clear-cut problems, each of them was a problem to the reader or to the audience.

The next significant comment on these plays was that of W.W. Lawrence in 'The Problem Comedies of Shakespeare' (1931). Lawrence found these plays "too serious and analytic" to be called plain comedies. Their seriousness and critical temper needed a separate category. He dropped *Hamlet* and thought that the three plays stood together in that in each "a perplexing and distressing complication in human life is presented in a spirit of high seriousness".[12] According to him, in each of them the theme is handled so as "to probe the complicated, interrelations of characters and action, in a situation admitting of different ethical interpretations".[13] The problem, as he saw it, was an ethical one—that of conduct. Since our ethical values have in some respects become more rigid compared to those in the Elizabethan age, what seems morally perplexing or ambiguous in these plays to our age, would not have seemed so to an Elizabethan audience.

E.M.W. Tillyard again changed the perspective with his "Problem Plays of Shakespeare" in 1951. He found that "We can infer from the plays themselves that he was especially interested in certain matters".[14] Tillyard elaborates the point specifying this preoccupation:

"First Shakespeare is concerned throughout with either religious dogma or abstract speculation or both. It may be retorted that so he was also when he wrote his later tragedies. Yet there is a difference in that dogma and speculation are less completely absorbed into the general substance of the problem plays; they are felt rather more for their own than for the drama's sake, as if, in this form at least, they were new and urgent in Shakespeare's mind, demanding at this point statement and articulation rather than solution and absorption into other material".[15]

Another point Tillyard notices in these plays is that Shakespeare's interest in human nature manifests itself differently here than elsewhere: "he was more content than at other times merely to record his observation without subordinating it to a great overriding theme".[16] In other words, we can say that Shakespeare's intellectual and critical faculty is more active than his imaginative faculty of fusing the matter into an organic whole. Hence there is something 'schizophrenic' about the plot of *All's Well* and *Measure for Measure*. On the other hand *Hamlet* and *Troilus and Cressida* display interesting problems which are complex and seem to be there for their own sake but are nevertheless connected with the main theme. For Tillyard, the two other plays are genuinely problematic.

L.C. Knights (1959) bringing out the cleavage in moral evaluations in *Antony and Cleopatra* implies this to be the play's problem:

"In *Macbeth* we are never in any doubt of our moral bearings. *Antony and Cleopatra* on the other hand, embodies different and apparently irreconcilable evaluations of the central experience".[17]

Another point he makes is the ambivalent impact of the energy which lends intensity to the play. "Shakespeare...evokes the passion of the lovers with the greatest possible intensity...but...he makes it impossible for us not to question the nature and conditions of that very energy that the lovers release in each other".[18]

The moral standpoint of the dramatist is thus in doubt and the total impact of the play leaves the reader or spectator unsure of his own moral bearings.

Perhaps in agreement with L.C. Knights, Ernest Schanzer, leaving out *Hamlet* and including *Antony and Cleopatra* and *Julius Caesar*, shifts the focus of the problem play to its moral centre and to the moral standpoint of the audience or the reader. But he does not think that the uncertainty regarding our moral bearings is enough to define the nature of a problem play.

"In watching a problem play our predominant state of mind during atleast part of the action is one of doubt of our moral bearings...What seems needed (in a problem play) is a concern with a central moral problem which will inevitably take the form of an act of choice confronting the protagonist and in relation to which we are in doubt of our moral bearings. The moral issue must not only be central but must appear problematic to the audience rather than to any of the characters".[19]

Ernest Schanzer then attempts a clear definition of a Shakespearean problem play:

It is "a play in which we find a concern with a moral problem which is central to it, presented in such a manner that we are unsure of our moral bearings, so that uncertain and divided responses to it in the minds of the audience are possible and even probable".[20]

The responses are so unstable that as Schanzer says, "What to one side of our minds appears as their (of characters) main flaws, to another side appears as their greatest virtues." To illustrate it he gives the example of the toy called a 'perspective' which presents two quite different pictures according to our angle of vision. Hence a two-fold or double vision is invoked in the spectator or the reader.

This brief survey of the changes in view points from Boas to Schanzer shows how indefinable the nature of the problem plays has been and when a definition nearest to its likely sense is evolved, there is a possibility of quite another viewpoint being evolved and presented with equal plausibility. Even the plays which belong to this category are not finally identified—while the three so-called dark comedies are invariably included. *Hamlet* is added to the group by some and dropped by others, while *Antony and Cleopatra* and *Julius Caesar* are added. It shows that the borderline of meaning as well as identity is shifting. There is undoubtedly some elusive quality in these plays which perhaps eludes us when we dissect them too critically and defies isolation. it may be worthwhile to attempt to explore the secret which has made the plays of such evanescent and changeful identity.

The secret lies in the double vision of the dramatist and the way it is projected in each play. It is at the root of the cleavage in impressions and it operates right from the point the dramatist envisions the character or situation in a certain way and communicates through words and images and other accessories of expression to the audience. The impact on the audience is also to evoke a double vision on their part towards that character and situation. Hence if the communication be perfect, the double vision of the dramatist transmits his two-fold imaginative apprehension in as much of its original form as possible. Then the darkness and light would darken or illuminate the character or situation and with a sudden shift of viewpoint, darkness may change to light and *vice versa*. This is the unusual beauty and charm which such ambivalence brings. It is responsible for the uncertain and divided responses on the part of the audience. It also knocks the bottom out of our moral bearings.

In this inquiry it will be our attempt to bring out how far this happens in our reading or witnessing of each of these problem plays and why should it be so. Is it a merit or defect of these plays? We shall also fix the number of plays falling in this category. Above all, each play will be discussed with reference to its characters and situations and it will be explored how far the double vision of the dramatist as projected on them, works those effects which we have already indicated as the peculiar attributes of Shakespeare's Problem Plays.

It is not an easy task to divide Shakespeare's plays into clear-cut groups. His first editors Heminge and Condell found it so hard that they grouped *All's Well* and *Measure for Measure* with the comedies while they put *Troilus and Cressida with the* tragedies. *Cymbeline* and *Pericles* were also put among the tragedies. The critics like Boas, Lawrence, Tillyard and Schanzer separated the tragi-comedies in a group and on basis of qualities which appeared problematic, included (or excluded) *Hamlet* and the Roman plays *Julius Caesar* and *Antony and Cleopatra*. A future critic may include any other play which, according to him, contains an insoluble problem. *Timon of Athens* with its excessive spiritual discord like that of *Hamlet* and *Henry IV Part I* with the problem of Falstaff's cowardice might be fair choices for the future. Timon's misanthropy of perverted love, Falstaff's real or affected cowardice might well appear to be one thing or the other as the angle of vision is changed. It is because Timon's spiritual flame brightens his end but a misanthrope's spiritual self is incapable of such fire and the other part of Falstaff's nature is inconsistent with cowardice, that their final evaluation might defy generalization and hence prove problematic.

For our immediate purpose we have chosen the traditionally regarded dark comedies—*All's Well, Measure for Measure* and *Troilus and Cressida* along with *Hamlet* which poses the general problem of duality as no other play of Shakespeare's does. *Julius Caesar* contains the problem of

Caesar's ambivalent characterization and *Antony and Cleopatra* a remarkable duality in character and action where the dramatist's own attitude remains enigmatic in spite of the positive, affirmatory final note in the play. There are certain baffling, unreconciled elements in Cleopatra's characterization as in Hamlet's, which cannot escape the attention of any reader or spectator. Above all, these plays written between 1600 and 1607, throw light on that phase of Shakespeare's development which is the richest in creativity and any baffling or enigmatic product of that time, must presumably be due to the excess of that creative power and not because of its deficiency. Or some other causes must be looked for.

We shall now consider these plays of Shakespeare as a part of the organic evolution of Shakespeare's dramatic genius in the light of the preceding and the following groups of plays. This will put them in a proper perspective and help in their evaluation.

REFERENCES

1. Aeschylus, *Agamemnon*, trans, E.D.A. Morshead, *Seven Famous Greek Plays* (Random House, New York, 1959) p. 77.
2. *Antigone*, trans. E.F. Watling: *Sophocles, The Theban Plays*, (Penguin Classics 1947) p. 144.
3. Ibid., pp. 145-146.
4. Aeschylus, Agamemnon, trans. E.A.D. Morshead, (Penguin Classics) p. 55.
5. Euripides, *Helen*, trans. Philip Vellacott (Penguin Classics 1954) p. 158.
6. Allardyce Nicoll, *World Drama* (George Harrap and Co. Ltd., London) 1962 Ed. p. 562.
7. Ibid., p. 562.
8. Ibid., p. 568.
9. Ibid., p. 569.
10. Fredrick S. Boas, *Shakespeare and His Predecessors*, (John Murray Ltd., London, 1896; Indian Edition Rupa and Co., Calcutta, 1963) p. 289.

11. Ibid., p. 289.
12. W.W., Lawrence, *Shakespeare's Problem Comedies* (1931) (Frederick Ungar Publishing Co., New York, 1960 Edition) p. 4.
13. Ibid., p. 4.
14. E.M.W. Tillyard, *Shakespeare's Problem Plays* (Chatto and Windus, London, 1950, Penguin Books, 1965) p. 11.
15. Ibid., p. 11.
16. Ibid., p. 13.
17. L.C., Knights, *Some Shakespearean Themes* (Macmillan and Company Ltd., London, 1959) p. 121.
18. Ibid., p. 122.
19. Ernest Schanzer, *The Problem Plays of Shakespeare*, (Routledge and Kegan Paul, Ltd., London, 1963) p. 6.
20. Ibid., p. 6.

11 Ibid., p.269.
12 [illegible] *[illegible] Papers in [illegible]* [illegible] [illegible] Publishing [illegible] 1950 [illegible] p.4
13 Ibid., p.8.
14 [illegible] *[illegible]* [illegible] 1950, [illegible] p.11
15 Ibid., p.11.
16 Ibid., p.13.
17 [illegible] *[illegible]* Macmillan and Company Ltd., London, 1959, p.121.
18 Ibid., p.182.
19 [illegible] [illegible] Ltd., London, [illegible] p. 6.
20 Ibid., p. 6.

CHAPTER II

Evolution of Shakespeare's Dramatic Art in The Problem Plays

Julius Caesar, the earliest play manifesting problematic features, does not strictly fall in the category of Problem plays and it has long been considered to be a flawless tragedy. It is Shakespeare's first tragedy of the kind which was developed to perfection in the subsequent tragedies. It stands at the threshold of the period of the four 'great' tragedies acknowledged to be his best and shares qualities with them which are common to the form associated with Shakespeare. The earlier tragedies, *Titus Andronicus, Richard III, Richard II* and *Romeo and Juliet* seem to feel the way to a form and we can discern a gradual progress. The first is crude and experimental and in spite of sustained characterization of Titus-a good, loyal man turned into a vengeful kind of Atreus - and that of Aaron the Moor, a prototype of Iago-the play is only a sequence of butcheries which seem to be there for their own sake. Jan Kott in *Shakespeare Our Contemporary* says that Richard III contains a prototype for Macbeth and the inner dimension of the character is enlarged but the extravagant butcheries and horror don't make him a truly tragic character and the tragic vision of Shakespeare has not yet evolved to the intensity and depth which later makes Macbeth tragic in spite of his deeds. *Romeo and Juliet* is a tragedy of an isolated kind - one of adolescent love-the like of which we do not encounter elsewhere in Shakespeare except in *Antony and Cleopatra* which is a tragedy of mature love. It is perfect in its own genre but it does not lead forward to any trend which develops later on. There is no complexity and Shakespeare's vision has a singleness just as in *Richard II. Richard II* is the first tragedy to evolve a truly tragic hero with an inner dimension. Shakespeare is definitely on his way to evolve a sensitive, poetic, speculative type of tragic character which appears in Brutus and Hamlet. We can say that Shakespeare's tragic art has reached a point which his comic art had reached in *A Midsummer Night's Dream.* There is no duality in Richard and from whatever angle we view him, we get the same impression of a king who failed because of his weakness. There is a spiritual depth in his nature which establishes him as a tragic hero, but he lacks the complexity of heroes of subsequent tragedies which arises from the duality of their natures. In other words, Richard II is always presented in the light of a single vision — there is a single-mindedness about him- and there is no contradiction or ambivalence anywhere in his character. There is no obscure corner of his being which Shakespeare does not illuminate for us. He is a perfectly transparent character.

With *Julius Caesar* the new type of presentation of character and situation is visible as a feature of Shakespeare's art. It is seen in a limited way in the complexity of Brutus. There are two parts of his nature which are shown to be at odds with each other and each is fairly presented. But there is something disjointed between Brutus the patriot and Brutus the friend of Caesar, — the talker and the doer—a split which is apparent on close reading. In Caesar the ambivalence is greater - his boastful and deluded nature designed to diminish the tragic effect, resembles a similar treatment of Agamemnon by Aeschylus and his power on the action after his death closely resembles the invocation of Agamemnon's spirit in the *Choephoroe* which somehow lends a moral strength to Orestes-but the two parts of his nature are as much inconsistent as the two aspects of Brutus. The only conclusion is that Shakespeare's double vision has started operating and we are made to see a character from two angles. The same is true of some situations which appear to be of different significance if seen from different angles. This incongruous gap is not wide enough to deprive the characters and situations of plausibility.

With *Hamlet* the play of double vision becomes so frequent and the resulting incongruities multiply to such a degree that the play can be seen as one vast spectacle of contrasts and paradoxes. The character of Hamlet is seen to have at least two incongruous facets and they appear in alternation in different situations. Apart from the fact that the play superimposes the qualities of a refined, poetic and sensitive nature (after those of the Earl of Essex or Philip Sidney, as it is conjectured) on the original barbaric, crude hero of Thomas Kyd or of Saxo Grammaticus, there must be something in the dramatic representation itself to account for it. The swift alternations in Hamlet's behaviour in the face of his ever-present subtlety of intellect and of "that capability and God-like reason", can only be accounted for by the double vision of the dramatist himself. His gentleness and kindliness with Horatio, the players and as revealed in the soliloquies, appear in a positive light, whereas his cruelty to Ophelia, Gertrude and Polonius appears in a negative light. It could as well be said that these two contradictory aspects of his character are presented in the light of the positive and the negative vision. It is a deliberate scheme of the dramatist and not a flaw arising from the imposition of a different concept on the original picture. If so, it is Shakespeare's changed vision which at a time presents him as an angel and at another time very nearly as a callous, unfeeling man, if not a brute.

Written after such a play, the dark comedies or the problem plays proper, must contain something of the dramatist's current technique. *Troilus and Cressida* which belongs almost to the same time as *Hamlet,* displays identical characteristics as regards the play of intellect and speculation. There is even an identity of imagery to a great extent. The spirit of iconoclasm which pervades the play is akin to that in *Hamlet*. The way ideals and values are dealt with indicates disillusionment and disgust. Even so, the Trojans and their values are presented in a positive light, while the Greeks and their values are presented in a negative light. The problems such as those of honour, degree and value, particularly the last, are left unresolved. The most outstanding irony is that no one acts in consistency with his own views. Most of all, the conclusion itself is inconclusive. The positive and the negative visions of the dramatist make characters and situations (of action there is little) abmirable or repulsive and the play mostly shows the working of the negative vision.

There is also much greater content of speculation in relation to effective action. In other words, most of this speculation is not integral to the plot and seems to be there for its own sake. It lends weight to the theory that the play was not intended for the stage and that it was written for a single private performance at White-Hall or for lawyers at one of the Inns of Court. Nevill Coghill rejects this idea and argues that *Troilus and Cressida* was originally acted at the Globe theatre and it was only later that it was performed at the Inns of Court with a prologue. He makes out a case for the play being a straight forward tragedy and not a problem play at all. If the mocking prologue and the epilogue are removed, it is seen to be as genuine a tragedy as any other.[1] Wilson Knight sees a simple polarity of good and evil, of the intuitional and the intellectual elements symbolized in the Trojans and the Greeks respectively.[2] But this does not defend the progressive coarsening of character and action which comes to a mocking, cynical point in Act V and appears to be inconsistent with tragedy. That might be the reason why the 1609 quarto introduced it as a 'history'. In the light of this, O.J. Campbell made out a case that the play derives from the contemporary vogue for satire. But the satirical note, which seems to be there most of the time, does not appear to be the final impression of the play. There is the appearance of genuinely tragic elements such as the death of Hector and the appearance of Cassandra. Even the disillusionment and despair of Troilus have a tragic quality. Shakespeare's general attitude of objectivity and detachment prevents the audience from entering into full sympathy with the tragic elements. It is now and then that genuine emotion is elicited and not uniformly as in Aeschylus's *Agamemnon*. The attitude is more of Euripides' *Orestes* with its combination of tragedy with irony and satire. Conjecturing that there is a possible influence of Euripides in translation, Anne Barton says :

"More speculative, but tantalizing, is the possible influence of Euripides. In play after play Euripides took up the matter of Troy. Elizabethans knew many of these plays in translation and adapted versions. If Shakespeare himself ever encountered the *Orestes* he would have found there an attitude towards the myth strikingly like his own. For

Euripides too, the Trojan war was an expense of spirit in a waste of shame. His Helen is a vain and lightminded flirt, manifestly not worth a fraction of the trouble she has caused, and the other 'heroes' are similarly debased. Everywhere, Euripides measures the epic grandeur of the story against the unlovely reality of these events and people when seen up close. Like Shakespeare's, his play is brilliant and savage, without any clear-cut moral or structural centre. It is also mixed in form, a combination of tragedy, comedy and satire so extreme that until recently, it was as much an embarrassment to the classicists as *Troilus and Cressida* was to the Shakespeareans of the eighteenth and nineteenth centuries."[4]

The identity with *Hamlet* in several respects—in bitterness of tone, fusion of irony and satire, gap between intention and action, the opposition between appearance and reality, the occasional coarseness, the disillusionment and disgust-establishes the fact that it shares all those problematic features with that play. In *Hamlet*, man's evaluation fluctuates between an angel and the quintessence of dust; in *Troilus and Cressida* men talk like Gods; they end up behaving like beasts. Chaos seems to be the final impression—in war, love and human relationship—a disintegration of values to the point of their final dissolution.

A tragedy presents a different picture of the human condition. Even *Hamlet* sounds a positive note towards the end although this does not indicate any upsurge of a new life. This absence of the note of regeneration of *Hamlet* among other things, makes Tillyard pronounce it a problem play. There is absolutely no positive note at the end of *Troilus and Cressida*. Whatever there was in flashes, is stifled by cynicism and satire. Nihilism was nowhere so dominant. Yet the play in some mysterious way, contains a grandeur, subdued and stifled though it be. As Anne Barton puts it, the play somehow gives us a 'feel' of something great and satisfying:

"....for all its pessimism and savagery, the experience of *Troilus and Cressida* is finally exhilarating. Despite the bleakness of the ending... this great play dismisses its audience fundamentally reassured."[5]

The secret of it can lie, as we have already suggested, in the double vision of the dramatist which projects, in turns, the baser side of human nature alternated by a glimpse of the positive redeeming side. A vision of evil presented with unmistakable clarity is alternated by a vision of as unmistakable good. The problem which emerges is not only of the resulting structure as drama but also of squaring this conflicting interpretation of human nature ranging between the angel and the beast. Without a sizable central figure, the elements of the play seem to move like electrons without a nucleus—a fair picture of a world without moral or spiritual cohesion. The two visions are obviously separately projected and the play becomes Shakespeare's most authentic portrayal of a disintegrated world.

All's Well that Ends Well, written after *Troilus and Cressida*, shows a different kind of spirit. It is no longer nihilistic or satirical, and in spite of the imperfection in execution which has been attributed to the incompatibility of different strands in the subject matter, the play shows a movement to positive values. It is partly due to the theme of love and its power to redeem, which looks forward to the last plays. Its tone contrasts sharply with that of *Hamlet* and *Troilus and Cressida*. But the problem which made Tillyard class it alongwith *Measure for Measure* as having "something radically schizophrenic" about it, is that of the incompatibility of the different elements of the play which were not completely fused by the poetic imagination. As Tillyard says :

"I have pointed out the difficulty, exceptional in his comedies, in which he involved himself : that of fitting a highly realistic set of principal actors into a plot belonging to the fantastic world of fairy lore. And it is quite possible that the difficulty explains the imaginative failure."[6]

Tillyard further concludes, "Shakespeare, knowing when he came to actual composition that he could not succeed, evaded the attempt and resorted, when the crisis came, to the conventional, the sententious, or the hieratic, never taxing his full imaginative powers."[7]

This line of argument, presuming that Shakespeare presents the realistic and the fairy-tale elments separately and fails to fuse them, overlooks the fact that Hamlet and Cleopatra (and even Falstaff) also embody two apparently irreconcilable aspects which are not completely fused. Yet they are Shakespeare's major triumphs. When Shakespeare wrote *All's Well*, he was in full possession of his creative powers. The same holds goods of the other two of the problem plays which go under the name of 'dark comedies'. So rather than resorting to such an explanation, we can attribute the apparent incongruity to the dramatic technique which he was adopting in these plays. In the plays written between the years 1600 and 1607, Shakespeare presents character and action from two angles. The same character is at one time virtuous and good and a little later, does something which is incompatible with this virtue. Hamlet shocks us by many such actions. So does Cleopatra. Helena too acts like a virtuous and innocent girl who has the single object of loving devotedly. But in her attempt to win the object of her love, she appears just the contrary-that she is not so innocent and can simulate, plot and resort to stratagems. If we look closely, it seems to be unnecessary to call the one self realistic and the other of fairy-tale. It is the 'mingled yarn' of human nature. To present it, Shakespeare used his double vision. He presumed the contrary elements as inseparable components of human nature and once any plot or character, however full of incongruities, was put in the crucible of his poetic imagination, it was transmuted by his vision. It is an important fact pertaining to all his plays whose plots were invariably borrowed with the exception of *The Tempest*.

Shakespeare's double vision has this characteristic quality of projecting plausibly all the elments—however discordant — of human nature. He didn't select with a view to harmonize, eliminate or mince them when it came to contradictions. They stirred his imagination. It is true that some such paradoxical character 'ran away' with his imagination. Falstaff did. Helena no doubt is a lesser character but in spite of the intractable matter, conceived on the same design as Falstaff, Hamlet or Cleopatra.

Thus Shakespeare's double vision-presenting positively and negatively the various movements of the characters - will be our cue. It will be our attempt to trace the 'unfused' parts and aspects, and each of them will be revealed as a projection by the positive or the negative vision.

It is not that there are two selves of the character or two unfused parts of the play unlinked with the theme. As Foakes says with reference to Helena's role as a divine agent:

"... it is rather that her combination of virtue, ambition, confidence in herself, and faith, bring success, so that indeed for this act she happens to become Heaven's agent."[8]

Thus for each act there is a link with the main concept. And this is provided by the positive or the negative vision which is highlighting this particular aspect of character which results in the act. From another point of view we can say that when a character is impelled by passion, he or she acts in a different way from that in which the same person would act when directed by reason. We cannot say that the one is from fairy tale or the other from the world of reality. As Northrop Frye puts it :

"In a world where action and passion are the same thing, there can be no union of the reason and the will on equal terms.[9]

The same technique of projection of either of the two visions accounts for, what Foakes calls 'the harsh polarities' in the action of *Measure for Measure*. Speaking of the three strains in the play (which fall in the two divisions of the flesh and the spirit) - "common vitality, license and lechery",[10] Angelo's "seeming" and Isabella's "chastity"— Foakes says,

"The harsh polarities established in the action and in the speeches... reflect... the oppositions which form the basis of the dramatic shaping of the play."[11]

It is the "dramatic shaping" which has to be observed under our eye in all the six plays under discussion. It will also reveal the way in which each character acquires its fuller shape in thought and action, as the dramatist's vision, in its two-fold way, lights it from different angles. This will determine our approach.

We can thus see the inadequacy of dramatic apprehension when Tillyard says of *Measure for Measure* :

"the play is not of a piece but changes its nature half-way through. It was partly through their correct perception of something being wrong that some earlier critics felt justified in making the Isabella of the first half of the play the scapegoat of the play's imperfections."[12]

This can be plausible only to those who think that the character of a person or the plot of a play must be of one piece. If Isabella seems to undergo a change and become passive, it is because the dramatist's attention is engaged by other aspects of the play, and the development of Isabella on the lines Shakespeare had adopted in the earlier part of the play, had reached the point necessary to the further development of the plot. Moreover, the play of the negative and the positive vision continues to shape the characters and their actions till a consummation is reached. The scenes between Isabella and Angelo and between her and Claudio had mostly presented the negative aspect of the characters and their actions in the light of the negative vision. The positive vision had highlighted the spiritual truth in the arguments of Isabella and the sheer power of life in the words of Claudio. Then the play had moved not only to show how a measure for measure is "meted out" but also to introduce the new value of forgiveness which is the culmination of the play's significance.

In this play as in the following one in our discussion — *Antony and Cleopatra* — Shakespeare has made a very deft use of his double vision to make us aware of good and evil, heights and depths and the infernal and divine aspects of human existence. The opposites are so juxtaposed and alternately focussed by the two visions that the sharpest contradictions are given a semblance of reality. All "discontinuities and contradictions in character and action"[13] can be shown to have been made parts of a total design by the dramatist's double vision. In the following chapters an attempt is made to illustrate this. Once this aesthetic and integrating quality is appreciated, it will be seen how futile it is to complain that there is a discontinuity in Isabella's character or that "the two Biblical demonic themes, Egypt and the serpent," make Cleopatra a "symbol of everything sinister,"[14] while at the same time "the holy priests bless her." It is by the operation of the double vision, where the negative and the positive appear to join each other in their fast alternation that the character of Cleopatra grows essemplastically.

William Rosen speaks thus of Shakespeare's play-world:

"It is a tangled skein; white and black merge; good grows up together with evil almost inseparably.. Opposing values .. are very often held in tenuous balance.. Shakespeare's unparalleled strength comes not only from the marvels of language but also from his penetration into the bewildering incongruities.. of human experience."[15]

Of *Antony and Cleopatra* the same critic says,

"Contradictions are to be found everywhere.. opposites play against each other.."[16]

It is to explain these contradictions and opposing values — the "tangled skein" of the problem plays — that this book proceeds to apply the idea of double vision as seen operating in the evolution of character and action in each of them. We shall consider these plays in a chronological as well as thematic order, generally concentrating on the affinity they have with one another while trying to evolve a meaningful interpretation of each. We have included the four plays initially styled as Shakespeare's problem plays, by Boas and subsequently included by Tillyard. To these, we have added *Julius Caesar* and *Antony and Cleopatra* included by Schanzer in his book. There is certainly a justification for treating them as problem plays as will be evident in our discussion. We shall begin our exploration with *All's Well* which thematically leads to *Measure for Measure*. Then the third of the traditionally acknowledged problem plays *Troilus and Cressida* — though earlier in chronological order — is taken up. This order of treatment is adopted to bring *Troilus and Cressida* as near *Hamlet* as possible. *Julius Caesar* precedes *Hamlet* and since both these plays have a great affinity with *Hamlet* in their own way, it makes identities more vivid when they are discussed in proximity. Thus the first two and the next three form two convenient groups. Finally, *Antony and Cleopatra*, which stands in a category apart and to which some of these earlier plays look forward, is discussed. This is followed by an exploration of features which are common to most of these plays—common ground as they are called—which provide a clue to their significance in the entire range of Shakespeare's works.

REFERENCES

1. Nevill Coghill quoted by Anne Barton in her introduction to *Troilus and Cressida* in *The Riverside Shakespeare*, p. 444. (Haughton Mifflin Company, Boston, 1974).

2. G. Wilson Knight, *The Wheel of Fire* (Mathuen and Co. London 1930) p. 48.
3. Jan Kott, *Shakespeare Our Contemporary* (Methurn and Co. Ltd. London, 1965) p. 68.
4. Anne Barton, in *Introduction to Troilus and Cressida* (Riverside Shakespeare) p. 445.
5. Ibid., p. 447.
6. E.M.W. Tillyard, *Shakespeare's Problem Plays* (Chatto and Windus, London, 1950) p. 102.
7. Ibid., p. 102.
8. R.A. Foakes, *Shakespeare, The Dark Comedies to the Last Plays* (Routledge and Kegan Paul, London, 1971) p. 11.
9. Northrop Frye, *Fools of time, Studies in Shakespearearn Tragedy* (University of Toronoto Press, O.U.P. London, 1967) p. 68.
10 R.A. Foakes, *Shakespeare, The Dark Comedies to the Last Plays*, p. 18.
11. Ibid., p. 23.
12. E.M.W. Tillyard, *Shakespeare's Problem Plays* (cf. 6) p. 123.
13. R.A. Foakes (cf. 9) p. 61.
14. Northrop Fyre, p. 72.
15. William Rosen, *Antony and Cleopatra*, an essay in *Shakespeare The Tragedies*, Ed. Cliffored Leech (University of Chicago Press, Chicago and London, 1965) p. 202.
16. Ibid., p. 202.

CHAPTER III

The Debile Minister

Most of the problems associated with the characters and actions of *All's Well* can be seen to be the result of the working of the double vision of the dramatist and they cease to be so if we examine them from this point of view. Shakespeare was at pains to show the evolution of these characters and accordingly, presents their actions in such a way as to make them as realistic as possible. When they do seem to break away from realism, it is due to the sudden turn given by the operation of the negative or the positive vision. These characters are those of Helena and Bertram while the others are completely consistent and seem to be created in the positive vision working uniformly. Only that of Parolles which is also consistent, is conceived (unlike that of Falstaff) entirely in the light of the negative vision.

The comedy succeeds or fails by the characterization of Helena and like Cleopatra, she displays antithetical poles of human behaviour. One of the main themes of the play (equally shared by Bertram) – that of appearance and reality–also explicates itself in her attitudes. She is in fact the key to the play's meaning. So, much would be revealed if we follow the development of her character. To understand the working of Shakespeare's double vision with reference to characterization, we have to see how sometimes a positive statement, even by way of rhetoric is preceded or followed by a negative one:

"...for where an unclean mind carries virtuous qualities, there commendations go with pity; they are virtues and traitors too. In her they are the better for their simpleness: she derives her honesty and achieves her goodness."[1]

The tone which creates a feeling of duality with reference to Helena's character and actions throughout the play has made its appearance. The positive vision is not without a tinge of the negative as is more explicitly seen in the Countess' words which genuinely seem to cast a doubt on Helena's sincerity in weeping as if she has some prescience of the truth:

"No more of this, Helena; go to, no more; lest it be rather thought you effect a sorrow than to have—"[2] (Act I Sc II *ll* 47-49)

This is preceded by a positive statement. And both are true as Helena asserts in her reply.

"I do affect a sorrow indeed, but I have it too."[3]

However, a subsequent disclosure in Helena's soliloquy shows that the negative vision had revealed the greater truth about Helena with reference to that particular action, that is of shedding tears. Helena was affecting a sorrow for her father but she was 'having' it for Bertram at the thought of his parting from her. It is clear from the words in the soliloquy which show that she had little feeling for her father comparable to what she had for Bertram, in spite of the tears she was shedding now:

"O, were that all! I think not on my father,
And these great tears grace his remembrance more
Than those I shed for him. What was he like?
I have forgot him; my imagination
Carries no favour in't but Bertram's.
I am undone; there is no living, none,
If Bertram be away;..."[4]

Both the positive and the negative vision have focussed this complex picture of Helena's character after that act of weeping. Another subtle device of making the Countess exit even before Bertram has departed from the scene is intended to make Helena's soliloquy possible which shows an interplay of the two visions and makes her subsequent actions explicable.

As already said, Parolles' character is unfolded entirely in the light of the negative vision and the image which exposes pretended virtue opens outwards and lingers in the mind till his final exposure in the Fourth Act. Helena says of him:

"Yet these fixed evils sit so fit in him.
That they take place when virtue's steely bones
Looks bleak i'th' cold wind;..."[5]

But where Shakespeare wants to correct perspective and sway our judgment in favour of a character we have a speech which is affirmatory and shows Helena gathering will and strength which finally culminates in that superhuman power with which she works the king's cure. There is no doubt that it is meant to be preparatory to her great exploits to come. It is a typical instance of how the positive vision conceives and projects a consistent movement of a character from one affirmation to another. She fixes her position as if to gain further momentum:

"Our remedies oft in ourselves do lie,
Which we ascribe to heaven. The fated sky
Gives us free scope; only doth backward pull
Our slow designs when we ourselves are dull.
What power is it which mounts my love so high,
...my intents are fix'd, and will not leave me."[6]

The "power" gathered up thus in relation to the "intents" does "mount" to a divine level.

It is by looking at Helena's movement from this vantage-point and at the positive vision of the dramatist which consistently projects the upward movement of that 'power' which impelled her that we can bridge the gap of plausibility between realism and fairy-tale which has been considered to be one of the 'problems' of the play. As Tillyard puts it,

"I have pointed out the difficulty, exceptional in his comedies, in which he involved himself: that of fitting a highly realistic set of principal actors into a plot belonging to the fantastic world of fairy-lore. And it is quite possible that this difficulty explains the imaginative failure".[7]

Both the conclusions of Tillyard are refutable because if the difficulty he points out can be shown to be superficial, then the imaginative failure, if any, is not due to it. It may lie in the comparatively unpromising nature of the theme of pursuit of a husband and the absence of a more complex motif which could spark off the poetic imagination. But even this is not fully correct because the character of Helena is no less a product of antitheses than that of Cleopatra, though on a smaller scale. And once we realize this—and the fact that, in terms of complexity, Shakespeare was successful in creating an enigmatic impression about her—we must try to analyse, as we proceed, how it is so, as she makes a way for herself, by that power which is manifested as superhuman and even as "divine" will. We shall, incidentally be also able to discover the subtle operation of the two creative visions as in the case of Cleopatra.

Helena immediately shows the growth of another dimension to her will in her reply to the demand of the Countess, "Come, come, disclose/The state of your affection, for your passions/Have to the full appeach'd."[8]

"Thus, Indian-like,
Religious in mine error, I adore
The sun that looks upon his worshipper..."[9]

The "religious" fervour develops naturally into "the hieratic tone" of Helena's later speeches to the King of which Tillyard says that "He (Shakespeare) is deliberately evading drama and substituting ritual and cloudy incantation."[10]

By the time Helena offered to cure the King, her will, exalted by love into a religious intensity, has become identified with God's will and she regards herself as only his "minister" - the word uniformly used for her in her religious role:

"He that of greatest works is finisher
Oft does them by the weakest minister
...Great floods have flown
From simple sources, and great seas have dried
When miracles have by the great'st been denied.........[11]

Miracles have always been associated with exceptionally intensified faith like the miracles of Joan of Arc or of Lazarus. Shaw and Eugene O'Neill have dramatically shown that the source of their miraculous power was their intense conviction that God's will was working through them. So it was with Helena who has so merged her will in God that she seems to herself to derive her inspiration from Him:

"Inspired merit so by breath is barr'd.
It is not so with Him that all things knows
As 'tis with us that square our guess by shows;
But most it is presumption in us when
The help of heaven we count the act of men.
Dear Sir, to my endeavours give consent;
Of heaven, not me, make an experiment."[12]

"not me" is significant. It is only God's grace—"The greatest Grace lending grace"—which is "lent" to her to work the cure. What could be more consistent than this movement from "will" to "grace"? We find the process in T.S. Eliot's *Murder in the Cathedral* which is as important as the main theme of that play. This is brought about by an unflagging working of the positive vision upto the point of the actual cure of the King.

The effect is announced in Lafew's words:

"They say miracles are past; and we have our philosophical persons to make modern and familiar, things supernatural and causeless. Hence it is that we make trifles of terrors, ensconcing ourselves into seeming knowledge when we should submit ourselves to an unknown fear."[13]

It is the dramatist's deliberate attempt to make the audience conscious of the fact that miracles must exist side by side with rational knowledge and both are as compatible as matter and spirit. Hence working by faith is unquestionable by reason. This prepares the way for the final, integrated statement:

"A Showing of a Heavenly Effect in an Earthly Actor", (with reference to the symbolic "dolphin" which points to the sound health of the king but also has implications of this integration.)

It is the general expectation, that this power (of God) would be useful in a universal manner after the recovery of the king, while the paradox between the weakness of human beings and the power of God is emphasized:

Very hand of heaven. in a most weak—and debile minister; great power, great transcendence, which should indeed give us a further use to be made than alone the recovery of the King, as to be—generally thankful."[14]

If the earlier will-to-possess and the subsequent miracle performed by Helena are not viewed as an organic growth of character and the action by which this growth is expressed, we are left with two isolated and irreconcilable aspects of character with equally implausible action which even the "clever wench" theory would not make convincing. The only residue of the fairy-tale conclusion with an impression of gross improbability would be left to bank upon. As the plot moves ahead with the performance of the impossible tasks, even the "clever wench" or "fairytale" theory would be inadequate to account for the diverging shades of character and action which seem to be a total contradiction of the spiritual transcendence which Helena achieves in the first part of the play. It is such a partial view of each action unintegrated with the growth of the character which makes it enigmatic by creating a lacuna between one phase and another as between one action and another. We have already suggested how this difficulty can be overcome.

Another point is that of disparate and often contradictory impressions created by a particular action and aspect of the character at a particular time. It is when two impressions, not easily reconcilable, coalesce in the same act and at the same moment. It is also possible that, like shot-silk, the same act appears to be justified or plausible from one angle but quite the contrary from another angle. This leads to a possibility of a double interpretation of the same act or experience and the uncertain and divided responses on the part of the audience or the reader.

We illustrate this with reference to Helena's speech beginning "Our remedies oft in ourselves do lie....", which I have referred to as a forward movement in the light of the positive vision. The words can be interpreted in a double way and then the response would be divided and uncertain. When Helena says that the remedies for our difficulties lie in ourselves which we attribute to God, her statement can be interpreted in an agnostic manner making a case that it is we ourselves who possess all the power which we wrongly think is God's. One might dismiss her as presumptuous. But an interpretation of the same lines from a different angle would reveal that Helena first wants the individual to awaken all his spiritual potentialities and thereafter to turn to God. Maybe, the difficulty can be solved without supplicating for Divine aid which, if invoked for little things, would make us incapable and "dull". This latter interpretation assumes an upward surge of the human spirit to meet God—only that it doesn't allow "dullness" to frustrate our ends which can be often easily achieved by us.

This is one category of situation where a statement can be interpreted positively or negatively according to the angle of vision. There is another category where the same action is simultaneously presented as good or evil, moral or immoral and both aspects have to be taken into account in any attempt to understand the situation. The situation is essentially ambivalent and the reaction of the audience or the reader would be one of complexity. This ambivalence or complexity would constitute a more important problem of the play in addition to the earlier problem of adjusting realism and fairy-lore as pointed out by Tillyard or that of divergent impressions of an identical situation or statement. Both of these latter categories have already been shown to be more superficial than real.

Before proceeding to these situations, let us trace the movement of the plot through incidents which show a working of the two visions alternatingly.

With the cure of the king there is an abrupt change of tone in the play. There is no more of the inspired or the hieratic quality in Helena's words and she again seems to become the realistic, matter-of-fact woman who had shed tears for the man she loved rather than for her father. The way she makes Bertram her choice with the words "This is the man", shows an utter disregard for his sentiments which should be a consideration in all matters of love. By any definition, even though she gives herself "into (his) guiding power",[14(a)] it is not the self-effacing love comparable with that of Viola ("She never told her love") or with that of Imogen who exiled herself with a complete surrender to the will of her husband. Here the negative vision shows her to be the possessive woman who is determined to become the wife of a man who would escape her. The same will which had moved to divine heights by identifying itself with God's is now working on a lower plane.

Just after, however, when Bertram is leaving without giving her the love due to a wife, the dramatist's positive vision has fixed her in an instant of utter humility and restraint which is free from possessiveness. When Bertram asks her, "Well, what would you say?" she replies :

"I am not worthy of the wealth I owe,
Nor dare I say 'tis mine-and yet it is;
But, like a timorous thief, most fain would steal
What law does vouch mine own."[15]

When Bertram further asks her, "what would you have?" She says with unparalleled restraint which matches that of any tragic heroine of Shakespeare:

"Something, and scarce so much; nothing indeed.
I would not tell you what I would, my lord.
Faith, yes:
Stranger and foes do sunder and not kiss".[16]

Unfeelingly, Bertram asks her to be on the move.

These are some of the deeply emotional lines and show the dramatist's involvement with the theme refuting the impression that his "imagination was not properly kindled".[17]

We now come to the instance of the two visions working almost simultaneously. To begin with, it is the positive vision which projects Helena's self-abnegation when she learns of Bertram's departure to Florence. It gives the impression that Shakespeare was deeply involved in Helena's characterization and he presents her on the point of an act which is clearly inspired by a spirit of sacrifice.

Learning of Bertram's conditions which were obviously impossible to fulfil and his decision to stay away from France, Helena's first thought is of herself being the cause of this unpleasantness followed by her decision to go away:

"Poor lord! is't
I That chase thee from thy country, and expose
Those tender limbs of thine to the event
Of the none-sparing war?.....O you leaden messengers,
That ride upon the violent speed of fire,
Fly with false aim;.....do not touch my lord...
I am the caitiff that do hold him to't;
...Better 'twere
I met the ravin lion when he roar'd
With sharp constraint of hunger;...
...I will be gone;..."[18]

But this is followed by an act to the contrary. The spirit of self-sacrifice which inspired her departure gives way to a will to follow Bertram to Florence and this 'act' — one of the most important acts in the play, (of the same importance as the healing of the King) — is conceived in a different key. We see the different nature of the vision and the entire tone changes again to pursuit and possessiveness. The clever wench is on her way to achieve the impossible tasks. From now onwards each of the acts she undertakes by wit and craft till the end of the play is capable of a double interpretation.

The desire to be gone is followed, without any lapse of real time, by her appearance as a pilgrim bound for the shrine of Saint Jaques. But although she does have the guise of a pilgrim, she has taken good care to carry enough gold to achieve her end. The words she writes in her letter are clearly meant to deceive and to conceal her real purpose.

> "I am Saint Jaques' pilgrim, thither gone.
> Ambitious love hath so in me offended
> That barefoot plod I the cold ground upon
> With sainted vow my faults to have amended...
> He is too good and fair for death and me;
> Whom I myself embrace to set him free."[19]

It is when we see that the "sainted vow" was to lead to the accomplishment of the tasks laid by Bertram, that we understand the real meaning of these lines. We admire her for her cleverness but more and more feel that somehow she is now being presented by the negative vision — the truly creative power of the dramatist does not come into play. The movement of the plot in a certain channel does not permit it.

Regarding Helena's further role in pursuing her end, all her actions, particularly the bed-trick, can be viewed as transpiring in a morally indifferent world where the positive vision does not any longer project her with an intensity as in the earlier part when she identified herself with God's will. Everything is now capable of a double interpretation. A case can be made for the operation of the positive vision as when Tillyard says, "Nor does the conception of Helena as a person specially favoured by heaven cease with her curing the king. The Countess, hearing that Bertram has cast her away, says, "What angel shall/Bless this unworthy husband? he cannot thrive,/Unless her prayers, whom heaven delights to her/ And loves to grant, reprieve him..." He adds, more significantly, "Nor does Shakespeare let the theme of Helena's divine agency drop."[20] Tillyard refers to Helena's words to Diana's mother

"Doubt not but heaven
Hath brought me up to be your daughter's dower,
And it hath fated her to be my motive
And helper to a husband."[21]

However, the words of the Countess can be said to have been inspired by her former opinion of Helena reinforced by the letter declaring that she is going as a pilgrim to the shrine of Saint Jaques, 'barefoot' and to likely death. We know this to be only a pretext for going to 'follow' Bertram. Thus the real situation was that the Countess herself was deceived by this 'act' of Helena, not knowing her real plan and so idolizing her. Accordingly Helena's act of departure becomes a revealing instance, pertinent to the point of this book, which becomes capable of a double interpretation and underlines another important theme, to be taken up separately—that of the divergence between appearance and reality.

The words spoken by Helena to the Widow could not otherwise be put for the desired effect because it was 'her' intention to make use of her daughter and compensate her for her help ('buying' it) by giving her the purse of gold and the promise to 'add' three thousand crowns for her dowry. This is what she says to widow:

"Take this purse of gold,
And let me buy your friendly help thus far,
Which I will over-pay and pay again
When I have found it."[22]

This is astute bargaining and it is difficult to imagine the hand of God behind it. As a matter of fact, there are two clearly different levels on which the character of Helena is conceived in the earlier and latter part of the play, which we have connected with the positive and negative vision of the dramatist. As G.K. Hunter puts it,

"True, in the first half of the play ("the healing of the king") Helena is a positive and competent figure, though to say she won the hand of Bertram "by a trick" is hardly fair to the facts of the play, in which virtue declares itself by divine favour and is found worthy of reward by the divinely allowed arbiter of destiny—the King. But in the second half of the play ("the fulfilment of the tasks") this assumption is clearly untenable".[23]

Taking the same view of Helena in the latter half, E.K. Chambers sees her development as a degradation of nobility. He says, "the meanness (of the bed-trick) ... is a measure of the spiritual straits to which the instinct of sex has reduced the noblest of women." He adds, "The only "problem" in it *(All's Well)* is Helena's problem of getting the man she wants for a husband.......It is a problem in wit....."[24]

It was perhaps the imperative need of the plot (of which the bargaining with the widow and the bed-trick were an intrinsic part) which left no room for a positive focussing of Helena's nobility and higher virtues. Her characteristics conforming to the idea of the 'clever wench' had to be brought into operation as best as this could be done and it made her acts inevitably fall short of expected moral propriety, or to use Hunter's epithet, become 'tasteless'.

Helena's appearance as a pilgrim outside Florence and her instant meeting with the Widow and her daughter just before Bertram was to pass that way with his troops, is designed as a multiple coincidence which is the first indication that it is the sole object of executing the plot and not developing the characters which is Shakespeare's immediate concern. The plot is now Helena's's plot and Helena's plot is her character in action. She moves the other characters like puppets and the widow and her daughter Diana do what she wants.

"Please it this matron and this gentle maid
To eat with us tonight;...
I will bestow some precepts of this virgin.
Worthy the note."[25]

In her second meeting she instructs the Widow:

"The count he woos your daughter
Lays down his wanton siege before her beauty,
Resolv'd to carry her;.
Let her in fine consent
As we'll direct her how "tis best to bear it."[26]

After Helena has told the Widow how her daughter can get Bertram's ring, the widow says

"Now I see
The bottom of your purpose."[27]

To this Helena, anxious to tell her that all this plotting is lawful, says,

"You see it lawful then; it is no more
But that your daughter, ere she seems as won,
Desires this ring; appoints him an encounter;
In fine, delivers me to fill the time, Herself most chastely absent. After,
To marry her, I'll add three thousand crowns
To what is pass'd already."[28]

It is apparent that Helena knows that the scheme is strictly speaking "immoral" — even sinful. And whatever she does can only be presented negatively. It is because the dramatist himself cannot give it a positive colour. But, paradoxically, as Helena herself argues, the deed is lawful though its nature and meaning may be wicked and sinful:

"Why then tonight
Let us assay our plot; which, if it speed,
Is wicked meaning in a lawful deed,
And lawful meaning in a lawful act, Where both not sin, and yet a sinful fact."[29]

Again there is room for two divergent interpretations, even if it is dominated by the negative vision.

The positive vision has been mostly absent in shaping the characters and their actions in the latter half of the play from the time of Helena's departure for Florence. In the exposure of Parolles which in a way, is the second important act on the scene next to the gulling of Bertram, we find the negative vision at work which strips him to the core. Bertram's exposure and the final reconciliation is now the act which has to take place back again at France in the presence of the king. This scene can be likened to the final scenes in *Cymbeline, Pericles* or *The Winter's Tale* where the hitherto-supposed dead person appears to be alive or as good as resurrected from the dead.

Accordingly, as usual in Shakespeare's comedies and last plays, the positive vision is again at work towards the end presenting Helena more favourably until her recognition.

Even before she is due to leave Florence, we find her in a new self-possession. She says to the Widow and Diana:

"You must know
I am supposed dead. The army breaking,
My husband hies him home, where, heaven, aiding,
And by the leave of my good lord the King
We'll be before our welcome."[30]

We are prepared for a scene of her supposed 'coming back to life' and also become aware that heaven would aid her in her plans. These words, however, don't come with that affirmation as the final symbolic words which show that some sort of new life is in the offing:

"Yet, I pray you;
But with the word: "the time will bring on summer"
When briars shall have leaves as well as thorns.
And be as sweet as sharp. We must away;
Our wagon is prepar'd, and time revives us.
All's well that ends well; still the fine's the crown.
Whate'er the course, the end is the renown."[31]

The imagery of rebirth is a clear proof that the positive vision is again projecting her actions and conditioning others' thoughts about her. To emphasize Helena's coming back to life from supposed death, the scene is prepared by the Countess' words: "it was the death of the most virtuous gentlewoman that even nature had praise for creating."[32] And in the court Lafew pays her 'memory' this tribute:

"He lost a wife
Whose beauty did astonish the survey
Of richest eyes; whose words all ears took captive
Whose dear perfection hearts that scorn'd to serve
Humbly call'd mistress."[33]

The king's words to Bertram, "All is whole",[34] are again an unconscious hint of a perfected state before actual reconciliation comes.

The accentuation of the religious element in the later part of the play had begun while Bertram's plan of seduction of Diana was going on and as if to underline that sin and to offset the impropriety of the 'bed-trick' certain statements of the French lords become relevant now. While condemning Bertram's conduct as 'rebellion' and human beings as 'traitors' to themselves, they had, as Tillyard says, made Helena represent heavenly grace and Bertram as natural unredeemed man. In the scene of the final recognition and reconciliation we find that the idea of redemption of Bertram is also implicit. The words of Diana which refer to Helena "one that's dead is quick" have also a suggestion of new life in which Bertram shares by his reunion with her.

Thus we see that as the heroine of a complex play with a combination of the divine agent and the clever wench with a task of pursuing and deserving the object of her love, passing through situations and undertaking acts which cannot be called altogether moral and even plotting and pretending, Helena creates uncertain and divided responses in the audience and the reader, which can be explained only by the double vision in the light of which Shakespeare habitually creates his characters particularly those whom he intends to partake of virtues and vices like "a mingled yarn".

Another character whose composite yarn mingles more of vices than virtues is Bertram. As such he is conceived mostly in the light of the negative vision. But not entirely. Bertram has a limit to his vices and Tillyard avoids the epithet "vicious" (which would mean "confirmed" in his vices and so beyond reformation). He says, "I did not include 'vicious'; and it is a triumph of art that Bertram can do so many selfish or mean things without incurring that epithet. Though never more than natural man, he is never, we feel, beyond the reach of grace. He (Shakespeare) keeps Bertram from positive viciousness by asserting from the first and then reiterating, his crude immaturity... Knowing that Bertram was under the discipline of Parolles, we can infer his shortcomings. Thereafter...the theme of his immaturity is maintained."[35]

The influence of Parolles on Bertram is certainly more evil than that of Falstaff on Prince Hal and the comparison has often been made and Shakespeare presumably invented the character of Parolles partly to provide a correlative to the atmosphere of moral degeneration which constitutes an important element of realism in the play. The other object was to mitigate the effect of his trespasses by adopting Parolles as a sort of scapegoat. But his fall from grace is unmistakable. As G.K. Hunter says,

"The problem of Bertram's role in the play involves much the same bifurcation of evidence. The plot requires him to be high-spirited, but faulty, rash and hasty, but admirable; Shakespeare, however, complicates our reaction to youthful impetuosity by considering in it the whole context of youth versus age, and by dwelling with moral weight on his flaws as typical of fallen humanity."[35]

'Two important facts emerge: his immaturity in the earlier half and his fall from grace in the later. Corresponding to these, his growth and redemption constitute an important theme of the play. At all those stages and in all those actions which display these defects, it is the negative vision which seems to be dominant. Only in flashes as when he appears as a valiant soldier, does he appear in the light of the positive vision and finally at the end when he accepts Helena.

Right from the opening of the play, an impression is given that Bertram is just a "boy" as he is often called. Being a minor, he was a ward of the King. As he is departing in response to the summons of the King, the Countess, his mother advises him, among other thing to "Do wrong to none", an advice he did not always keep. Even Helena, who sheds tears at his departure, says that the court would be a learning-place for him.

Curiously enough, the King, when he sees Bertram, wishes that just like his father's face, he may inherit his "moral parts" as well. The impatience of Bertram to be sent on the Florentine wars and his fretting on being commanded to remain at the court shows his adventurous spirit as well as his immaturity:

'.....kept a coil with
'Too young', and
'The next year' and
'Tis too early'.
to which Parolles replies,
'And thy mind stand to't, boy, steal away bravely.' [37]
'Boy' is reminiscent of 'lad' of Falstaff.
This is Parolles' prescription for a valiant career:

"Use a more spacious ceremony to the noble lords;...they wear themselves in the cap of the time;...and though the devil lead the measure, such are to be followed."[38]

Bertram responds: "And I will do so."

The above two instances show that the positive and the negative visions are operating simultaneously; Bertram's fiery spirit and his tameness to Parolles and his influence show the two sides of his nature and foreshadow much of what follows.

One of the best-known incidents in the play is that of Helena's choice of Bertram to which the King was bound by a solemn promise. It is a rare instance of moral ambivalence where the viewpoints of all three who are connected with the choice can be justified. Most so, that of Bertram. When the king says, "Why then, young Bertram, take her; she's thy wife," Bertram gives a plain answer:.

"My wife, my liege! I shall beseech your highness.
In such a business give me leave to use
The help of mine own eyes."
The King's argument is rather lame:
"Know 'st thou not, Bertram,
What she has done for me?"
Bertram more plausibly replies,
"Yes, my good lord;
But never hope to know why I should marry her."[39]

Later he gives his reason more explicitly," I cannot love her nor will strive to do't."[40]

But when he had said giving another reason:
"A poor physician's daughter my wife! Disdain
Rather corrupt me ever!"[41]

He displays an untenable presumption and deserves the King's rebuff," Proud, scornful boy".

So he is right and wrong and we see how the dramatist envisions him positively and negatively at the same time. The response of the audience is divided and uncertain.

Of this situation, Tillyard says, "By modern standards the King acts very hardly to Bertram in forcing Helena upon him... (but) by Elizabethan standards, the King is less hard... Bertram was his ward, and at his disposal... and; Elizabethan audience would have accepted the plea (of the king) and have considered Bertram to have had as fair a deal."[42]

Nevertheless, the situation permits of a double interpretation.

It is when Bertram, having duly married Helena, sends her away and himself going to Florence, informs her of his conditions ("When thou canst get the ring upon my finger... and show me a child begotton of thy body that I am father to"),[43] that he gives another indication of his obdurateness and immaturity not realizing that Helena could be up to the challenge. He makes way for further scheming, schemes himself only to be easily gulled and somehow emerges not as wiser but only as a person to be redeemed or admitted into grace by the virtue of his wife who herself had emerged as rightfully one by a 'sinfully sinless' manoeuvre. No wonder most of this, except the end, seems to be projected by the negative vision of the dramatist. Still as Tillyard says, "the crises through which Bertram passes in the last half of the play at once form the gist of the plot and reveal his nature."[44]

Throughout, the impression of Bertram's boyishness is maintained even in the bed-trick in which he is so easily colted, although the sense of his 'fall' with the sin of adultery is not mitigated on that score. He has the worst of it both ways while Helena who engineered the latter is honourably acquitted. The difference is clearly not in the deed but in the intention and form the point of his departure to Italy, each of his actions is marked by moral error and is seen to be so by other characters.

When the Countess learns of his desertion of Helena, she says,

"This is not well, rash and unbridled boy...
By the misprizing of a maid so virtuous.."[45]

and when she learns of Helena's going away as a pilgrim, she says,

"What angel shall
Bless this unworthy husband?"[46]

In a more severe and religious vein, there is the criticism of his supposed seduction of Diana. The second Lord says, "He hath perverted a young gentlewoman here in Florence, of a most chaste renown, and this night he fleshes his will in the spoil of her honour; he hath given her his monumental ring, and thinks himself made in the unchaste composition."

The First lord:

"Now, God delay our rebellion! As we

are ourselves, what things are we!"
The second Lord: "Merely our own traitors."[47]

Clearly, the planned adultery and fall of Bertram becomes, in a more universal way, an instance of the fall of the natural man. The bleakness of the negative vision here is unequalled in the whole play. There is no hope until redemption comes.

There is one more instance of how the two visions can be seen to operate simultaneously.

As the Widow of Florence, Diana and others are waiting to see Bertram's victorious troops pass, Diana says of Bertram, "They say the French count has done most honourable service."

The Widow says, "it is reported that he has taken their great'st commander, and that with his own hand he slew the Duke's brother."[48]

This is positive praise and should elicit admiration for Bertram's valour, however, in the same breath there is talk of another kind. Mariana, a friend says, "Well, Diana, take heed of this French earl... one Parolles, a filthy officer he is in those suggestions for the young earl... all these engines of lust, are not the things they go under;..."[49]

There is an immediate turn of opinion to the negative view of such a man. The response is uncertain particularly because Bertram's fault is lightened by the idea of insinuation of Parolles. Even when the actual 'fall' comes, the idea of his being 'gulled' by his own wife acts as a mitigating factor, again making the final response uncertain. The bed-trick has been played 'upon' him and there is always some allowance made for the victim.

Hence it is that the essential quality of ambiguity and uncertainty arising from the characters and their actions in the problem plays is very markedly seen in the case of both Helena and Bertram.

The third important character of the play is Shakespeare's own invention without any counterpart in the 'source' — William Painter's 'Giletta of Narbona'. It is not without its own significance. Just as Falstaff was conceived to act as a corrupter of Hal almost like Vice, a morality-figure, similarly, Parolles is introduced in the scheme of *All's Well*. As G.K.

Hunter says: "Parolles serves to define the reality of Bertram: at the same time he acts as a scapegoat and takes at least some of the blame for Bertram's faults'.[50] The entire sub-plot of Parolles and exposure is also invented by Shakespeare and when Shakespeare did so (which was rare with him) it was with an important function in mind.

Hence the character of Parolles and the incidents associated with him are not be dismissed lightly. What is noticeable however, is that whereas Falstaff can be said to have been conceived in the positive vision (with a little of the negative only when some of his acts pass the bounds of admiration) and even in his running away at Gadshill, he is not positively a coward, Parolles is either a corrupter or a coward throughout the play without any redeeming trait whatever, hence he is uniformly presented in the light of the negative vision.

The description of his character by Helena right in the beginning of the play is very much to the point.

"And yet I know him a notorious liar,
Think him a great way fool, solely a coward;
Yet these fix'd evils sit so fit in him."[51]

It is the aptness with which the inner emptiness of Parolles is exposed in spite of his being well-dressed. A parallel that attaches itself to Bertram who is guided by him is that his fine exterior conceals an inner emptiness — both in wisdom and experience. This is how a multiple effect moves in a ripple-like fashion from some of the statements in Shakespeare.

The witty skirmish on virginity shows how Parolles would 'instruct' Helena ('Little' Helena whom he equates with the 'boy' Bertram) and it also brings out a real indifference to that virtue in his mind as against a pretended one in Helena's.

However, the cynicism of Parolles as regards virtue is quite alien to the humorous tone of Falstaff on honour; it is near that of Iago who calls virtue 'a fig'. Although Johnson says that "Parolles has many of the lineaments of Falstaff". Peter Alexander has corrected the perspective by saying that "Falstaff for all his vices belongs to another order of character".[52] So it is only in the morality mode that they are akin.

The characters in a morality play were either black or white - they were presented by the positive or the negative vision and Vice certainly in the stark negative. Parolles more nearly approaches Vice than any other character does in Shakespeare.

To take an instance of his Iago - like cynicism, here is the advice he gives Helena on virginity:

"Virginity, like an old courtier, wear her cap out of fashion, richly suited but unsuitable, just like the brooch and the toothpick, which wear not now. Your date is better in your pie and your porridge than in your cheek; and your virginity, your old virginity, is like one of our French wither'd pears: it looks ill it eats drily; marry 'tis a wither'd pear; it was formerly better;..."[53]

It is Lafew who 'finds him out' at first and says so:

"I did think thee for two ordinaries to be a pretty wise fellow; thou didst make tolerable vent of thy travel; it might pass. Yet the scarfs and the bannerets about thee did manifoldly dissuade me from believing thee a vessel of too great burden. I have now found thee; when I lose thee again I care not. Yet art thou good for nothing but taking up, and that thou'rt scarce worth."[54]

After his exposure and humiliation, Parolles admits to Lafew, "O my good lord, you were the first that found me."[55]

Unlike Falstaff whose cowardice at Gadshill has been left so "gingerly" in doubt by Shakespeare, Parolles' cowardice in the episode of fetching his drum is so callously brought out that there is no doubt that here Shakespeare was trying to conform to the Jonsonian type of comedy. This time he was in no mood to let a comic character run away with his imagination. In spite of this intention to "limit" him, Shakespeare yet gives him a memorable expression which points to the essence of his character. After his discomfiture Parolles says:

"Yet am I thankful, If my heart were great,
T would burst at this:
Captain I'll be no more.
But I will eat and drink and sleep as soft
As captain shall. Simply the thing I am
Shall make me live.

Who know himself a braggart,
Let me fear this; for it will come to pass
That every braggart shall be found an ass.
Rust, sword; cool, blushes; and Parolles live
Safest in shame; being fool'd, by fool'ry thrive."[56]

There is no ambivalence about him except that he too, like Bertram, becomes wiser by experience and his self-knowledge places him above the scum to which he is reduced. He has turned from a knave to a fool — whose vocation he wants to adopt now with a conviction that "Simply the thing I am/Shall make me live". Here 'am' has a ring of affirmation.

It is well known that Shakespeare always adds a positive touch (however slight) in the characterization of his villains except in Iago. Even Edmund has his dying confession. Although, strictly speaking, Parolles does not belong to that class, his presentation is uniformly in the light of the negative vision. However, in his self knowledge and affirmation at the end there is a momentary gleam of the positive.

It was not without some such feeling that Charles I substituted "Parolles" for "All's Well" as the play's title in his copy of the Second Folio.

From the above discussion regarding the three main characters of *All's Well* it is clear that whatever appears to be baffling or incongruous in these characters or in their actions can be explained by the operation of the double vision of Shakespeare.

REFERENCES

1. *All's Well That Ends Well*, Act I, Sc I, *ll* 38-42.
2. Ibid., Act I, Sc I, *ll* 47-49.
3. Ibid., line 50.
4. Ibid., *ll* 78-83.
5. Ibid., *ll* 100-102.
6. Ibid., *ll* 216-225.
7. E.M.W. Tillyard, *Shakespeare's Problem Plays* (Chatto and Windus, London 1950, Penguin Books, 1965) p. 102.

8. *All's Well*, Act I, Sc. III, *ll* 184-86.
9. Ibid., *ll* 199-201.
10. E.M.W. Tillyard, *Shakespeare's Problem Plays*, p. 102.
11. All's Well, Act II, Sc. I, *ll* 135-140.
12. Ibid., *ll*. 147-153.
13. Ibid., Act II Sc III, *11*.1-6.
14. Ibid., *ll*, 30-38. 14(a) Ibid, 1 104.
15. Ibid., Act II, Sc V, *ll*. 79-82.
16. Ibid., *ll*. 85-86.
17. E.M.W. Tillyard, *Shakespeare's Problem Plays*, p. 92.
18. *All's Well*, Act III, Sc II, *ll* 102-122.
19. Ibid., Act III, Sc IV, *ll* 4-17.
20. E.M.W. Tillyard, *Shakespeare's Problem Plays*, p. 107.
21. Ibid., p. 107.
22. *All's Well*, Act III, Sc VII, *ll*. 14-17.
23. G.K. Hunter, *Introduction to the Arden Edition of All's Well*. (Methuen and Co., London, 1962) p. xxxi.
24. Arden Edition of *All's Well*, p. xlix.
25. *All's Well*, Act III, Sc V, *ll* 96-100.
26. Ibid., Act III Sc VII, *li* 17-20.
27. Ibid., *ll* 28-29.
28. Ibid., *ll* 30-36.
29. Ibid., *ll*. 43-47.
30. Ibid., Act IV, Sc IV, *ll* 10-14.
31. Ibid., *ll*, 30-36.
32. Ibid., Act IV, Sc V, *ll* 8-10.
33. Ibid., Act V, Sc III, *ll* 15-19.
34. Ibid., *l* 37.
35. E.M.W. Tillyard, *Shakespeare's Problem Plays*, pp. 112-113.
36. G. K. Hunter, *Introduction to the Arden Edition of All's Well*, p. x/ v.
37. *All's Well*, Act II, Sc I, *ll*. 27-29.
38. Ibid., *ll* 49-55.
39. Ibid., Act, II, Sc III *ll* 106-111
40. Ibid., *l*. 145.
41. Ibid., *l*. 115-116.
42. E.M.W. Tillyard, *Shakespeare's Problem Plays*, p. 97.
43. *All's Well*, Act III, Sc II, *ll*. 26-30.

44. E.M.W. Tillyard, *Shakespeare's Problem Plays*, p. 110.
45. *All's Well* Act III, Sc. II, *ll*. 26-30
46. Ibid., Act III, Sc IV, *ll*. 25-26.
47. Ibid., Act IV, Sc III, *ll* 18-20
48. Ibid., Act III, Sc V, *ll*. 5-7.
49. Ibid., *ll* 11-20.
50. G.K. Hunter, *Introduction to the Arden Edition of All's Well*, p. xxvii.
51. *All's Well*, Act I, Sc I, *ll* 98-100.
52. G.K. Hunter, *Introduction* to *All's Well* (Arden), p. xlvii.
53. *All's Well*, Act I, Sc I, *ll* 151-158.
54. Ibid., Act II, Sc III, *ll* 200-207.
55. Ibid., Act V, Sc II, 41.
56. Ibid., Act IV, Sc III, *ll*. 319-327.

CHAPTER IV

The Angel With Horns

Measure for measure is the other 'problem' play which has been subjected to the charge that it shows a split in the middle so far as the poetic imagination is concerned. We shall leave this controversy to be resolved at the end. To begin with, we shall try to establish that it is the most effective comedy in its own genre and a problem play of the most provoking and stimulating kind.

The extreme effectiveness of this play can be accounted for by a sustained interplay of Shakespeare's double vision which manifests itself in a manner which unites in the most heightened form all the subsidiary themes knit together appearance and reality, justice and mercy, body and spirit, life and death and even heaven and hell. To these polarities may be added those of virtue and vice, forgiveness and revenge, Providence or divine order and disorder, folk-lore and realism and finally, that of 'surface design' and the 'deeper evaluations' which come home to us from the totality of the play. The play is so complex and the pattern of antitheses so tightly knit that with every 'point' we encounter a 'counterpoint' almost simultaneously. It is particularly in this instant counterpointing in *Measure for Measure* that the role of the dramatist's double vision is more vital and significant than in any other play. That there is any resolution at the end - partial or complete - is again made difficult by the half lights and shadows for ever 'teasing us out of thought' in the texture of this play.

There is more to it than meets the eye on the surface. As seen in almost all the plays of Shakespeare, there is something Janus-like in his genius which reveals to us more than one side of a question alternately or at the same time and there always seems to be a layer of meaning below the surface and sometimes yet another layer. As for characters, there is often a process of unmasking as the real self of the character is revealed to us. Conversely, there is a process of growing up with self-knowledge and the revelation of his own self to the character. Both these processes are seen in the problem plays and hence the characters and their actions naturally lead to uncertain and divided responses in the audience or the reader. The total effect is one of inconsistencies and paradoxes which make the play baffling in its effect. Ernest Schanzer suggests this quality in Shakespeare's art by saying that he is 'alternately engaging and alienating our feelings' on moral issues 'in such a manner that we are unsure of our moral bearings', so that there are 'uncertain and divided responses to it in the minds of the audience'. J.W. Lever speaks of the consequent effect in this play :

"*Measure for Measure* is made up contrasts, and antinomies juxtaposed and resolved, and the process is incorporated in its dramatic form. The characters evince too many human inconsistencies, the themes too many contradictory aspects.."[1]

Coleridge found *Measure for Measure* 'profoundly disturbing' partly because of this quality. W.W. Lawrence perceived the result in psychological incongruity : "Shakespeare's art oscillates between extreme psychological subtlety and an equally extreme disregard for psychological truth."[2]

No attempt however, has been made to trace these disparities and contradictions to their very origin in the dramatic vision of Shakespeare. Once this process is apprehended, they become quite plausible and fall in their place as aspects of very complex characters and situations which, as an integral part of Shakespeare's comprehensive imagination, are dramatically projected, as they could only be, in the light of his double vision.

So we can embark on this exploration by taking into account how it comes about from the very beginning of the play.

As the play opens we find the stage set for the complete delegation of the power of the duke to Angelo to rule and administer justice in Vienna in his absence. He has 'lent him [his] terror and drest him with [his] love.' As the Duke later says to Friar Thomas, it was because

"We have strict statutes and most biting laws,
The needful bits and curbs to headstrong jades,
Which for this fourteen years we have let slip;...
For terror, not to use, in time the rod
Becomes more mock'd than fear'd : so our decrees;
Dead to infliction, to themselves are dead,
And Liberty plucks Justice by the nose,
The baby beats the nurse, and quite athwart
Goes all decorum."[3]

The intention is not limited to the enforcing of these dormant laws; it is also to see "If power change purpose, what our seemers be."[4]

His eye is equally on this ethical problem as to how power can affect a man, which is the first problem posed in what becomes a sequence. What is relevant is to note that both the intentions of the duke become the starting point and everything ensues from them. A 'providential' plan which critics have noticed from the Third Act onwards, is already there from the beginning.

The Duke's original purpose was not only to restore moral health to the state by enforcing order and justice through his deputy, but also to establish a norm of virtue and goodness and both are accomplished by his choice of Angelo. As he says to Escalus in the disguise of a friar,

"...there is so great a fever on goodness, that the dissolution of it must cure it;"[5]

The point of 'dissolution' apart from the seething immorality of the underworld of Vienna, is more sharply in the change in Angelo from a saint-like figure to a bargainer for lust. It is also the unmasking of virtuous hypocrisy to bring out lurking vice in a fair exterior which was as much a symptom of moral decay as liberty turned to licence:

"O what may man within him hide,
Though angel on the outward side ! "[6]

So both plans are seen to be one and are so pursued. As Wilson Knight says : "As the play progresses and his plot on Angelo works he assumes an ever-increasing mysterious dignity, his original purpose seems to become more and more profound in human insight, the action marches with measured pace to its appointed and logical end."[7]

But had the working out of this double intention of the Duke been the sole preoccupation of the play, it would not be a problem play in the sense we are intending to discuss it - intriguing and baffling in the doubleness of its moral implications, particularly with reference to certain situations and actions of the characters. Once the designs of the Duke set the plot in motion, these chameleon moral shades start moving out from each situation and action like ripples from a stone thrown in still water. These constitute the most fascinating aspect of the play giving rise to 'uncertain and divided responses', contrasts and antinomies.

Not that the unmasking of Angelo is in itself not a powerful illustration of the play's preoccupation with the duality in human nature—of the Jekyll-and-Hyde strains or the Apollonian and the Dionysian elements which were existing in a precarious balance in him. But the response to the unfolding (with an ironical point in the Duke's words to him "to the observer doth thy history/Fully unfold") is unequivocal. The angel was after all, no better than a beast, and certainly worse, for all his hypocrisy, than the one whom he condemns. But no one is morally intrigued at this. It is in what accompanies this process of exposure that reveals the subtler shades capable of diverse interpretations.

The central theme, in terms of events apart from the abstract polarities, is the unmasking of the seemer -Angelo. Allied to it is the 'chastity' of Isabella and the 'adultery' committed by Claudio. The 'immoral' underworld of Vienna represented by Lucio, Pompey and Mistress Overdone is the background which is indirectly but organically connected with these three characters and what they do. It is to remedy the licence of this world that the Duke has appointed Angelo as his duputy and it is as a part of it that Claudio has acted 'immorally' and we can even conjecture that Isabella's decision to enter a convent was in a way inspired by the degeneration and corruption around her. This is the apparent situation. The Duke has intended to purge the evil through Angelo and wants to observe the way he does it including any possible change in him.

Had the play been preoccupied with this ethical purpose alone, going so far as to punish Angelo for committing the same offence for which he had sentenced Claudio, it would have been entirely second-rate, unworthy of Shakespeare. We know that Shakespeare never wrote a play with an exclusively ethical purpose. What we actually have is a play with multiple suggestions of facets of characters and varied significances of the same actions which seem to create intriguing ambiguities regarding these characters and actions.We begin to develop a feeling that the dramatist implies much more than a simple categorization of Vice and Virtue till we are unsure of our own moral reactions. What emerges is an ambivalence so that the same character or action can be looked upon as ethically right or wrong. This is the most fascinating quality of Shakespeare's dramatic art in his problem plays and it leaves the 'problems' almost insoluble. This can be traced, as we have already attempted to show, to the working of Shakespeare's double vision.

Ernest Schanzer puts this quality of a problem play mainly as a moral problem which involves a choice creating uncertain response in the audience or the reader:

"In watching a problem play our predominant state of mind during at least part of the action is one of our moral bearings...What seems needed as well in a problem play is a concern with a central moral problem which will inevitably take the form of an act of choice confronting the protagonist, and in relation to which we are in doubt of our moral bearings."[8]

He goes on to provide the definition of a Shakespearean problem play in the light of this ambivalent quality:

"A play in which we find a concern with a moral problem which is central it, presented in such a manner that we are unsure of our moral bearings, so that uncertain and divided responses to it in the minds of the audience are possible and even probable."[9]

It is a split of a different kind which Tillyard means when he applies the term 'schizophrenic' to *Measure for Measure* and *All's Well* as problem plays which are 'genuinely abnormal'. If we apply it as organic artistic unity to the characters, we find the double strain in each of them even though they don't reveal schizophrenia in the psychological sense. That accounts for the change in behaviour—of these characters in action--from one stage of the drama to another and also for the simultaneous presence of antithetical traits which make for a complexity which W.W Lawrence traced to a combination of "extreme psychological subtlety and an equally extreme disregard of psychological truth."[10]

Making it clear how it is the ambivalent quality of the characters and their actions which accounts for the problematic nature of the play, we can proceed to illustrate it and probe deeper for other factors which combined with character and action, lead to divided responses. As already suggested, all the above characteristics emerge due to the operation of Shakespeare's double vision.

We have already said that it is the central theme of Angelo's unmasking which brings in the associated actions and reactions of Claudio and Isabella involving some of the representative characters of the underworld of Vienna while the Duke who has set the main plot in motion, actively participates in disguise conditioning their actions. So Claudio on whom Angelo's `measure' first operates can first be considered.

As he speaks of the sentence of death to Lucio, he seems to view his sin in a wider context :

"From too much liberty, my Lucio, Liberty,
As surfeit, is the father of much fast;
So every scope by the immoderate use,
Turns to restraint. Our natures do pursue,
Like rats that ravin down their proper bane,
A thirsty evil; and when we drink, we die.[11]

Here is an objective view of moral trespass leading to one of the most characteristic images of the operation of evil on human nature. The instinctive, almost animal responses of Claudio (which appear later with greater effect) can be seen in the 'rat' image and in the implicit absence of reason driving the victim to self-annihilation. There is something Dionysian in Claudio and shows a natural drift to tragedy which would be his fate in spite of his animal-like struggle to escape but for the interference of the Duke.

But just afterwards he contradicts that he has sinned and asserts that it was a true marriage contract but for a formal announcement. Perhaps to remove all suggestion of sin, he omits any mention of the need of a church ceremony:

"Thus stands it with me: upon a true contract

I got possession of Julietta's bed.
You know the lady; she is fast my wife,
Save that we do the denunciation lack
Of outward order. This we came not to
Only for propagation of a dowe'r
Remaining in the coffer of her friends,..."[12]

Moral licence had already dispensed with the need of church ceremony. The further suggestion which Claudio gives to Lucio, shows that he does not rule out the possibility that his sister Isabella can "make friends/To the strict deputy "saying that" in her youth/There is a prone and speechless dialect/Such as move men, "[13] which shows that he expects her physical charm to soften Angelo.

Thus we find a double strain in Claudio. One part of him knows that he has sinned and deserves punishment even under "the drowsy and neglected act, "[14] while the other asserts the propriety of his act and wants to escape at any cost.

L.C. Knights, discussing the presentation of Claudio expresses his belief that "it is the slight uncertainty of lattitude in Shakespeare's handling of him that explains some part, at least, of this play's disturbing effect."[15] He finds the source of this uncertainty in "feelings at war with themselves " in the poet, the result of a temporary 'emotional bias' that seems to blur some of the natural positive values which in *Macbeth* and *Lear* are vividly realized as the vision of evil.

To this, Schanzer says "It seems to me that the contradictions in Claudio's attitude towards the actions for which he has been sentenced are not, as L.C. Knights has suggested, the result of 'feelings' at war with themselves' in the poet, but rather spring from Shakespeare's exploitation, for his own purposes, of contradictions interent in the church's edicts relating to the marriage contract".[16] As Schanzer further suggests, one of the set purposes of the dramatist was to underline Angelo's "adherence to the letter rather than the spirit of the law, which is one of the main concerns of the play. "[17] It is an ironical comment that Claudio who had dropped the form in his relationship with Juliet is being tried by a man who has dropped the spirit for the strict form of the law.

There are in fact two great temptation scenes in the play—one is the famous scene of the temptation of Angelo, while the other is the less noticed temptation scene which shows Claudio tempted by life—by the desire to live, prompted both by the love of life and the fear of death. It is generally viewed in the relationship of Isabella's firm resolve to live in chastity and the ignominious desire of Claudio to buy his life out of his sister's shame of which the only proper reaction seems to be Isabella's outburst of her brother's denunciation. However, there is no other scene in the play which creates such uncertain and divided responses in the minds of the audience and where Shakespeare's double vision is so much at work. Being so simple in suggestion and response, it is difficult to see why it should evoke mixed reactions. To understand it we must delve fairly deep into Shakespeare's sources and also understand Shakespeare's artistic manner—the way the dramatist went to work when such contrary points of view had to be presented.

The entire problem is differently presented in George Whetstone's play "Promos and Cassandra", Shakespeare's nearest dramatic source. Promos who is appointed to rule over the city of Julio, reviews a defunct law and sentences Andrugio to death for immorality of the same dubious kind as that of Claudio. Andrugio's sister, Cassandra, weeps over the hard fate of her brother who appeals to her to plead with Promos. She meets Promos and obtains a postponement of the execution. Meanwhile, Promos like Angelo, develops an infatuation for Cassandra and on a second meeting, makes his infamous proposal which amazes and horrifies her as in the case of Isabella. Even though Promos promises to make her his wife, she refuses and goes to her brother's cell to inform him of Promos' vile condition and to prepare him for death. Andrugio, surprised that a judge of Promos, integrity had been corrupted by the same lust for which he would condemn another, appeals to his sister to accept his terms and thereby save his life. They argue and finally Cassandra consents.

After seducing her, Promos breaks his promise and orders Andrugio's execution. As in Shakespeare's play a substituted head is brought to affirm the death and the judge is exposed to the king who orders the marriage of Promos with Cassandra and his subsequent execution. The turning up of the brother ensures forgiveness for Promos and all ends well.

It is a story of a sister's love for her brother and as the price of his life she sacrifices her honour — a plausible situation which is the same in other works which could be cited as Shakespeare's sources such as Cinthio's *Hecatommithi* and *Epitia* which are in the form of prose fiction. Shakespeare has sharply diverged from his sources in this respect with the resulting ambivalences and divided responses whereas there are none in Whetstone or Cinthio. It is of the same moment as the change in the Hamlet story when he made Ophelia an altogether different girl from her original. The results of this change were so far-reaching as to affect the entire structure of *Measure* for *Measure*.

But before we consider these effects, we may see how Claudio himself ambivalently reacts to the situation. Even here Shakespeare has prepared for a very complex reaction instead of the simple natural desire of a youngman to live as in Whetston's or Cinthio's story.

Contrary to depicting a simple situation, Shakespeare prepares for a complex one which reveals more than one facet of each character and prepares for equally two-faced action. Its importance can be guaged from the fact that it is placed in the third act which is seminal in determining the trends of the upshot. It begins with the Duke, in the disguise of a friar, preaching to Claudio to be prepared for death, stressing the futility and meaninglessness of life in imagery which, at many points, resembles that of Hamlet's musing in his famous soliloquy on death :

> "Be absolute for death : either death or life
> Shall thereby be the sweeter
> ...Thy best so rest is sleep;
> And that thou oft provok'st, yet gorssly fear'st
> Thy death, which is no more. Thou art not thyself;
> For thou exists on many a thousand grains
> That issue out of dust...
> ...Thou hast nor youth, nor age,
> But as it were an after-dinner's sleep
> Dreaming on both;..What's yet in this
> That bears the name of life? Yet in this life

Lie hid moe thousand deaths; yet death we fear
That makes these odds all even."[18]

Being presented with such a prospect of death-in-life even if he lives, Claudio appears reconciled to death:

"I humbly thank you.
To sue to live, I find I seek to die,
And seeking death, find life. Let it come on."[19]

It is like Hamlet's " let be". It seems to be final acceptance. Just then Isabella enters and while the Duke overhears, she informs Claudio of Angelo's condition. It is to be noted that she does it gradually withholding the main point and at each step, while suggesting it obliquely, she sharpens Claudio's sense of honour:

"O, I do fear thee, Claudio, and I quake
Lest thou a feverous life shouldst entertain,
And six or seven winters more respect
Than a perpetual honour..."[20]

It evokes the necessary response. Claudio is prepared to die and positive imagery is used which leaves no doubt about its being a final choice:

"If I must die,
I will encounter darkness as a bride
And hug it in mine arms."[21]

And when Isabella puts the stark fact that it is her virginity that Angelo wants as a price, Claudio categorically says, " O heavens, it cannot be!"[22]

However, some mysterious process is going on while Isabella yet reiterates her resolve to sacrifice her life except her chastity and perhaps the sudden instrinct that nature can be so strong in an unfeeling man like Angelo as to risk damnation of his soul, which makes him revert to a clutching back at life in the face of the imminent darkness of death. It is not moral cowardice but a sudden Dionysian urge which Nietzsche calls one's being lost " in the vast onward Dionysian sweep of life " which makes him utter the words:

"Sweet sister, let me live.
What sin you do to save a brother's life,
Nature dispenses wiith the deed so far
That it becomes a virtue."[23]

We find nowhere a better instance of Shakespeare's double vision which makes a character see the same predicament at the same time from two different angles in such a way that the audience is immediately 'taken in' by each point of view, so that when Isabella's denunciation follows, its sympathies are divided and even a moral consideration on one side does not sway the balance. It is not that Shakespeare has endowed Claudio with greater human feeling than Isabella. It is because the dramatist himself is more deeply involved with what Claudio says. The earlier speech expressing the fear of death is a clear proof of this involvement and put in his mouth as if to justify what he says later so that the words seem to be a logical outcome:

"Ay, but to die, and go we know not where ;
To lie in cold obstruction, and to rot ;
This sensible warm motion to become
A kneaded clod; and the delighted spirit
To bathe in fiery floods, or to reside
In thrilling region of thick-ribbed ice;
To be imprison'd in the viewless winds
And blown with restless violence round about
The pendent world : or to be worse than worst
Of those that lawless and incertain thought
Imagine howling, - 'tis too horrible!"[24]

It is also a fine example of Shakespeare's negative capability-of recreating the 'present' experience of the man waiting for imminent execution as if he were himself in the condemned place. The imagery has an immediacy which drives each of the states with its sensation in space deep into the consciousness of the reader. Curiously enough, the entire condemnatory speech of Isabella which follows, does not contain a single authenticating image and does not have that effect on the audience or the reader.

This is what makes this scene so memorable, apart from the fact that it marks the climactic point in the poetry of the play and nothing what is said or done (in terms of character or action) later seems to have that 'poetical' validity. Much that is thematically significant follows ; but it does not add to our poetic awareness. It is clear that in what Claudio says for either of his 'choices' the double vision of Shakespeare is deeply engaged.

Taking this scene to be a representative example of interaction of characters and their revelation, Walter Pater says : "But the main interest in *Measure for Measure* is not, as in *Promos and Cassandra*, in the relation of Isabella and Angelo, but rather in the relation of Claudio and Isabella."[25]

He adds: "...the skill with which Isabella plays upon Claudio's well-recognized sense of honour, and endeavours by means of that to insure him beforehand from the acceptance of life on baser terms, indicates no coming laxity of hand... It was rather that there rose in Shakespeare's conception...something of that terrror the seeking for which is one of the notes of romanticism...The stream of ardent natural affection, poured as sudden hatred upon the youth condemned to die, adds an additional note of expression to the horror of the prison... From behind this group with its subtle lights and shades, its poetry, its impressive contrasts, Shakespeare conveys to us a strong sense of the tyranny of nature and circumstance over human action... Called upon suddenly to encounter his fate, looking with keen and resolute profile straight before him, he gives utterance to some of the central truths of human feeling, the sincere, concentrated expression of the recoiling flesh. Thoughts as profound and poetical as Hamlet's arise in him...the most eloquent of all Shakespeare's words... "[26]

In Claudio's case, it is in his two attitudes towards death, that the double vision—we could call it the positive and negative vision—of Shakespeare can be seen focussing them. Just allied to these is the double vision in relation to Isabella, focussed on her single action—that of dismissing Claudio's entreaty to save his life by surrendering her virtue. This act is even more critically discussed with wide divergences among critics. There is no more intriguing aspect of the play and none over which, in the whole canon of Shakespeare's works, are critics and readers more at divergence. Hence it is a more baffling instance of the operation of double vision which makes the same act appear in a different light when seen through different angles. It has the effect like that of shot-silk and fits exactly into Schanzer's definition of a problem play eliciting uncertain and divided reponses from the audience and the readers.

Before referring to the opinions of critics, let us take a view of the exact situation. When Claudio, quite overcome by his love of life and fear of death solicits Isabella, "Sweet sister, let me live", offering a view of sin and virtue with which she cannot agree, the reaction on Isabella is sudden and there is a hysterical outburst of condemnation which, apart from her desire to preserve her chastity, shows a ferocity much greater than warranted by her cause. It is clearly inspired by her puritanical revulsion from the kind of man who wants to live at the cost of her virtue and treats the very suggestion as an injury which has to be paid back. Her virtue seems to have suffered by the foulness of this thought on the part of her brother as Hamlet's body seemed to him to have become contaminated by the sin of his mother (we have to remember that the two plays, written with little interval, are so allied in thought and feeling that the drift of one seems to run into the other). This alone can explain the vehemence of Isabella's reaction.

This act of Isabella, of cruelly refusing a charitable act, even at the cost of her virtue for a greater (or smaller ?) cause of saving the life of her brother, has defied the judgment of readers and critics to 'place' it ethically. She has denied charity —a christian virtue—to save a human being which was incumbent on her. She has denied mercy herself while a little before she had argued in such powerful terms to Angelo to show it. She has given way to anger — a vice. She has even cast an aspersion on her mother. On the other side, having been on the point of entering a convent she was in a frame of mind severely hostile to corruption and meanness and it can even be conjectured that her decision was prompted by the excessive moral corruption—the fever on goodness—as the duke puts it—which she saw around her and from which she wanted to escape. And now like a lurking snake it was just beside her in the form of her own brother. Her surprised and shocked reaction is the same as of one who has seen a snake up one's sleeve.

But when all is said, her intolerance is indefencible. In face of sin and evil a true Christian, whether of the religious order or a layman, is always patient and tolerant. But the very point begets another defence for Isabella—she was but a novice and a would-be initiate who had already shown too much earnestness in demanding "a more strict restraint/ upon the sisterhood."[27]

The ambivalence of Isabella's act recalls the ambivalence of Antigone's act of stealthily burying her brother in Sophocles' play of the same name and courting death for it. Antigone, in an almost similar situation, had shown supreme sacrifice for her 'dead' brother and there is no doubt what she would have done to save a 'living' one in the situation of Isabella.

Sophocles' play is the archetype of all problem plays. Antigone's action and her notion of love is pitched against Creon's determination to keep duty to the state above any personal consideration. There are two sides of the question and as the Chorus says, much can be said on both sides. The moral dilemma is simply insoluble and clashes of love and duty have always proved to be so. Critics are still divided on the point whether Creon or Antigone was right. In fact both were right and underneath the very theory of tragedy (which Hegel formulated) lies this conflict of wills. But the other element which was introduced by Sophocles for the first time in tragic drama — that of love — is beyond doubt a basic positive value and would justify sacrifice of anything in any situation. And Antigone is first in the line of all such sacrificers for love. "I cannot share in hatred, but in love."[28]

But with all the opposition of the two ethical values, there is no ambivalence in *Antigone* and no uncertain or divided response with reference to the same act. It is because Sophocles' vision was fixed on a single, sharp, burning zone of human action with an intensity and absoluteness which did not permit an alternative angle of vision whereas Shakespeare, by the very nature of his artistic mode, often directed a double vision towards the same character or the same act without appreciably diminishing the intensity at least in the tragedies. Obviously, *Measure for Measure* being a comedy (however 'dark'), there was no question of maintaining a pitch of intensity in the two-fold point of view.

Now let us adduce opinions of critics who have been led by the two modes in which Shakespeare has envisioned the act of Isabella, either to justify her or to disapprove of her 'choice'.

Ernest Schanzer puts the problem of ambivalence in Isabella's act as follows:

"I am maintaining that throughout the play Shakespeare is ...manipulating our feelings towards Isabel by alternately engaging and alienation our affection for her, and that he is doing all this mainly to make us question her decision to sacrifice her brother rather than her virginity. He makes us question it without forcing an answer upon us. The majority of critics have, in fact, felt that Isabel could have acted in no other way than she did. R.W. Chambers, who must speak for all these, declares that "whether she remains in the Convent or no, one who is contemplating such a life can no more be expected to sell herself into mortal sin than a good soldier can be expected to sell a stronghold entrusted to him." (By taking it for granted that it would be a moral sin, Chambers begs the question. Hence analogy with the soldier is a false one.) There have been others —a miniority among critics, but much more numerous...among... Shakespeare's readers— who have thought that Cinthio's Epitia and Whestone's Cassandra made the more admirable choice. The manner in which Shakespeare manipulates his material, as the evidence of his other plays, suggest to me very strongly that he, too, preferred Cassandra's choice.. By depicting first the inhumanity of Angelo's legalism by numerous parallels between Isabel's and Angelo's characters, and then showing Isabel's legalistic view of Divine Justice, Shakespeare is... strongly suggesting his own attitude towards her choice. But he leaves it sufficiently unobtrusive to allow the audience to respond to it in an uncertain, divided or varied manner."[29]

Schanzer finds this play and its characters and actions the most characteristic ones fitting into his concept of a Shakespearean problem play:

"*Measure for Measure* is thus seen to conform to the definition of a Problem Play.... We have found in it " a concern with a moral problem which is central to it, presented in such a manner that we are unsure of our moral bearings, so that uncertain and divided responses to it in the minds of the audience are possible or even probable."

R.W. Chambers, to whom Schanzer already refers, devoted an entire lecture to the vindication of the point of view of Isabella. He implies that Isabella's sense of purity was

Christian to the core: "Christianity could never have lived through its first three hundred years of persecution, if its ranks had not been stiffened by men and women who never hesitated in the choice between righteousness and the ties to their kinsfolk. We may call this fanaticism : but it was well understood in Shakespeare's day .... Now it is open to us to say that we are not Christians: it is open to us to say that Isabel is un-Christian..I am amazed at the way critics condemn Claudio, when he breaks down...And I am even more amazed at the dislike which the critics feel for the tortured Isabel... Claudio is asking for what she cannot give, and she bursts out in agony."[30]

Regarding the idea of any deliberate design on the part of Shakespeare to create moral ambivalences in the minds of the audience by this encounter of brother and sister, R.W. Chambers quotes the words of Kittredge with reference to Shakespeare's art: "However much the dramatis personae mystify each other, the audience is never to be perplexed."[31]

So it could also be said of Sophocles that when he wrote *Antigone* he didn't intend to leave his audience in any doubt as to who was right. And the dramatist's own sympathy was clear enough. Creon was punished for his "stubborn will", while Antigone's sacrifice is emphatically brought out and evokes sympathy:

"On every side I hear voice of pity
For this poor girl, doomed to the cruellest death,
And most unjust, that ever woman suffered
For an honourable action - burying a brother..."[32]

To justify her forbidden action for her brother, Antigone says:

"O but I would not have done the forbidden thing
For any husband or for any son...
But, father and mother lost, where would I get
Another brother ?"[33]

This raises Antigone in the esteem of the reader and the dramatist's attitude is unequivocal. Yet *Antigone* is a problem play because Creon's case for duty to the state has been so presented as to create a feeling of validity for his point of view.

Similarly, Claudio's case has been presented evoking sympathy for his point of view but Isabella's seems to demand equal consideration. What is more, Shakespeare's double vision is at play not only as *between* the two points of view pitching one against the other, but as between two *angles of vision* as regards the same object, action or person. Claudio's wish to live at the expense of his sister's honour, by itself, seems to be right or wrong and Isabella's decision "More than our brother is our chastity" seems to be equally so. It is what we can call a two-fold operation of positive and negative vision on the same character and action giving rise to uncertain and divided responses. Hence what Kittredge states can be better modified to suit the problem plays by saying that even if the dramatis personae don't mystify each other—and normally what they say is unequivocal—the audience is perplexed by the divergence between the apparent and implicit meaning.

For a different manner of handling two sides of a problem we can go back a little and take up the famous argument between Angelo and Isabella on the respective claims of justice and mercy. Here the oppositions are neatly balanced and there is no ambivalence in character or action either of Angelo or Isabella. The action of Angelo in condemning Claudio is consistent with his idea of Justice and expresses his character with its apparent austerity which, however, has a quality of 'seeming' but does not, for the time being detract from the soundness of his arguments. Isabella's arguments for Mercy are consistent with her religious bent of mind and since there is no strain of 'seeming', her conviction is greater and has the force of human as well as divine love. In this opposition of the secular and the spiritual, the austerity of Angelo proves to be skin-deep and it is in the bringing out of the two strains in his nature—the seeming austere and the repressed sensual — that the double vision of the dramatist is at work.

In this case of the opposition between Angelo's 'seeming' fairness as a judge and his repressed sensuality, the same operation of the double vision of the dramatist is perceptible. It is a double picture of the man which emerges from the whole encounter which is continued in two interviews—that of an angel and a beast—and it is part of the plot to expose him till a measure for measure is meted out. It is in other words, a double image of Angelo which the two fold vision focuses on the minds of the audience creating a 'divided problematic response.' As Schanzer puts it:

"The image which these presentations suggest is not the web woven of "a mingled yarn, good and ill together", but rather the toy which the Elizabethans called a 'perspective', presenting two quite different pictures, according to our angle of vision."[34]

Since this two-fold image of Angelo is at the heart of the play, we can proceed to analyze how it is projected in the great temptation scene of the play which is also the scene of the great debate between the claims of Justice and Mercy.

It is noteworthy that a subtle hint of Angelo's susceptibility is seen in his response to the information of the servant that 'the sister of the man condemned' wanted to see him. His repressed nature instinctively brings out the query "Hath he a sister"? and the Provost's words "a very virtuous maid / And to be shortly of a sisterhood"[35] introduce a subconscious appeal which develops during the subsequent dialogue to the point when he says in his soliloquy "O cunning enemy, that, to catch a saint, / with saints dost bait thy hook!"[36]

Here lay Angelo's fallibility—in his artificially imposed rigour upon himself which made the Duke say

"Lord Angelo is precise
Stands at a guard with Envy; scarce confesses
That his blood flows....,"[37]

and which made him think of himself "a saint".

The two aspects—the hard ascetically made up man of reason and the lurking, repressed sensualist—the Jekyll and the Hyde—were already present in his nature when the Duke made him his deputy. What Nietzsche calls the Apollonian and Dionysian elements existed, in a balance which could be upset only by an encounter with a woman who was truly more Apollonian than himself and by whose impact his Apollonian mask would come off. Naturally, the other part would be released—the seeming angel betrayed by the devil's horns into his true identity.

We can see the role of the dramatist's double vision till the culmination of this process.

Whatever Angelo says in strict defence of the law is unanswerable on the level of its secular operation. His defence of the law is comparable to Creon's in *Antigone* and shares his conviction. When Angelo says,

"Condemn the fault, and not the actor of it?
Why, every fault's condemn'd ere it be done:
Mine were the very cipher of a function
To fine the faults, whose fine stands in record,
And let go by the actor,"[38]

He speaks as much out of pure conviction as does Creon:

"To transgress
Or twist the law to one's own pleasure, presume
To order where one should obey, is sinful,
And I will have none of it.
He whom the State appoints must be obeyed."[39]

Isabella almost gives up, prepared to go but Lucio's encouragement warms her suddenly carrying her entirely to a spiritual pitch to which she is lifted partly by her love for her brother but more by her religious zeal which provides her the analogy of sin and redemption by Divine Grace. Angelo finds no effective argument to counter in support of a purely secular act and his moral force being progressively weakened by his subconscious susceptibility to Isabella's virtue, the negative vision starts operating. It is seen in his laconic argument which is explicated by the single image of a prophet's glass:

"The law hath not been, dead though it hath slept:
Those many had not dar'd to do that evil
If the first that did th' edict infringe
Had answer'd for his deed. Now 'tis awake,
Takes note of what is done, and like a prophet
Looks in a glass that shows what future evils,
Either new, or by remissness new conceiv'd,
And so in progress to be hatch'd and born,
Are now to have no successive degrees,
But ere they live, to end."[41]

The effect is of multiplication and not enlargement or a new awareness. It is not backed by the positive vision which alone can lend a spatial dimension. Envisioning future evils if an act is left unpunished, it makes no appeal to the imagination. More than anything, the evils in the abstract are not backed by a concrete word and the process of being "conceived", "hatched and born" is not visualized by anything concrete.

On the other hand, Shakespeare's positive vision endows Isabella's plea for Mercy with all the concrete richness of Biblical imagery, the source to which this virtue could be naturally linked. And it makes his imagination glow with a white incandescent heat which can be felt as a tangible presence in Isabella's words:

"Alas, alas!
Why, all the souls that were, were forfeit once,
And he that might the vantage best have took
Found out the remedy. How would you be
If he, which is the top of judgment, should
But judge you as you are? O, think on that,
And mercy then will breathe within your lips,
Like man new made."[41]

The imagery spans the process of redemption and spiritual transformation by using the concrete image of breathing on two levels. To borrow the interpretation from J.W. Lever: "As Adam was given a soul when the Creator breathed life into his nostrils, so the new Adam is redeemed from first Adam's sin by the breath of divine mercy in Christ, which moves on his lips when he speaks mercifully to his fellow men."[42] Thus the idea of breath, of sin and of mercy is communicated on two levels reinforcing the present idea of sin and mercy in the immediate context, thereby suggesting that Angelo's act showing mercy to Claudio will be divine and Christ-like. This is what may be called an evolving use of imagery — the earlier connotations imparting significance to the present situation.

It is obvious that Shakespeare's creative imagination is deeply engaged on this theme of mercy. He had already put in the mouth of Portia in *The Merchant of Venice* a plea for mercy linking it with the grace of God. In the present play another idea which is implicit is that any kind of justice must go with mercy and without it, the most extreme justice may warp itself into injustice. The other argument of Isabella juxtaposing four concrete images as symbols of justice, with the abstract quality of mercy whose power of grace overweighs all these, is an example how the positive vision can knit together many objects around one idea:

"No ceremony that to great ones, longs,
Not the king's crown nor the deputed sword,
The marshal's truncheon, nor the judge's robe,
Become them with one half so good a grace
As mercy does."[43]

Roland Mushat Frye says of this :

"Such references are equally Senecan and Christian,...Thus, in connection with mercy and justice, it is well to note...a condemnation of excessively rigorous justice...it has been well said...the most extreme justice is the greatest injustice...What is uniquely Christian is the denial of man's ability to be sufficiently just to satisfy God, along with the corollary doctrine that man's only ultimate hope is in the mercy of God."[44]

Shakespeare was not a theologian but a poet and he has given this theological concept a validity through poetry. Another instance of this process where the positive vision fuses multiple images and classical with Christian connotations, is Isabella's third and most inspired speech which calls up more powerful contrasts to illustrate the hybris of the authority—drunk man, reminding of the Duke's apprehension: "If power change purpose...."

"Could great men thunder
As Jove himself does, Jove would ne'er be quite,
For every pelting petty officer
Would use his heaven for thunder; nothing but thunder.
Merciful Heaven,
Thou rather with thy sharp and sulphurous bolt
Splits the unwedgeable and gnarled oak,
Than the soft myrtle. But man, proud man,
Dress'd in a little brief authority,
Most ignorant of what he's most assur'd-
His glassy essence - like an angry ape
Plays such fantastic tricks before high heaven
As makes the angels weep; who, with our spleens,
Would all themselves laugh mortal."[45]

The contrast betwen "pelting" and "bolt", between "myrtle" and "oak" and between "ape" and "angels", lends its force to the contrast between "proud man" and "Merciful Heaven"—all adhering around "authority"—brief like man's and eternal like Jove's. The man misusing it can learn its proper use from God but he cannot do it because while he possesses his "little brief authority" he remains ignorant of his "glassy essence"—his spiritual entity or his soul—which is an image of God and like a glass, mirrors God. At the same time "glassy" also implies brittleness, transience, a short-lived brilliance and the idea of mere appearance as against reality—all applicable to man's brief authority.

Here, in contrast to Angelo's static image of a prophet looking into his glass, we find the same with multiple connotations which converge, like spokes of a wheel to the central idea of God.

As already remarked earlier, there is no ambivalence in character or action in this encounter between Angelo and Isabella which, in two stages, completes the process of unmasking of Angelo. The double vision has been at work in Angelo's vindication of his own version of Justice while a powerful positive vision irradiates Isabella's pleas for mercy with an increasing intensity.

REFERENCES

1. *Measure for Measure*, ed. by J.W. Lever (Arden Edition, 1965) Introduction, p. lix.
2. W.W. Lawrence, *Shakespeare's Problem Comedies* (Frederick Ungar Publishing Co., New York, 1931) P. 118.
3. *Measure for Measure*, Act I, SC III, *ll.* 19-31.
4. Ibid., *1*. 54.
5. Ibid., Act III, Sc II *ll.* 216-17.
6. Ibid., Act III, Sc II *ll.* 264-5.
7. G. Wilson Knight, *The Wheel of Fire* (Methuen and Co., London, 1930) p. 79.
8. Ernest Schanzer, *The Problem Plays of Shakespeare* (Routledge and Kegan Paul, London, 1963) p. 6.
9. Ibid., p. 6.

10. W.W. Lawrence, *Shakespeare's Problem Comedies*, p. 118.
11. *Measure for Measure*, Act I, Sc. II *ll.* 117-120.
12. Ibid., *ll.* 134-140.
13. Ibid., Act I, Sc II, *ll.* 170-171.
14. Ibid., *l.* 159.
15. Ernest Schanzer, *The Problem Plays of Shakespeare* (quoted) p. 126.
16. Ibid., p. 126.
17. Ibid., p. 126.
18. *Measure for Measure*, Act III, Sc I *ll.* 5-41.
19. Ibid., *ll.* 41-43.
20. Ibid., *ll.* 73-76.
21. Ibid., *ll.* 82-84.
22. Ibid., *l.* 98.
23. Ibid., *ll.* 132-35.
24. Ibid., *ll.* 116-127.
25. Walter Pater, *Appreciations*, quoted in Signet Classic Edition (New American Library, 1960), p. 152.
26. Ibid., p. 153.
27. Ibid., Act I, Sc IV, *ll.* 4-5.
28. Sophocles, Antigone, translaed by E.F. Watling (Penguin Classic, 1947) p. 140.
29. Ernest Schanzer, *The Problem Plays of Shakespeare*, pp. 104-5.
30. R.W. Chambers, *Man's Unconquerable Mind* (Jonathan Cope, London, 1939) p. 287.
31. Ibid., p. 150.
32. *Antigone*, trans. E.F. Watling (Penguin Classics) p. 226.
33. Ibid., p. 150.
34. Ernest Schanzer, *The Problem Plays of Shakespeare*, p. 226.
35. *Measure for Measure*, Act II, Sc II, *ll.* 19-22.
36. Ibid., *ll.* 180-81.
37. Ibid., Act I, Sc III, *ll.* 50-52.
38. Ibid., Act II, Sc II *ll.* 37-41.
39. *Antigone*, trans. E.F. Watling (Penguin Classics) p. 144.

40. *Measure for Measure*, Act II, Sc II, *ll*. 91-98.
41. Ibid., *ll* 74-79.
42. J.W. Lever, Introduction to Measure for Measure (Arden Edition 1965) p. xlvii.
43. *Measure for Measure*, Act II, Sc II, *ll*. 59-64.
44. Roland Mushat Frye, *Shakespeare and Christian Doctrine*, (Princeton University Press, 1963) pp. 206-7.
45. *Measure for Measure*, Act II, Sc. II, *ll*. 111-124.

CHAPTER V

The Fragments of Faith

Troilus and Cressida is a play which has defied a clear understanding not merely as regards the content but primarily as regards the form. It is the one play which, to this day, remains a puzzle for those who want to place it in a category with well-defined groups. The editors of the Folio placed it between the Histories and the Tragedies implying perhaps that it belonged to the intermediate ground between history and tragedy while it was neither. Later, it was classed with the comedies and grouped with what are called 'the dark comedies'. But it does not have any of the essential qualities of a comedy — a happy ending, romantic atmosphere and a concept of the hero, heroine or the fool—which should be integrated into the spirit of comedy. On the other hand, it tends to be anti-romantic (that is why liked by Shaw) and there is a bitter spirit of cynicism, disillusionment and disgust pervading the play. For the first time we find Shakespeare as an iconoclast and determined to demolish the 'heroism' of the inflated Homeric figures. It is certainly not a history play because the entire action rests on the Greek myth of the Trojan war and it was not history even to Aeschylus, Sophocles or Euripides when they wrote plays mostly based on this myth. That was their strength because it provided them an unexploited field to give a shape to their tragic visions. It is intriguing therefore, that Shakespeare who was a dramatist of equal, if not greater capabilities, should have made such a hybrid play while working on a part of the same material when he could have written a tragedy like *Agamemnon, Electra, Philoctetes, Hecuba* or *The Trojan Women*? Was his genius not up to writing a genuine tragedy when he went to this rich repository of classical myth? He who could even make a silk purse out of a sow's ear, could certainly have done that. Then why did he waste so much artistic energy in writing a "still-born" play (as we could call it atleast with reference to its stage history) which remained one of the least acted and the least popular plays of his canon till the twentieth century? The question is unanswerable particularly when we consider that Shakespeare's imagination was heavily charged with the Greek myth and references to it are so abundant from *Titus Andronicus* onwards through *Henry VI* (a play very rich in close parallels in imagery which can be traced to Aeschylus) to *Hamlet*. One who could envision the player "with tears in his eyes, distraction in his aspect" could certainly write a great tragedy on the Trojan War.

The explanation must lie in Shakespeare's frame of mind when he took up the myth or part of it for dramatic treatment. To arrive at a clear understanding of this connection between the dramatist's attitude to life and his works, we would do well to take a view of what the following two critics have said about the group of plays called the Dark Comedies to which *Troilus and Cressida* belongs. What they say is particularly applicable to this play.

Dowden, writing on these plays as early as 1875 and dividing Shakespeare's career into four well-marked phases, puts these 'comedies' in the third phase—"In the Depths" — and noting their utter difference from the early light and jovial comedies, accounts for it by saying that by this time Shakespeare had ceased to be able to smile genially, and had either to be ironical or else to take a deep, passionate, tragical view of life. Boas, writing in 1896, stresses 'abnormal conditions of brain and emotion' in these plays which give rise to 'intricate cases of conscience'. This, coupled with what Dowden says, is enough to account for the fact that Shakespeare, while treating this tragic material, could not make a tragedy out of it. Due to whatever circumstances, his view of life became too ironical as it is apparent in Hamlet whose tone is ironical to a great extent. This tendency, in this play which almost immediately followed it, becomes the very stuff of his thoughts and it is not possible to make a tragedy only out of an ironical or a satirical attitude. But Dowden also hints that Shakespeare had developed a deep, passionate, tragical view of life and so each of these plays, particularly

Troilus and Cressida is imbued in the tragic spirit. Now an authentic tragedy can be written only when the tragic spirit can be forged into an organic form by an essemplastic power which synthesizes the multilateral apprehensions into a single unity which makes them merge into a single burning zone around the protagonist. As Boas suggests, there was some split or even an abnormal condition of brain and emotion due to some emotional crisis in Shakespeare's personal life. Although this theory has since been exploded by critics like C.J. Sisson, in 'The Mythical Sorrows of Shakespeare', the presence of a split can not be denied which might have been incidental to Shakespeare's middle age. Hence the synthesis which is necessary even in a tragedy which presents more than one point of view (such as *Antigone*) could not be effected. We find, now and again, dramatic inspiration kindled almost to white heat and then petering out into musty uncertainty till the end is as cold and casual as the beginning.

It does appear that Shakespeare's creative imagination was not so deeply engaged in *Troilus and Cressida* as to effect a unity of aesthetic impression. That is why Troilus cannot be called a protagonist. As Steiner says, "It is the triumph of rationalism and secular metaphysics which marks the point of no return."[1] What he implies is that whenever rationalism and a metaphysical point of view which adopts secular considerations as its basis begin to dominate, tragedy declines. He levels this charges not against Shakespeare whom he considers to be in line with Sophocles and Euripides but against the dramatists attempting to write tragedies after the seventeenth century. But *Troilus and Cressida* is the only play of Shakespeare which presents a predominance of the rationalistic and metaphysical element which-at least on the Greek side-manifests itself in a greater importance to intellect, policy and secular evaluations. The Trojan side is seen to be equally liable to false reasoning and illusory values.

Interpenetrating all these is a bitter, almost cynical spirit of anti-romanticism and iconoclasm. Naturally, the tragic spirit not only declines but becomes anti-climactic till instead of pity and terror we feel nauseated with revulsion and disgust. All are 'anti-heroes' except Hector at whose death we do not experience tragic catharsis because the effect is one of revulsion and the dramatist does not make any attempt to present it 'tragically'.

Since three great tragedies of Shakespeare were to be written shortly after, we cannot assume that he was devoid of the dramatic genius to write a great tragedy out of the Homeric material. It was because the play was not organically conceived and the positive and negative visions were more engaged in 'aspects' of the dramatic situation than with the situation as a whole. These aspects were so far enlarged by a rationalistic, intellectual treatment that a point when tragic denouement could have been reached was crossed and the divergent themes were not integrated by the dramatic vision. A point of no return was reached and at the end Shakespeare seems to have left it at that, winding up the heterogeneous elements as well as possible. The two themes seem to proceed almost parallel to each other and the positive and the negative visions—powerful to the last—illuminate this split and the disintegrated state of things. Naturally, there was never a play in which there were more uncertain and divided responses on the part of the audience and the reader.

Let us examine the role of the double vision with reference to the characters and their actions in the light of our conclusions.

It is a remarkable characteristic of the play that right from the beginning, a 'metaphysical' quality which we have not noticed in the earlier plays of Shakespeare, begins to appear in the thought and the images and an intellectual element which generally suffuses metaphysical imagery (as for instance of the metaphysical poets) begins to manifest itself. The working of dramatic vision can be seen more and more in the nature of the imagery.

Hardly fourteen lines are spoken when the food imagery—one of the dominating images in the play—makes it appearance. Its use to illustrate spiritual effects, particularly of love, is a metaphysical quality which identifies the most disparate objects. Its use for physical appetite is invariably in the light of the negative vision.

The imagery of grinding of wheat followed by bolting, leavening, kneading, baking and cooling sets the figurative tone of the nature of Troilus' passion. The metaphysical conceits exhibit an intellectual element and a strain which shows a comparative lack of spontaneity. This is evident in the affectation in the images by which Troilus expresses his love for Cressida. They lack the urgency of driving passion:

"...when my heart,
As wedged with a sigh, would rive in twain",[2]
and one that looks like a school boy's conceit:
"I have, as when the sun doth light a storm,
Buried this sigh in the wrinkle of a smile."[3]

The sun lighting a storm and its light being 'buried' by it being likened to a smile burying a sigh in its wrinkle is far-fetched association not properly integrated. It doesn't serve to validate the emotion and argues for an immaturity in Troilus which seems to be the dramatist's purpose at this stage. It is clearly the negative vision exposing the present shallowness of the emotion.

The following speech of Troilus shows again a play on opposites-'all whites are ink', 'spirit of sense/Hard as the palm of ploughman'.[4] The latter image could have been cited as an example of a metaphysical simile. They don't validate and the positive vision does not come into play.

But the soliloquy of Troilus uttered after Pandarus' departure shows suddenly a more mature view because it is objective and a subsequent use in the same speech of elemental images. Troilus sees in an intuitive flash the illusion under which Helen has put the Trojans as well as the Greeks:

"Fools on both sides, Helen must needs be fair,
When with your blood you daily paint her thus.
I cannot fight upon this argument;
It is too starv'd a subject for my sword."[5]

The image in the second line is intrinsic to the sense which multiplies in significance. The food image in the fourth line is equally integrated into the under-meaning. Hence, in a flash, the immature vision of Troilus becomes positive. It is because an objective view of the "issue" of the war raises him above his own immature state. Thus as we see during the play, the character of Troilus is presented alternately in the positive or the negative vision. Sometimes indeed the two visions operate so closely that, as we shall see, the same act or speech can be interpreted in two different ways-positive and negative—giving an impression of ambivalence leading to divided responses. Every tragedy is a kind of 'schooling' of the tragic hero which illustrates the saying of Aeschylus in *Agamemnon*, "Man shall learn wisdom by affliction school'd".[6] Even though Troilus is not presented as a tragic hero in the same sense as Hamlet or Antony, we find that he had some title to be called the protagonist. It is partly implied in the title and the play presents his vicissitudes in love. And even though the focus of the play changes too often and the play fails to become a genuine tragedy, we find that Troilus is schooled by suffering and becomes wiser in the crucible of suffering. This process is also presented and intensified by the two visionary modes.

Troilus' next appearance is the crucial council scene in which Priam and his sons debate whether to deliver Helen to the Greeks and end the war or to keep her at the possible cost of destruction to them all. If "choice" is at the heart of tragedy, here is the critical scene of the play because with the choice to keep Helen once made, the fortunes of the Trojans decline steeply. And although the choice is collective, it was Troilus who had intervened to prevent Hector's proposal from being accepted. Hence it was his choice and if Shakespeare had developed the theme presenting the consequences of this with Troilus as the central figure, the play would have been a tragedy like *Antony and Cleopatra* or *Hamlet* - plays with which it has great affinity. But as we shall see, this great scene shifts the emphasis to the respective claims of honour and reason and the basic question of 'value' ending on a wrong decision. In tragedy, again, the responsibility for the choice and its consequences is fixed on a single character, the protagonist. Here, by the yielding of Hector to the arguments of Troilus and Paris, they all, including Priam, become responsible for not using their judgment in favour of reason in spite of the repeated warnings of Cassandra. So the tragic catastrophe descends on all of them. Troilus' choice then, does not play a part vital enough to make the play a tragedy. But as Tillyard says, "The irony of Troilus arguing that value rests in the valuer and not in the thing valued is terrible when we apply his argument to his own fate at the hands of Cressida".[7] And this is his personal tragedy.

However, the divided emphasis on the two points of view does show how the two visions interact. The Trojan council scene is a typical example. It can be treated as the crisis of the play because the subsequent course of the war and the fate of all the Trojans leading to the final burning of Troy hinges upon the slight turning of the scales between the two opposite notions of 'value'. One is the chivalric but fallacious evaluation of Helen which in the context of the anti-romantic tone of the play, is clearly in the light of the negative vision. The other is the rational and realistic view putting forth a proper evaluation in the light of the positive vision. We shall consider them in the order they are put forth till the one superimposes itself on the other. It is remarkable that Hector, who is the true embodiment of all chivalric values, puts forth the rationalistic view:

"Let Helen go.
Since the first sword was drawn about this question,
Every tithe soul, 'mongst many thousand dismes,
Hath been as dear as Helen;
I mean, of ours.
If we have lost so many tenths of ours To guard a thing not ours nor worth to us,
Had it our name, the value of one ten,
What merit's in that reason which denies
The yielding of her up?[8]

This is no other but an evaluation of the destructive role of Helen which, in spite of the prevailing romantic notion of Helen's beauty, is ultimately more plausible against the background of the flames which engulfed Troy. S.L. Bethell remarks of this: "The Helen whose face had launched a thousand Marlovian ships, is subjected to a remorseless Shakespearean "debunking" — the inadequate object of so much misplaced idealism".[9] As Cassandra prophesies:

"Let us pay betimes
A moiety of that mass of moan to come.
Cry, Troyans, Cry! Practice your eyes with tears!....

Cry, Troyans, Cry! A Helen and a woe!
Cry, cry! Troy burns, or else let Helen go".[10]

Here Shakespeare is more in line with the Greek dramatists — particularly Aeschylus and Euripides — who did not aggrandise Helen and on the other hand, referred to her as an agent of destruction. Aeschylus compares her to a lion-cub which the Trojans, by a false evaluation, had reared thinking it to be harmless:

"Troy! thou hast fed and freed to roam
A lion-cub within thy home!
A god sent pest invincible,
A minister of fate and hell".[11]

Euripides goes to the extent of implying that what the Trojans had falsely valued at such a cost was actually Helen's shadow and not the real Helen.

So Hector's conclusion appears as the sanest statement in the whole play:

"Tis mad idolatry
To make the service greater than the god;
And the will dotes that is attributive
To what infectiously itself affects,...."[12]

This is juxtaposed with the illusory romantic view upheld by Troilus who, as we have seen, helps to make the choice of keeping Helen.

"Why, she is a pearl
Whose price hath launched above a thousand ships
And turnd crown'd kings to merchants........"[13]

As D.A. Traversi says, "The Trojans follow a false idealism, which deceives itself with talk of 'honour', but is really based on 'blood' and ends in a pathetic and helpless realization of its own insufficiency;"[14]

Hector's yielding to the plea for honour made by Troilus and Paris, is a kind of apostasy of conviction and what was worse, a conscious acquiescence in what was bound to bring bloodshed and suffering to all. Therefore, his death is a logical consequence of 'his' choice and its cruelty can be accounted for as a kind of nemesis. His change of opinion fails to convince particularly when it is abruptly followed by a consciousness of doing wrong.

"Thus to persist
In doing wrong extenuates not wrong,
But makes it much more heavy, Hector's opinion
Is this in way of truth. Yet ne'ertheless,
My spritely brethren, I propend to you
In resolution to keep Helen still;
For, tis a cause that hath no mean dependence
Upon our joint and several dignities."[15]

Troilus' own change of conviction is less glaring. As against his earlier refusal to fight for Helen who was painted 'fair' only by blood, he now calls her a pearl and 'a theme of honour and renown'. Besides being in keeping with the other and more powerful illusion about Cressida, it makes his own suffering worse when he is shorn of his idealism. Thus Troilus' fallacious evaluation of Helen as well as of Cressida, combines his personal tragedy with that of the Trojans as a whole and provides the play a unity of theme.

It is obvious that while Hector's earlier argument to return Helen in order to prevent death and suffering, was in the light of the positive vision, his sudden catapulting and Troilus' illusory valuation are in the light of the negative vision. The one had revealed Helen as an object of ruin from one angle and the other had shown her as a priceless symbol of honour.

The Greek council reveals an equally dubious approach to truth. It is clear that in spite of the brilliant rhetorical quality of Ulysses' speech, the dramatist's genius is not deeply engaged in the argument. It is devoid of the intensity of feeling which we find in Hamlet's speech on man infused with the same kind of rhetoric. While the dramtist's interest seems to enliven the rational arguments of Hector, we feel an aridness about Ulysses rationality. As D.A. Traversi puts it: "the Greeks elaborate endlessly on 'judgment' that is out of touch with the instinctive sources of action."[16] On an over-all view, we find that the Greeks are throughout presented with an iconoclasm which can only be consistent with a negative vision. It is also ironical that whatever Ulysses says about 'degree' is altogether ignored by the Greek heroes like Achilles' and Ajax right till the end. Even the high-flown speech is ultimately succeeded by a plot to prick Achilles' vanity. It is remarkable how devoid of imagination the speech is and it moves only by a linear progression:

"Degree being vizarded,
Th' unworthiest shows as fairly in the mask.
The heavens themselves, the planets, and this centre.
Observe degree, priority, and place,
Insisture, course, proportion, season, form,
Office, and custom, in all line of order.
And therefore is the glorious planet Sol
In noble eminence enthroned and spher'd
Amidst the other; whose med'cinable eye
Corrects the influillnce of evilplanets,
And posts, like the commandment of a king,
Sans check, to good and bad. But when the planets
In evil mixture to disorder wander,
What plagues, and what portents, what mutiny,
What raging of the sea, shaking of earth,
Commotion in the winds! Frights, changes, horrors,
Divert and crack, rend and deracinate
The unity and married calm of states
Quite from their fixture?"[17]

We can compare this picture of the violence of the elements with that of King Lear's outburst on the heath where the dramatist's interest is deeply engaged, and we shall see that it is the negative vision which projects the speech of Ulysses and fails to involve us emotionally in what he says.

As we have said, the positive and the negative visions alternately focus the situations and actions and the characters partake of their quality.

Our next sight of Troilus shows him deeply in love and in spite of the illusory nature of the image of Cressida which he cherishes, his emotion is authenticated by its pitch and the imagery which explicates it:

"No Pandarus. I stalk about her door
Like a strange soul upon the Stygian banks
Staying for waftage. O, be thou may Charon,
And give me swift transportance to these fields,
Where I may wallow in the lily beds
Proposed for the deserver."[18]

This is followed by an equally exalted mental state when the 'imaginary relish' and an anticipation of fulfillment are explicated through the imagery of fainting and death. It puts to mind Othello's outbrust that he would choose to die at the moment of greatest exaltation when he sees Desdemona arriving in Cyprus or Keats' wish to 'cease upon the midnight with no pain' at the pitch of joy while he hears the song of the nightingale. The positive vision makes the experience live on the timeless plane irrespective of the quality of the object of love:

"I am giddy; expectation whirls me round.
Th'imaginary relish is so sweet
That it enchnats my sense.
What will it be When that the wat'ry palate tastes indeed
Love's thrice-repured nectar? Death, I fear me;
Swooning destruction, or some joy too fine,
Too subtle, potent, tuned too sharp in sweetness
For the capacity of my ruder powers.
I fear it much; and I do fear besides
That I shall lose distinction in my joys,...."[19]

But at the same time there is an underlayer of meaning which suggests an immaturity in his feelings - they are liable to change as soon as the truth about Cressida's lack of constancy dawns upon him and creates a doubt regarding the very identity of the object of his love. We could even say that just as his earlier advocacy was for Helen's shadow (as Euripides implies in *Helen*), his present love is also for a shadow which is not the real Cressida. So a streak of negative vision operates at the same time and this creates an ambivalence which makes it possible to judge Troilus' speech from two angles at the same time. Speaking of such an effect with reference to the History Plays of Shakespeare, A.P. Rossiter says:

"I mean by 'ambivalence' that two opposed value-judgments are subsumed and that both are valid".[20]

Thus Troilus' expressions of his love can be evalued in two opposed ways as shown above and both evaluations are valid. The positive one is more obvious while the negative one is implicit and detected on a better understanding of the character and the subsequent actions.

Daniel Seltzer's comment is relevant in this context pointing to the dramatist's intention.

"The Trojan lover dotes upon his own ideal of faith as much as he dotes upon his faithless woman, and is blinded to a true perception of worth."[21] In the broader context of the play, Seltzer says, "(Shakespeare) desired to indicate a parallel between the betrayal of love that ends the former (the romantic story) and the disintegration of heroism that ends the latter (the historical story).[22] Here Seltzer suggests, the play's problem is also that the ideal cannot be made a part of reality. In fact the ideal hardly bears out the reality as it might emerge under his 'sensuous enchantment'. R.A. Foakes remarks with an eye on this contrariness: "The romantic ardours of Troilus and his pose as lover bear little relation to what he really intends to do, namely to seduce Cressida. Both the passion and the intention are real and convincing, but we are aware, as Troilus is not, of the disconnection between them....."[23]

Thus we find that the same situation, with reference to character and action, yields a double meaning and the two do not integrate. Troilus as a lover is seen from two angles and so also Cressida and the two views reveal quite opposite sides of their natures. This leads to uncertain and divided responses according as the audience sees the faithful lover or the immature, illusioned adolescent in Troilus. The same responses arise when Cressida, in what follows, can be either seen as a faithful lover or a potentially shallow, faithfless woman. There is no doubt that in Shakespeare's presentation of Cressida, the two facets of her character are more unmistakably presented.

The very first meeting of Troilus and Cressida is so skillfully presented that it reveals at every step not only the characters of the two lovers but also foreshadows what is going to follow. What is more, almost every speech seems to yield a double meaning. Obviously, the two visions — the positive and the negative — are at work almost simultaneously.

When Troilus asks her a few moments after their meeting "What too curious dreg espies my sweet lady in the fountain of our love?", she replies; "More dregs than water, if my fears have eyes".[24]

These words are capable of a double interpretation. Cressida not only feared that the course of their love could never run smooth in the uncertain time of the war, but she also doubted the very authenticity of Troilus' love. A flame kindled by idealism, might not withstand the harsh winds of reality. When Troilus says "This is the monstrosity in love, lady, that the desire is boundless and the act a slave to limit",[25] it brings out the repartee which underlines the contrast between word and deed and ironically foreshadows the contrast between her own words and her subsequent change. And all through, she seems to act on the assumption that their love has more dregs than water. When she confesses her love, she qualifies it by a return of doubt by adding:

"Perchance, my lord, I show, more craft than love,
And fell so roundly to a large confession
To angle for your thoughts."[26]

What follows seems to be an excessive bid to assert constancy. Psychologically, it shows a desire to cover up a subconscious fear of change. In no other play do we find so much extravagant assertion (in *Hamlet* Gertrude's remark "The lady doth protest too much"[27] is uttered after a lighter assertion of faith than Cressida's) on the part of lovers.

With this we can consider the reiterated assertions more critically.

What strikes us is the strained and almost rugged movement of the lines in the two speeches of Troilus. It is not the strong adolescent emotion which finds it hard to express itself fully. It is because, as Tillyard puts it, "Shakespeare was not writing in the full passion of earnestness, was not quite sunk in what he did...."[29] In other words he was not inspired as he was in *Romeo and Juliet* or even in *As you Like it*. There was a dark streak of scepticism and disillusionment which interfered with the pure lyricism of this love and he seems to overload the verse with protestations in place of images which would have essemplastically shaped the speeches. As we shall see, only the last two lines of the first speech come off spontaneously. The whole speech deserves quoting:

"O that I thought it could be in a woman —
As, if it can, I will presume in you —

To feed for aye her lamp and flames of love;
To keep her constancy in plight and youth,
Outliving beauty's outward, with a mind
That doth renew swifter than blood decays;
Or that persuasion could but thus convince me
That my integrity and truth to you
Might be affronted with the match and weight
Of such a winnowed purity in love:
How were I then uplifted! but, alas,
I am as true as truth's simplicity,
And simpler than the infancy of truth."[29]

The unspurred imagination of the dramatist is reflected in the lack of spontaneity which is made worse by a hypothetical way of expounding of 'integrity, truth and purity' of love. The words 'persuation could but thus convince me' hint at doubt and lack of conviction. We somehow feel that there could be a less affected and more powerful and 'positive' way of explicating the emotion and we never doubt that Shakespeare was capable of it if anyone ever was, but something was impeding the flow and we can only attribute it to a disillusioned and sceptical mood which permitted the negative vision to operate. Even the last two lines seem to be marred by a touch of tautology and the second of them is clearly illogical because truth does not lose simplicity if it 'grows up'.

The second speech is certainly 'truth tired with iteration' which for the benefit of other 'true swains in love' Troilus caps with numerous homely similes till he calls himself 'truth's authentic author'[30] and seems to have moved away from the immediate object of his love in his desire to serve for other's edification. This draws an appropriate remark from Cressida, "Prophet may you be!" We begin to doubt whether, as Tillyard suggests generally, Shakespeare did not have 'his tongue at least part way in his cheek' in this 'method of inflation and deflation."[31]

Cressida's response to this avowal of his love by Troilus, is in a slightly different vein. She doesn't find it hard to affirm her faith which she earnestly means for the time being. But like Cleopatra, with her vision of how she would be parodied into "some squeaking Cleopatra..../I'th' posture of a whore"[32] by some boy-actor in Rome, Cressida, more prophetically than she has given Troilus credit for, envisions her own denigration by future generations if she proves false.

However, there is some lack of authenticity in her piling up of similes instead of a plain affirmation. The rhetorical flourish is suspect. To put a genuine thing with as much adornment is not Shakespeare's usual way. It is rather Viola's "She sat like Patience on a monument, /Smiling at grief. Was not this love indeed?"[33] So short and rendered by a concrete image. There is no concrete image in the whole speech of Cressida - only time's waste and similies to illustrate but nothing to validate:

"If I be false, or swerve a hair from truth,
When time is old and hath forgot itself,
When waterdrops have worn the stones of Troy,
And blind oblivion swallow'd cities up,—
And mighty states characterless are grated
To dusty nothing,— yet let memory,
From false to false among false maids in love,
Upbraid my falsehood! When they've said, "As false
As air, as water, wind or sandy earth,
As fox to lamb, as wolf to heifer's calf,
Pard to the hind, or stepdame to her son,"—
Yea, let them say, to stick the heart of falsehood,
"As false as Cressid,"[35]

One thing is noticeable in the assertions of eternal fidelity on the part of both Troilus and Cressida. They seem to take account of some unforeseen power which might wrench them apart. The mode of avowal is almost hysteric. They are conscious of living in insecurity and the dramatist, knowing that the story must develop to Cressida's violation of faith, seems to emphasize this as the only absolute value in the relationship. But in Cressida's mental make-up some suggestion of fickleness must be left in order to make her future behaviour plausible. Jan Kott calls it self-distrust. It conditions her avowal of faith and the dramatist's negative vision infuses every word with it. Jan Kott says:

"Cressida is one of the most amazing Shakespearean characters, perhaps as amazing as Hamlet... bitter and ironic....she distrusts herself.....There is no place for love in this world."[35]

That is why, due to inner apprehension that love may not last, she caps her assertions with hyperboles and similes as Troilus also does, and it betrays a tenseness which lies at the heart of the play. In the play's world of flux, uncertainty and insecurity, no value is secure while everyone is fighting for values. This is what Tillyard means when he speaks of "the difficult and complex unease by which Troilus and Cressida is characterized."[36]

It is the negative vision throughout as it presents the lovers in this world of uncertainty, flux, distruct and apprehension. The question of doubt as regards one's very identity is but one step from it and it comes almost as a logical development as the chaos and dissolution assert themselves on both planes—external events or actions and inner consciousness of characters.

All characters and actions in the play appear morally warped and it is because the negative vision gradually becomes all-pervasive. Positive values which were so far symbolized by the Trojans are shrinking. This can be seen by a consideration of the war-plot which serves as backdrop to the love-story. Here Thersites, albeit a clown, is the dramatist's chief spokesmen, and he is only an instrument of the negative vision, illuminating what is most despicable in human nature.

R.A. Foakes remarks: "Thersites...provides a sardonic chorus... his comments accentuate the critical detachment with which the central figures are displayed."[37]

Mark Van Doren says: "The role of Thersites is to cheapen the heroes. But Achilles and his brach Patroclus are such boors, Hector is so stuffed and so stupid an orator, Agamemnon is such a mouther, Nestor......is so tiresomely prolix, and Ulysses in spite of his golden tongue is so politic a rogue, that in order to sink beneath them Thersites must bubble in eternal mire.....And no blasphemer in Shakespeare has surpassed him in brute competence."[38]

Van Doren adds, "But there is nothing for him to accomplish. The heroes have accomplished their own degradation, they have shouted themselves too hoarse and deaf to hear any wisdom out of this filthy mouth."[39]

The clown actually has the last word. The whole panorama shows him only this and from the vantage point of the negative vision it is nothing more than what he sees:

"Here is such patchery, such juggling, and such knavery. All the argument is a whore and a cuckold."[40]

He notices that "Ajax....wears his wit in his belly and his guts in his head"[41] and a great deal of Achilles' wit lies in his sinews. That with the two much- vaunted heroes. Of Agamemnon and Menelaus, the two eagles of Aeschylus, he says as if he has dissected them:

"Here's Agamemnon, an honest fellow enough, and one that loves quails, but he has not so much brain as ear-wax; and the goodly transformation of Jupiter there, his brother, the bull, the primitive statue and oblique memorial of cuckolds.....To an ass, were nothing: he is both ass and ox, To an ox, were nothing; he is both ox and ass. To be a dog, a mule, a cat, a fitchew, a toad, a lizard, an owl, a puttock, or a herring without a roe, I would not care: but to be Menelaus, I would conspire against destiny. Ask me not what I would be, if I were not Thersites; for I care not to be the louse of a lazar, so I were not Menelaus."[42]

Of Troilus and Cressida, the lovers who would have been more at home in an atmosphere like that of the early comedies or the Last Plays, Thersites says like an iconoclast who can't brook a shred of romance:

".......That same young Troyan ass that loves the whore there....;"[43]

Ulysses, Nestor and the two Greek heroes again come in for scathing criticism that has a grain of truth: "A th't'other side, the policy of those crafty swearing rascals — that stale old mouse-eaten dry cheese, Nestor, and that same dog-fox, Ulysses - is not prov'd worth a blackberry. They set me up, in policy, that mongrel cur, Ajax, against that dog of as bad a kind, Achilles; and now is the cur Ajax prouder than the cur Achilles..."[44]

This is like a roll-call of honour turned inside out by the negative vision which Shakespeare endowed Thersites with as a part of the design of the play. At least it partly shows the dramatist's own point of view as always a chorus does and Thersites has some authenticity of an all - seeing chorus. What he says towards the end just before his comments quoted above, may serve as the anti-romantic's fling at love and war — the two heroic themes—which even Shaw could not have equalled:

"Lechery, lechery! Still wars and lechery! Nothing else holds fashion. A burning devil take them![45]

T.S. Eliot's vision of the Waste land appears tame beside this. Ofall the Problem Plays, *Troilus and Cressida* is the only one where, in the general darkness, the positive vision irradiates a few limited moments on crucial occasions. It shines forth in those moments when Troilus first speaks of his love for Cressida or when Cressida first learns that she must leave. It also irradiates two or three more of their speeches on the occasion of their final leave-taking. In addition, Hector's well-judged view of Helen whose timely return would have saved Troy, is also projected in the light of the positive vision.

Apart from these flashes, we hardly find a play of the positive vision in this dark and dismal play. It seems to partake of the qualities of a tragedy except in the unity and a proper denouement. That is why the editors of the folio prefaced the tragedies with it. As it is, the play is harsh and bitter, without a like in the Shakespeare canon-one vast picture of disintegration and desolation illuminated by the negative vision. The disintegration is because of the complete collapse of values and the desolation is due to the desertion of everything good and virtuous. Even the clown has lost his humour and laughter as much as the lover his prospect of union which we find in the two other 'dark' comedies.

Of this main theme of the lovers who were the archetype before *Antigone* was written, Shakespeare does not seem to have cherished a romantic or medieval concept. It is clear in the light of the development of the theme which seems to bring a search-light to the question of identity and cast a doubt whether the object of love was the same Cressida or not. It is like finally taking off the base and let the building tumble to a debris.

The meeting of lovers at Calchas' house in Troy is immediately followed by the decision of both sides to exchange Antenor, a Trojan prisoner for Cressida whose father,

Calchas, had already gone over to the Greeks. it provides as crucial an occasion for reiteration of faith as the earlier confession of their love to each other.

This is Cressida's first reaction to the sudden compulsion to go:

"I will not, uncle. I have forgot my father;
I know no touch of consanguinity-
No kin, no love, no blood, no soul so near me
As the sweet Troilus. O you gods divine,
Make Cressida's name the very crown of falsehood
If ever she leave Troilus ! Time, force, and death,
Do to this body what extremes you can;
But the strong base and building of my love
Is as the very centre of the earth,
Drawing all things to it. I will go in and weep-"
And she adds:
"- Tear my bright hair, and scratch my praised cheeks,
Crack my clear voice with sobs, and break my heart
With sounding Troilus. I will not go from Troy."[46]

In contrast to the earlier protestation of her faith to Troilus, this speech is shot through by the positive vision,- the only occasion in the play when the dramatist presents her entirely dominated by the spirit of the moment as Troilus is when he is giddy with expectation. There is nothing hypothetical or inflated about the emotion. There is no rhetoric. The two lines "Make Cressida's name the very crown of falsehood / If ever she leave Troilus" have more effect than her earlier speech on falsehood. But the quality which makes it poetically effective is the appearance of concrete images which are missing in the former speech. "the strong base and building" coupled with the image of the "centre of the earth" give her love a firm and dynamic quality. All ideas seem to be subsidiary to it and even time, force and death cannot shake it. On the other hand, they would all be drawn by the spirit of her love irrespective of the fact of what they do to her body. The impact of the verse is a positive uplifting of her love above the secular and temporal plane.

All this has a full validity with reference to the moment when it is spoken. However, it is the central irony of the play that once she is forced to leave, as she was determined not to, she undergoes an unaccountable change. Even this does not invalidate the positive emotion of the moment.

Regarding the subsequent change in Cressida, it is an act which is uniformly taken to be morally reprehensible and Cressida, in myth and tradition, became a prototype of infidelity in love. It is presented in the light of the negative vision and Shakespeare as usual in such cases, presents it as an instance of the divergence between appearance and reality.

But some critics diverge from this view, not inclined to put all the blame on Cressida. Even so, the negative character of her transformation cannot be denied. Before making this assessment, let us consider the gradual progression of the situation as revealed by the text.

Cressida's grief at the prospect of parting from Troilus is longer-drawn than would be supposed by those who judge her by her subsequent change. What is more striking is that its expression is sensuously rendered. This is the quality which Keats picked up from Shakespeare and it is a perfect example of what could connect the master with the far-removed younger poet. The grief of Cressida is rendered in terms of taste (as seen in Keats' *Ode on Melancholy*):

> Why tell you me of moderation?
> The grief is fine, full, perfect, that I taste,
> And violenteth in a sense as strong
> As that which causeth it. How can I moderate it?
> If I could temporize with my affections,
> Or brew it to a weak and colder palate
> The like allayment could I give my grief.
> My love admits no qualifying dross;
> No more my grief, in such a precious loss."[47]

The above speech could stand as a fine poem in its own right, on the futility of moderation. It is written almost at the peak of Shakespeare's power as a poet and no charge of diminution of poetic power can be made. As remarked before, it is true that he was not completely sunk in the theme all the time as at the present moment he was. And there is no doubt that it is the positive vision of the dramatist which is projecting this grief. The second line anticipates the best of Keats.

Troilus' avowal of his love is in a more conventional vein but there are no hyperboles or conditional epithets as before:

"Cressid, I love thee in so strain'd a purity,
That the blest gods, as angry with my fancy,
More bright in zeal than the devotion which
Cold lips blow to their deities, take thee from me."[48]

The speech which follows expresses the intense emotion of a final leave-taking. It is now Troilus' unstrained and natural intensity which expresses itself with the same sensuous ease which distinguished Cressida's 'immoderate' grief. Such poetic outbursts of both Troilus and Cressida are marvels of lyricism suffused with the radiance of the positive vision.

"And suddenly, where injury of chance
Puts back leave-taking, justles roughly by
All time of pause, rudely beguiles our lips
Of all rejoindure, forcibly prevents
Our locked embrasures, strangles our dear vows
Even in the birth of our own labouring breath.
We two, that with so many thousand sighs
Did buy each other, must poorly sell ourselves
With the rude brevity and discharge of one.
Injurious time now with a robber's haste
Crams his rich thievery up, he knows not how;
As many farewells as be stars in heaven,
With distinct breath and consigned kisses to them,
He fumbles up into a loose adieu,
And scants us with a single famish'd kiss,
Distasted with the salt of broken tears"[49]

Such unimpeded lyricism alongwith the superb quality of the lyrical speeches of Cressida and Troilus quoted earlier, argues against the hypothesis that in *Troilus and Cressida* Shakespeare's imagination was not fully engaged; that the dramatist was not quite sunk in the theme or with the same material as Homer and Aeschylus wrote on, Shakespeare, who was a master dramatist of as much genius, could not have written a play like *Agamemnon*. However, the contention still holds because it was Shakespeare's poetic genius which was touched to the same fine frenzy as in *Romeo and*

Juliet or the *sonnets* and equals the great comedies and tragedies in lyrical quality, but his dramatic genius was not stirred to an equal degree. And we only find passages of exquisite beauty which are radiant with the positive affirmatory vision of the dramatist. For a specimen, we may put a sonnet embodying a somewhat identical emotion beside the leave-taking speech of Troilus quoted above:

"If the dull substance of my flesh were thought,
Injurious distance should not stop my way;
For then, despite of space, I would be brought
From limits far remote, where thou dost stay.
No matter then, although my foot did stand
Upon the farthest earth remov'd from thee,
For nimble thought can jump both sea and land
As soon as think the place where he would be.
But ah! thought kills me that I am not thought,
To leap large lengths of miles when thou art gone,
But that, so much of earth and water wrought,
I must attend time's leisure with my moan,
Receiving nought by elements so slow
But heavy tears, badges of either's woe.[50]

Irrespective of the fact that the sonnets were addressed to 'my lovely boy', the emotion at the prospect of separation of the loved person is common to both and beside the sonnet, the address of Troilus reads compactly like another sonnet except that it is sixteen lines and not bound in the three quatrains - and - couplet form. But the progression of the emotion is overwhelming and the last two lines clinch the entire content by juxtaposing the 'simple famished kiss' against and as the equivalent of 'locked embrasures', 'many thousand sighs' and 'as many farewells as be stars in heaven'. It is a miracle of spontaneous emotional progression. We can only wonder how such gems could be embedded in what is a saga of passion run awry by some unaccounted bitterness and disillusionment which created a Thersites to counterblast all romanticism.

The conclusion is inescapable that counterpointing is one of the unmistakable techniques of Shakespeare's Problem Plays — a quality common to the three plays we have been considering. And as a counterpointing to the affirmations of love and eternal fidelity on the part of the lovers, comes the final scene of this love — episode which reveals Cressida "as false as air, as water, wind or sandy earth" and corrodes Troilus' heart so much that to him "all untruths" seem glorious by her strained name, and challenges identity itself.

Clearly the negative vision of the dramatist is at work projecting a Cressida who would be a by-word for faithlessness and also to evolve a version of this affair which would conform both to his attitude to love and to the well-known tale versified from Homer to Chaucer. Helen was one paradigm of this who emerges as anything but "a theme of honour and renown"[51] and Cressida another for whom, as it appears in retrospect, Troilus was waiting on the Stygian banks to have his soul wafted to the abysm of despair. But before we see that there are two sides (a counterpointing within a counterpointing as is Shakespeare's way) to the question even here, we may view the progression to the final stage as it comes to be.

It is said that Cressida begins to change as soon as she enters the Greek camp; that she allows herself to be kissed by one and all. But it was the suggestion of Ulysses when she was welcomed by Agamemnon with a kiss on behalf of the Greeks, that "T'were better she were kissed in general".[52] It was inexplicable unless it was intended as a way to initiate her to a completely different way of life and make her break from the Trojans, final. There seems to be an implicit intention to put her as a Trojan woman to this vulgar treatment in the light of what had been done to Helen. There is a suggestion of this when Menelaus offers to kiss and Cressida refuses. But whether naturally or as a matter of policy, Cressida had begun to appear liberal enough to warrant the remark of Ulysses:

> "There's language in her eye, her cheek, her lip;
> Nay, her foot speaks; her wanton spirits look out
> At every joint and motive of her body."[53]

It is but a short way from this to the complete transformation as it is observed by Troilus, when Cressida appears completely different from what he thought she was. Again we have to tread this ground with caution lest we take one point of view to be final. Intending this to be the most crucial scene of the love-plot, Shakespeare has shown it from three different points of view thereby implying that none of them is fully valid and that there might be a fourth point of view as well—that of the dramatist. All these would elicit different responses on the part of the audience. So before we consider the implications of all these viewpoints, let us see the actual progress of the action.

As Troilus and Ulysses approach Calchas' tent, Thersites follows them. The former two watch together but from different points of view; the standpoint of Thersites--the sardonic-cynical—is already a staple of the play.

All three watch the responses of Cressida to the approaches of Diomedes. Though Diomedes can at the most extract a promise to meet later, the fact that Cressida gives him Troilus' sleeve betokens the truth that Dimoedes has supplanted Troilus in her affections or would do so very shortly. It is finally clear in Cressida's speech that she has abandoned the memory of Troilus' love and has proved false in such an ironical contrast to her former protestations that Troilus feels his very cognition challenged. A very complex question of identity ensues and it also reveals the limits of reality the human mind can bear. Cressida's words tear aside the veil of idealism which at this point dissolves like a mist

"Troilus, farewell! One eye yet looks on thee,
But with my heart the other eye doth see.
Ah, poor our sex! this fault in us I find,
The error of our eye directs our mind.
What error leads must err. O, then conclude,
Minds sway'd by eyes are full of turpitude."[54]

Troilus is almost stunned with the shock of disillusionment. When Ulysses sensing his reaction, says, "All's done my lord", he only says, "It is". Then he gives vent to the fiercest sense of disgust which resembles that of Hamlet, but expresses itself, unlike Hamlet's moral outbursts, in terms of appearance and reality. Discrediting all "attest of eyes and ears", he says,

"Was Cressid here?"[56]

It is like Lear's, "Are you our daughters?" The very question of identity on which all recognitions of act are based, is raised by a mind under assault by an unbearable sense of reality. It is a recoil of an idealist's mind questioning the validity of his own senses and of his subjective perceptions, ultimately concluding that the subject "is, and is not".

"This she? No, this is Diomed's Cressida.
If beauty have a soul, this is not she;
If souls guide vows, if vows be sanctimonies,
If sanctimony be the gods' delight,
If there be rule in unity itself,
This was not she. O madness of discourse,
That cause sets up with and against itself!
Bifold authority! where reason can revolt
Without perdition, and loss assume all reason
Without revolt. this is, and is not, Cressid.
Within my soul there doth conduce a fight
Of this strange nature that a thing insperate
Divides more wider than the sky and earth;
And yet the spacious breadth of this division
Admits no orifex for a point as subtle
As Ariachne's broken woof to enter.
Instance, O instance! strong as Pluto's gates;
Cressid is mine, tied with the bonds of heaven.
Instance, O instance! strong as heaven itself;
The bonds of heaven are slipped, dissolved, and loos'd,
And with another knot, five-finger-tied,
The fractions of her faith, orts of her love,
The fragments, scraps, the bits, and greasy relics
Of her o'ereaten faith, are given to Diomed."[56]

This is the most comprehensive expression of disillusionment which makes the play unique in the Shakespeare canon. Of a state when faith in virtue has completely crumbled, leading to a state like nihilism, we find an instance in Othello's frame of mind when overcome by doubt. A state of mind when rooted faith is suddenly snapped or 'deracinated' (a seminal word in *Troilus and Cressida*) leading to a loss of basic identities and revealing the mental upheaval in which a contrary belief seeks to be implanted, can be seen in his outburst to Iago:

"By the world,

I think my wife be honest, and think she is not;
I think that thou art just, and think thou art not.
I'll have some proof. Her name, that was as fresh
As Dian's visage, is now begrim'd and black
As mine own face."[58]

Troilus' state of mind shows a similar upheaval in which uprooted faith almost reverses the tide of consciousness creating a loss of the basis of identity. If the virtue by which he knew Cressida is gone, the recognition of Cressida is gone too. The Cressida without virtue is another Cressida as Desdemona without virtue was another Desdemona and Othello in all earnestness murdered this 'other' one. Similarly, Troilus is faced at the same time with the old Cressida and the 'other' one and cannot decide who of these is the 'real' Cressida.

Shakespeare's imagination was here concerned not so much with the 'pity' of it as it was in *Othello* where it was backed by the tremendous dramatic irony that Desdemona was really chaste when Othello apparently thought her to be otherwise. On the other hand, it is concerned here with the irony in the contrast between appearance and reality in an opposite situation — that Cressida who appeared to be chaste is now proved to be otherwise. As Troilus says, 'instance, strong as heaven itself[58] was there to prove that Cressida was true and now those same bonds are 'slipped, dissolved, and loosed' revealing that her faith 'a thing inseparate/Divides more wider than the sky and earth'.[59] A chasm has opened before his consciousness obliterating almost all established values. The food imagery which follows envisions the transformation of virtue into mere appetite and the disintegration of that unbreakable unity to pieces, 'relics' which, like scraps of food soiled by greasy lust, are now given to Diomed.

In this picture of a chasm in belief resulting from a complete collapse of faith and disintegration of old established values, Shakespeare has come nearest to anticipating the twentieth century consciousness, which is just a point to be noted in passing. As for the question of its relevance in the dramatic context, we find that it presents the 'inverted', anti-romantic conclusion of the love-plot, which, as indicated by the title, is the play's central theme. Hence it is likely that Shakespeare has implied, as usual in his art, more than one layer of meaning.

REFERENCES

1. George Steiner, *The Death of Tragedy* (Faber and Faber, London, 1963) p. 192.
2. *Troilus and Cressida*, Act I, Sc I, *ll.* 36-37.
3. Ibid., *ll.* 39-40.
4. Ibid., *ll.* 58 and 60-61.
5. Ibid., *ll.* 94-97.
6. Aeschylus, *Agamemnon*, translated by E.D.A. Morshead, *Seven Famous Greek Plays* ed. by Oates and O'Neill Jr. (Random House, New York, 1950) p. 55.
7. E.M.W. Tillyard, *Shakespeare's Problem Plays* (Chatto and Windus, London, 1950) p. 71.
8. *Troilus and Cresida* Act II, Sc II, *ll.* 17-25.
9. S. L. Bethell, *Shakespeare and The Popular Dramatic Tradition* (Staples Press, London, 1944) from extract in the Signet Classic edition, p. 233.
10. *Troilus and Cressida* Act II, Sc II, *ll.* 106-12.
11. Aeschylus, *Agamemnon*, trans. E.D.A. Morshead, *Seven Famous Greek Plays* (Random House, New York, 1950) p. 75-76.
12. *Troilus and Cressida* Act II, Sc II, *ll.* 56-59.
13. Ibid., *ll.* 81-84.
14. D.A. Traversi, *An Approach to Shakespeare* (Doubleday and Company, New York, 1956) from extract in Signet Classic Shakespeare, 1963) pp. 226-27.
15. *Troilus and Cressida* Act II, Sc II, *ll.* 186-93.
16. D.A. Traversi, *An Approach to Shakespeare* from extract in Signet Classic Shakespeare, 1963) p. 227.
17. *Troilus and Cressida* Act I, Sc III, *ll.* 83-101
18. Ibid., Act III, Sc II, *ll.* 7-12.
19. Ibid., *ll.* 16-26.
20. A.P. Rossiter, *Angel with Horns and other Shakespeare Lectures*, ed. Graham Story (New York, 1961) p. 51.
21. Daniel Seltzer, *Introduction to Troilus and Cressida* (Signet Classic Shakespeare, The New American Library, 1963) p. XXXVIII.

22. Ibid., p. XXXIX.
23. R.A. Foakes, *Shakespeare, The Dark Comedies to the Last Plays* (Routledge and Kegan Paul, London, 1971) p. 52.
24. *Troilus and Cressida* Act III, Sc II, *ll.* 66-69.
25. Ibid., *ll.* 82-85.
26. Ibid., *ll.* 154-56.
27. *Hamlet*, Act III, Sc II, *1.* 224.
28. E.M.W. Tillyard, *Shakespeare's Problem Plays*, p. 58.
29. Troilus and Cressida Act III, Sc II, *ll.* 159-172.
30. Ibid., *l.* 182.
31. E.M.W. Tillyard, *Shakespeare's Problem Plays*, p. 58.
32. *Antony and Cleopatra*, Act V, Sc II, *ll.* 218-19.
33. *Twelfth Night*, Act II, Sc IV, *ll.* 113-14.
34. *Troilus and Cressida*, Act III, Sc II, *ll.* 185-97.
35. Jan Kott, *Shakespeare Our Contemporary* (Methuen and Co., London, 1965) p. 65.
36. E.M.W. Tillyard, *Shakespeare's Problem Plays*, p. 51.
37. R.A. Foakes, *Shakespeare, The Dark Comedies to the Last Plays*, p. 54.
38. Mark Van Doren, *Shakespeare* (George Allen and Unwin, London, 1941) p. 207.
39. Ibid., p. 208.
40. *Troilus and Cressida* Act II, Sc III, *ll.* 68-70.
41. Ibid., Act II, Sc I, *ll.* 76-77.
42. Ibid., Act V, Sc I, *ll.* 52-67.
43. Ibid., Act V, Sc IV, *l.* 6.
44. Ibid., Act V, Sc IV, *ll.* 9-15.
45. Ibid., Act V, Sc II, *ll.* 192-4.
46. Ibid., Act IV, Sc II, *ll.* 98-111.
47. Ibid., Act IV, Sc IV, *ll.* 1-10.
48. Ibid., *ll.* 24-27.
49. Ibid., *ll.* 33-48.
50. Sonnet 44.
51. Ibid., Act II, Sc II, *1.* 199.
52. Ibid., Act IV, Sc V, *1.* 21.
53. Ibid., *ll.* 55-57.
54. Ibid., Act V, Sc II, *ll.* 105-109.
55. Ibid., *1.* 121.
56. Ibid., *ll.* 134-157.
57. *Othello*, Act III, Sc III, *ll.* 387.
58. *Troilus and Cressida* Act V, Sc II, *1.* 152.
59. Ibid., *11.* 145-46.

CHAPTER VI

The Noblest Roman of Them All

Julius Caesar is the first tragedy of Shakespeare which presents a tragic hero in the light of the double vision. The year 1590 when the play was written, marks a well-known change in Shakespeare's art. In a word, it becomes serious and marks a turning point to tragedy. It cannot be necessarily attributed to a personal misfortune unless it was his son's death. But it was more a change in his artistic methods showing a natural evolution from comedy to tragedy. The last of the 'happy' comedies — *Twelfth Night* — shows a slight tendency to incorporate a tragic sense of life even if it sweeps past like an evanescent shadow. The history plays like *Richard II*, *Richard III*, and earlier, the three parts of *Henry VI* are all tragic and the former two, alongwith *Romeo and Juliet* and *Titus Andronicus* could be classed as authentic tragedies. So *Julius Caesar* was not a new form to the Shakespeare canon—only the consummateness which evinced itself in the presentation of Brutus and his inner self was in itself a new step in tragic complexity which reaches a point of perfection in *Hamlet*. So what was new to this mode, was the use of double vision in displaying alternately or at the same time, conflicting impressions about the tragic hero in addition to a sustained use of either the positive or the negative vision creating an effect of intensity.

Apparently, *Julius Caesar* appears to be a play without much complexity. Shakespeare does not depart from the historical truth as narrated by Plutarch except in very minor details. As Charlton says :

"Shakespeare's dramatic mood when he made this Roman matter into a play was not primarily the tragedian's. It was rather the point of view of the dramatist who had found a way of giving dramatic validity to the political material of chronicle-history without constraining it to the patterns of either tragedy or comedy. They (the Roman Plays) enacted a history which permitted a more dispassionate scrutiny and a calmer imaginative apprehension. *Julius Caesar* seems to have provided Shakespeare with some such extension of his political or historical awareness."[1]

Thus, while remaining faithful to history as recorded by Plutarch, Shakespeare incorporated a new awareness which implies an objectivity and detachment and sets both Caesar and Brutus 'on this side idolatry' as Charlton puts it. But he was not satisfied with presenting them from a single point of view. There are invariably two angles of vision and they persist till the end. Thus the total impression of the play is not without a sense of ambiguity. At every step the spectator or the reader perceives one apparent and the other implied meaning in the words and acts of these characters. This permits two moral standpoints creating uncertain and divided responses. The issues of good and evil and right and wrong are left so doubtful by the dramatic vision that we are inclined to look at the same person or act as good or evil, right or wrong. This moral ambivalence is the essence of the play's technique and it is brought about by the operation of the double vision of the dramatist at every point.

In *Julius Caesar* this ambivalence shows itself right from the beginning. It is one of basic assumptions of some characters that Caesar had grown a vain, conceited man who could be a threat to the liberty of the Roman people. This idea is developed by the conspirators till the assassination. The behaviour of the living Caesar seems to reinforce it. But as soon as he is dead, the idea is shown to be fallacious and a shadow of doubt is cast upon the assumptions of these characters in the beginning. There is, thus, an implicit counterpointing in the basic ideas which deprives the stand of the conspirators of the validity which they claim from the beginning and yet the sequence of the presentation and the intensity of their conviction seem to make it convincing. It is thus an interesting artistic presentation which projects the idealistic movement of Brutus' thought to the point of his commitment to the assassination. It is a uniform positive vision highlighting the important stages of his mental process with intermittent flashes of the negative vision which show the fallacies in many of his arguments or convictions.

Charlton puts this technique of presenting Brutus in another way, attributing his positive aspects to the influence of Plutarch and negative ones to Shakespeare's critical judgment :

"To many, however, Brutus is the tragic centre of the play. Mr. G.B. Shaw declared that Shakespeare wrote Caesar down for the technical purpose of writing Brutus up. But though Shakespeare's Brutus is not so degraded from his Plutarchian original as is his Caesar, he is nevertheless set much more on this side idolatry than is Plutarch's. For Brutus was a man after Plutarch's own heart."[2]

Charlton quotes lines from North's translation of Plutarch which show a higher unequivocal estimate of Brutus than we get from Shakespeare's play. The idea of its being unequivocal is important because in Shakespeare it is not so. There is, in *Julius Caesar*, a hint of a double estimate of Brutus—one apparent and the other implied. We can put the two side by side and detect a note of ambivalence.

Plutarch says : "Brutus .... for his virtue and valiantness, was well-beloved of the people and his own, esteemed of noblemen, and hated of no man, not so much as of his enemies: because he was a marvellous lowly and gentle person, noble-minded, and would never be in any rage, nor carried away with pleasure and covetousness, but had ever an upright mind with him, and would never yield to any wrong or injustice."[3]

This is unmixed praise. Now let us see one or the many references, in the play to Brutus' virtue and nobility. In Act I Sc ii, after having initiated the idea of Caesar's inclination to tyranny, Cassius speaks in a soliloquy how far Brutus can be influenced :

"Well, Brutus, thou art noble; yet, I see
Thy honourable metal may be wrought
From that it is dispos'd. Therefore it is meet
That noble minds keep ever with their likes;
For who so firm that cannot be seduc'd?
Caesar doth bear me hard; but he loves Brutus.
If I were Brutus now and he were Cassius,
He should not humour me."[4]

It is clear that Shakespeare implies that Brutus' nobility

and judgment can be 'wrought' from its natural quality. Later on his idealism is presented in all earnestness as a genuine quality but the implication is maintained that there is something illusory about it. This creates an uncertainty or ambiguity of response in the audience or the reader and as we shall see later, it is due to the interpretation or the scope for such an interpretation - that a royalist like Shakespeare would have to leave open while treating a tyrannicide like Brutus. Thus, this aspect of the characterization of Brutus constitutes a problem which masks the real attitude of the dramatist. We find that the positive and the negative visions alternately focus the really noble and virtuous and the illusory and impractical facets of Brutus' character. This process can be seen right from the moment Brutus is first presented on the stage.

It is characteristic that the first words spoken by him are in the light of the negative vision and the words which follow create a sense of uncertain responses. When Cassius asks him whether he would go to see the race on the feast of Lupercal, he says,

> "I am not gamesome: I do lack some part
> Of the quick spirit that is in Antony."[5].

It marks the intellectual and unsportive bent of mind without the "quick spirit" which is not only physical but a temperamental trait. In other words, he lacks the agility and quickness of action and thought which ultimately makes Antony get the better of him. This is evident in the prompt use which Antony makes of his opportunities and the equally striking lack of promptness, physical and mental, on the part of Brutus which prevents him in making the best use of his own opportunities. It is also manifested in his inability to take quick and right decisions. Throughout the play, the vacillations and delays ultimately followed by wrong actions, are seen to be responsible for this failure. All these are presented in the light of the negative vision. It is only the moments when the higher ideals and instincts raise him almost to an absolute plane irrespective of this flaw, that the positive vision redeems him and makes him the tragic hero that he is.

His next utterance to Cassius creates an effect of uncertainty even though it brings out the inner landscape which remains the focus of the spiritual action of the play for some time :

"Vexed I am
Of late with passions of some difference,
Conceptions only proper to myself......."[6]
These are followed by the words

".. Brutus, with himself at war," which introduce an unprecedented trait - that of spiritual conflict - in Shakespeare's conception of tragedy which marks all his tragic heroes down to Coriolanus.

It is interesting to note that to the indirect suggestion of Cassius that "many of the best respect in Rome—Have wish'd that noble Brutus had his eyes"[7] Brutus protests speaking against the presumption of that which is not in him implying thereby the leadership of the rebels against Caesar. But shortly after, he expresses a commitment to anything which is in the interest of the people :

"What is it that you would impart to me ?
If it be aught toward the general good,
Set honour in one eye and death i' th' other,
And I will look on both indifferently;
For let the gods so speed me as I love
The name of honour more than I fear death?[8]

It is clear that Brutus had a desire to lead the people to freedom although he had not a mind to kill Caesar. As it appears later, he wanted to achieve the impossible task of killing the spirit of Ceasar and let Caesar live. Paradoxically, what he does achieve is to kill the body and activate the spirit of Caesar till it becomes his "evil spirit" dogging him to defeat and death—an agent of retribution. It is one of the greatest ironies in tragedy that the protagonist seems to aim at one thing while performing an action but as it is done, it turns out to be the very opposite of what was intended. A classical example is in *Oedipus Tyrannus* where Oedipus trying to trace his birth in order to clear himself of the suspicion of parricide and incest, happens to confirm it. Or earlier, by running away from Corinth to escape the Oracle's prophecy he comes to Thebes and unwittingly kills his father and marries his mother. The result of these actions is just the opposite of what was intended. Similarly the result of Brutus' action is the opposite of what he intended. To refer to the actual lines :

"Let's be sacrificers, but not butchers, Caius.
We all stand up against the spirit of Caesar,
And in the spirit of man there is no blood.
O that we then could come by Caesar's spirit
And not dismember Caesar."[9]

Apparently, it is an idealistic thought but the unrealistic, fallacious and immature way of argument ultimately turns everything which Brutus says or does with such feeling into its opposite.

If we analyse it still more deeply, we find that Brutus' fallacious way of reasoning arises from a lack of balance between emotion and reason, between the heart and the head and between ideal and reality. The two aspects of his personality are at odds, he is "at war with himself". What is most intriguing is that his ideals are presented in a positive light as traits of character but in a negative light in action-in their being put into practice. This results in uncertain and divided responses on the part of the audience or the reader.

The lack of equilibrium between the two faculties of reason and emotion, makes for a split or disjointed state at the moment when a decision has to be taken by the operation of both the faculties particularly as regards Caesar who appeals to Brutus' emotion as a friend but whom his reason makes him think dangerous to the liberty of the Roman people. This intensifies the inner conflict when he is faced with a choice and the resulting state of mind is a turmoil and the "phantasma" is akin to the schizophrenic and paranoiac states put together which make for a mental split leading to severe delusions. It is a temporary state but it continues as a strain in his divided nature appearing finally in his vision of Caesar's ghost before the battle of Philippi. Here, as later on, it is accompained by sleeplessness pointing to a strong similarity with Macbeth :

"Since Cassius first did whet me against Caesar, I have not slept.
Between the acting of a dreadful thing

And the first motion, all the interim is
Like a phantasma or a hideous dream.
The Genius and the mortal instruments
Are then in council; and the state of man,
Like to a little kingdom, suffers then
The nature of an insurrection."[10]

It is characteristic (what has been little noticed) that the movement of Brutus' thought has been rendered by likening his mind to a kingdom in the state of insurrection - precisely what he was going to do in Rome. We frequently find such underlayers of correspondences in Shakespeare.

In the secret conference of the conspirators, there is further proof that it is not one stuff in the idea of killing Caesar - the motive has strains. The love for the city combines with the desire for "redress" for personal wrongs. This seems to contradict Brutus' words in the preceding soliloquy that "for my part/ I know no personal cause to spurn at him".[11] Here when he says, "Till each man drop by lottery", he doesn't exclude himself from this apprehension.

With this in mind, it is more illuminating to examine the famous soliloquy in which Brutus has just resolved to kill Caesar. The soliloquy is supposed to be thought-in-process but Brutus is already resolved since it opens with the words: "It must be by his death". It is only later that Brutus ratiocinates as if to justify his decision. The further statement, "And since the quarrel/Will bear no colour for the thing he is/Fashion it thus",[12] clearly shows that Brutus wants to devise a plausible ground to kill Caesar while as he says "I know no personal cause.." But the very desire to invent a viable cause by resorting to a hypothesis, "So Caesar may" or "How that might change his nature" shows that he was not fully convinced of his grounds but was still determined to kill him. Something like reassurance is sought by the arguments. Moreover, Brutus doesn't seem to state the whole truth about his feelings towards Caesar. There doesn't seem to be any objection to Caesar being crowned if that does not change his nature. This puzzled Coleridge who thought Brutus' line of thought illogical or at best, evasive :

"... Surely nothing can seem more discordant with our historical preconceptions of Brutus, or more lowering to the intellect of this stoico-platonic tyrannicide, than the tenets here attributed to him, the stern Roman republican; viz., that he would have no objection to a king or to Caesar, a monarch in Rome, would Caesar be so good a monarch as he is now disposed to be. How too could Brutus say he finds no personal cause; i.e. none in Caesar's past conduct as a man? Had he not passed the Rubicon ? Entered Rome as a conqueror ? Placed his Gauls in the Senate ? Shakespeare (it may be said) has not brought these things forward. True, and this is just the ground of my perplexity. What character does Shakespeare mean his Brutus to be ?"[13]

Contradictions — apparent and implicit — continue to show themselves between the words and actions of Brutus to the very end. And yet Shakespeare has so presented Brutus that his appraoch to the entire problem of the assassination appears to be positive because he leaves no doubt about his virtues like nobility, patriotism and sacrifice. But it is when they are 'applied' to the task there are, as we have pointed out, undertones or 'underlayers' of contrary implications too subtle to detect at first sight. This was again detected by Coleridge :

"This is singular - at least I do not at present see into Shakespeare's motive, the rational or in what point he meant Brutus' character to appear."[14]

N.H. Hudson is similiarly intrigued by Brutus' soliloquy and the speech to the co-conspirators. The combination of unmixed idealism with mixed motives makes him uncertain of his own moral bearing regarding Brutus' character :

"Upon the supposal that Shakespeare meant Brutus for a wise and good man, the speech seems to me utterly unintelligible. but the poet, I think must have regarded him simply as a well — meaning, but conceited and shallow idealist; and such men are always cheating and puffing themsleves with the thinnest of sophisms; feeding on air and conceiving themselves inspired, or as Gibbon puts it mistaking the giddiness of the head for the illumination of the spirit" [15]

The explanation seems to lie in what Charlton says about Shakespeare's typically Elizabethan attitude to a man who was, in spite of his virtues, more or less a regicide. This developed an ambivalence regarding his thoughts and actions which made Shakespeare present him in the light of his double vision — a positive light for his virtues and ideals and a negative light for an 'underlayer' disclosed by subtle hints and for most of his actions. As Charlton says :

"An Elizabethan, however, would not look with the same philosophic detachment (as Plutarch) on a man whose actions were those of Brutus. Rebellion had a different set of implications ; assassination, and especially the assassination of a ruler, appeared in a different order of ideas. Hence Shakespeare's Brutus has puzzled many wise critics."[16]

This explains why there is an implicit condemnation of conspiracy in the words of Brutus when he is going to meet the conspirators after he has himself resolved to kill Caesar "in the shell" :

"O Conspiracy,
Sham'st thou to show thy dang'rous brow by night,
When evils are most free ? O, then by day
Where wilt thou find a cavern dark enough
To mask thy monstrous visage ?
Seek none, conspiracy ;
Hide it in smiles and affability !
For if thou path, thy native semblance on,
Not Erebus itself were dim enough,
To hide thee from prevention."[17]

Of this, Charlton remarks :

"There is, too, a suspicion of the Pharisee's smirk in Brutus' ideal recoil from conspiracy at the moment when he is about to welcome his fellow—conspirators. Neither is his conviction of assured intellectual superiority an engaging trait, when he puts aside the military dispositions of Cassius' more practical strategy. And these are broadly obstacles to admiration. On the top of them, to Shakespeare, Brutus was politically a regicide in act, if not in name; and his own plea in claiming justifiable homicide was explicitly built on no more than a speculation about what the victim might possibly have aspired to. The victim, too, was one from whom he had himself enjoyed particular favour. Killing, surely, needs more excuse than this, and Brutus' murder of Caesar is a killing which excites faint or overt suspicions of murder, patricide and regicide linked in one dread deed."[17]

It is in fact Shakespeare's initially positive attitude to Brutus and a lack of subjective analysis of the effects of crime - which prevents him from presenting him as he does another regicide, Macbeth, a few years after. Both of them are presented as tragic heroes but the imaginative intensity which focuses Macbeth's inner world, is missing in the case of Brutus due to Shakespeare's desire of presenting him as an idealist who is not converted to evil in spite of any insinuation and yet performs a deed similar to Macbeth's.

It is interesting to note how this double strain in Brutus subsequently bifurcates and embodies itself in such characters as Hamlet and Macbeth. It provides a fine glimpse into what Yeats called "The rag - and - bone shop of the heart"[19] of the the great dramatist.

To Charlton's diagnosis, Frank Kermode combines yet another factor. He suggests that the mental process of Brutus in deciding to kill Caesar includes three strains of thought and that Shakespeare combines these to conform to Brutus' possible idealistic motives. With his singular aversion to 'the crowning of Caesar', combines a deep sense of ritual which was an essentially pagan characteristic. It appears in his idea of presenting a savage murder as a ritual or sacrifice. The third of these strains is the Elizabethan attitude to regicide and the dilemma of obedience (which Shakespeare anticipates) if a king, in the future, set himself above the Parliament. Kermode remarks :

"He (Brutus) is, in short, a Roman considering with a pagan conscience a problem to which he cannot know the answer; but he thinks about it in terms not unfamiliar to the Elizabethan student of politics, which is why the offer of a crown seemed more important to him than the crossing of the Rubicon. Shakespeare treats him with delicate sympathy, but cannot have thought his act a right one, however much he may prefer him to Cassius, Octavius and Antony. What he does make clear is that, quite apart from his tactical mistakes in trusting Cassius and Antony, Brutus faced a real problem, of exactly the kind an Englishman might have to face — did have to face — when a king, some time in the future, might set himself above Parliament and confuse his mortal body with his Dignity. [20]

Even the portents before the death of Caesar can be interpreted as a sign of the greatness and power of Caesar's spirit which Brutus was up against. They are also a cosmic manifestation of the disorder which is soon going to overtake the secular world with the end of that power which held it together. Wilson Knight, identifying the disorder-symbolism in *Julius Caesar* and *Macbeth* emphasizes this point and relates it also to the disorder in Brutus' soul as the storm in *King Lear* is related to the upheaval in Lear's mind :

"... the murder of Caesar is heralded by varied unnatural phenomena. Not only do 'birds and beasts' break from all habits of their 'quality and kind'; all laws of nature are interrupted." Casca narrates how

"A common slave - you know him well by sight—
Held up his left hand, which did flame and burn
Like twenty torches join'd, and yet his hand,
Not sensible of fire, remain'd unscorch'd,
Beside - I ha' not since put up my sword -
Against thc Capitol I met a lion,
Who glared upon me and went surly by,
Without annoying me."[22]

He further tells how

"Men all in fire, walk up and down the streets
An yesterday the bird of night did sit
Even at noon-day, upon the market place,
Hooting and shrieking."[22]

In addition to this, a lioness "hath whelped in the streets," graves have opened, the dead walk forth shrieking. All things have changed "from their ordinance / Their natures and performed faculties / To monstrous quality."[23]

There is no heart within the sacrificial offering. Wilson Knight adds,

"In *Julius Caesar* all order is inverted : 'old men, fools and children calculate'. And all this shadows vaguely the terrors and dangers of an act against the symbol of order and authority : an act of destruction directed against the state, a rough tearing of the woven fabric of society and order and peace."[24]

Interpreting the disorder as an objective equivalent of the disorder in the soul, Wilson Knight says:

"The poetic symbolism and imaginative atmosphere of these two plays (*Julius Caesar* and *Macbeth*) tend to mirror the spiritual significance. The outer conflict is a symbol of an inner conflict ... I shall ... attempt to show why the disorder - symbols of *Julius Caesar* must be related to Brutus, and not elsewhere... it is exactly this (Brutus') incertitude, this wavering between two aspects of reality, which is at the root of disorder. It is this which torments Brutus; it is this twofold fated necessity and yet rational absurdity of Caesar's assassination which the play as a whole, gives the reader... the poetic experience .. created, and ... induced by the attendant symbolism of storm, blood and chaos in nature."[25]

Thus whatever reveals the underlayer of conflict and contradictions to his ideal with the entire disorder - symbolism with its account of ill-omens, is presented in the light of the negative vision. The impression of the power of Caesar's spirit is also conveyed in a negative light since it emphasizes the futility of Brutus' arguments and actions. As this process leads up to the decisive point of the assassination, the positive vision of the dramatist appears less and less and when it does, it is to light forth the simple, loving and devoted nature of Portia, Brutus' wife, to reveal the genuine love between Brutus and Cassius in the reconciliation after their quarrel and finally in the suicide of the two after the battle of Philippi. Before we proceed to examine these scenes, let us take a view of Shakespeare's presentation of Caesar which is even more enigmatic than that of Brutus.

Julius Caesar is the only play of Shakespeare (except *Cymbeline*) which is named after a character who does not remain on the stage for any considerable time in the whole play. Actually he appears in only three out of eighteen scenes and dies before the play is half-way through. Yet he seems to dominate the play and what is more important, the spiritual landscape of the play. The consciousness of all characters is dominated by him and he remains spiritually present almost till the end. The play is about him-his assassination, its causes, its course and its effects. Brutus is more of a tragic hero, Caesar is a tragic presence. That is why there are as many readers who would call Brutus the protagonist of the play as there are who would like to assign that part to Caesar. Shakespeare, apart from presenting Brutus a little more positively and Caesar almost wholly negatively, does not give any hint as to whom he considers the central figure unless we take our cue from the title.

One of the recurring themes in most plays of Shakespeare is that of ingratitude which he considers to be the most heineous of vices. If it is coupled with the crime of murder as in *Macbeth*, he could write a great tragedy to match with *Agamemnon* or *Oedipus Tyrannus*. In *Julius Caesar* too, there is the murder of as great a figure as Agamemnon and there is ingratitude on the part of one of the chief assassins but Shakespeare has not created a tragedy of that order. He could have done it more naturally. As Charlton says:

"Even nearer to Shakespeare than are we with our readiness to forgive those who assassinate to bring about a vague sort of enfranchisement was Dante; and Dante on a political and theological rather than a personal and human issue, had no doubt whatever that the place of Brutus in eternity was in the ice-bound grip of Satan's mouth."[26]

The reason why Shakespeare chose to devalue Caesar and endow Brutus with redeeming ideals is not merely that he was following Plutarch or that he had a distaste for a world — conqueror and dictator like Caesar. If we judge from the other references to Caesar in *Hamlet* or *As you like It*, we find that Caesar dominated Shakespeare's consciousness as a symbol of secular greatness and also as a paradigm of its ultimate futility. The reason seems to lie in his predilection for the type of romantic tragic hero whose first sketch was drawn in Brutus. This type was endowed with virtues "as pure as grace" and "as infinite as man may undergo" but he also bore "the stamp of one defect" and due to it all his qualities or the chiefest of them, acquired the nature of defects in their working. So is it in Hamlet—a type just an elaboration of the sketch of Brutus. So it is in all the subsequent tragic heroes each with his particular "fault". And with the sceptical temper evinced by the tragedies and the problem plays, Shakespeare was more concerned with "flaying" established values and reputations. Brutus appeals to him more than Caesar, as later, Antony appealed to him more than Octavius or Cleopatra more than Octavia. The "writing down" of Caesar is attributed by Charlton to "some dramatic reason" (which we have analyzed above); otherwise his assessment is exact :

"Certainly in Shakespeare's play, Ceasar is not shown as the empire-builder controlling the world by the might of his own personality. On the contrary, for some dramatic reason or other, he is deliberately written down. With Plutarch's portrait before him as he wrote, Shakespeare made his Caesar very different, a Caesar who has been a consummate actor with the forum for his stage and the world for his theater, but now a ranting shadow of his former self, senile, vainglorious, deaf, timid and superstition-ridden, a very parody of Plutarch's figure. This is no Shakespearean tragic hero; nor is he even given the space which any hero requires in his own play."[27]

Mark Van Doren thinks that in the play, Caesar has been presented only as a 'presence' and when he speaks, it is not like a Roman but like a conceited Elizabethan :

"Caesar was the foremost man of all the world, but it (his blood) remains a metaphor, a political metaphor, distant from the experience of our senses... There is as much real blood (in him) as there is in stone... Caesar is not a noble Roman, not one of Plutarch's men. He is that rarity in the play, an Elizabethan personality; he is one of Shakespeare's men. While he lasts he reveals himself in his irregularity, not in his symmetry, in picturesqueness rather than in pose... He appears, indeed, only in his singularity; and he appears but briefly before he falls at the hands of men so completely unlike him that the difference alone might pass as motive for their hatred."[28]

What Van Doren says can be put in the fewest words that Caesar does not come to life in the play as other characters do. We do not know how Shakespeare wants to present him because he does not seem to set about seriously at the task. Actually, Shakespeare parts company with Plutarch and puts the historical details about Caesar without allowing the character any organic growth. This results in a disjointed characterization creating divided impressions. As Ernest Schanzer says :

"The complex and divided attitude to the Caesar story found in Shakespeare's play.. however much it may be a reflection of what he had read and felt about the matter, it is used by him as a deliberate dramatic device."

What Schanzer wants to make out is that Shakespeare's treatment of Caesar has a deliberate intention - that of giving an enigmatic character to the whole play. He goes on to establish it :

"Throughout the first half of the play, we are given a series of images of Caesar none of which bear much mutual resemblance, though some of them are not irreconcilable. But doubt is thrown in one way or another on the validity of most of them. And to these Shakespeare adds his own presentation of Caesar, a presentation so enigmatic and unrevealing that none of the other images are really dispelled by it. It is a dramatic treatment of Caesar in the manner of Pirandello. Which of these is the real Caesar ? Shakespeare seems to ask... making us feel that perhaps there in no real Caesar, that he merely exists as a set of images in other men's minds and his own."[23]

Let us see how far Schanzer's idea serves to throw light on the enigmatic nature of Caesar's portrayal and what accounts for the complex and divided attitude which we find in the play. Why does Caesar appear to be like a parody of Plutarch's figure ?

The most plausible answer, as already suggested, can be given in the light of Shakespeare's evolution as a tragic dramatist from 1599 onwards. The tragic hero as conceived from this year to 1608 when he wrote *Coriolanus*, was of a type which does not conform to the pattern of Caesar. Rather it conforms to the pattern of Brutus. From a broader point of view, Brutus, Hamlet, Othello, Lear, Macbeth, Antony and Coriolanus have more in common with each other than with the historical Caesar. Now against any of these, each of whom was endowed with a typical tragic flaw, Julius Caesar like Octavius Caesar in *Antony and Cleopatra* would stand more for the head than for the heart - for reason than for passion. True, in the play his anti-type Brutus is also a man of reason but he has a strong susceptibility for emotion which Caesar doesn't have. The historical Caesar doesn't have it too.

So he did not appeal to Shakespeare's imagination. Once Shakespeare had chosen a protagonist like Brutus, there was a dramatic necessity of devaluing Caesar in order to bring Brutus to prominence, otherwise he would have been utterly overshadowed by Caesar and the balance of the characters could not have been maintained. Hence whereas Brutus is an outcome of Shakespeare's organic or essemplastic imagination, there is no such quality in evidence in the portrayal of Caesar who does not show any growth at all which a tragic character must have. Thus while appearing to be the central character of the play he remains static because his dramatic function was more symbolic than human. It is true that Shakespeare with his creative genius of which the meanest character appearing in single scenes (like the porter in *Macbeth* or the clown in *Antony and Cleopatra* or the Grave-diggers in *Hamlet*) partake in plenty, could have touched him to immortality. But it did not come off. Or perhaps presuming that his historical status would be enough to ensure an identity, Shakespeare adhered to the barest details of his later career without bothering to transmute them. The greatest reason of all was that Shakespeare projects him throughout in the light of the negative vision and a character could not acquire much life in a negative light. It was enough for his scheme of the play as he envisioned it and Caesar was given no more elaboration than Achilles who in spite of being the greatest hero on the Greek side, was mostly presented in a negative light in *Troilus and Cressida*.

To make this argument further plausible, let us take the exactly parallel instance of *Agamemnon* (the first play of the trilogy 'the Oresteia') by Aeschylus where in spite of the fact that the play is named after Agamemnon, he like Caesar, is mostly presented in the light of the negative vision while Cassandra who has a minor role is presented in the light of the positive vision. In a brief scene, her stature grows to prophetic heights and she is utterly human representing the predicament of those who knowingly enter the house of Death. On the other hand Agamemnon is almost impersonal like Caesar and does not grow. Paradoxically, we feel greater pity and fear at the death of Cassandra for whom the dramatist has evoked our sympathy. Agamemnon who is going to be murdered as a retribution for the sacrifice of his daughter and for hybris does not evoke our sympathy. Clytemnestra who, like Brutus, murders him, is also presented as a dynamic character and she is no less powerful in the creative imagintion of the dramatist than Cleopatra in *Antony and Cleopatra*. It is because, it spite of the fact that Aeschylus intended to present Agamemnon with the awe and majesty due to a great conqueror of the magnitude of Caesar, he did not find his creative imagination so deeply engaged. On the other hand, by recounting his sin in the Choruses and by making him walk on the crimson carpet, he positively wrote him down, as Shakespeare is supposed to have done with Julius Caesar. It is inevitable even with mighty characters who fail to engage the dramatist's imagination. An interesting example of a minor character coming to life (as any of those already pointed out by Shakespeare) is that of the nurse in *the Choephoroe* the second play of *The Oresteia*.

A view of the development of the theme of *Julius Caesar* from the beginning of the play would show us the attitude adopted by the dramatist. The play opens with the artisans crowding the streets to see the triumph of Caesar. The second citizen says to the tribunes:

"But indeed, sir, we make holiday to see
Caesar, and to rejoice in his triumph."

To this Marullus answers with a rebuke :

"Wherefore rejoice ? What conquest brings he home ?
What tributaries follow him to Rome,
To grace in captive bonds his chariot wheels ?
You blocks, you stones .....
O you hard hearts, you cruel men of Rome,
Knew you not Pompey.....
And do you now strew flowers in his way
That comes in triumph over Pompey's blood?[30]

After sending the rabble away from the streets Flavius asks Marullus to disrobe the images hung with Caesar's trophies and remarks :

"These growing feathers pluck'd from Caesar's wing
Will make him fly an ordinary pitch,

Who else would soar above the view of men,
And keep us all in servile fearfulness."[31]

When Caesar enters, the first words we hear from him show his leaning to superstition—a trait which can be seen in constant opposition to the impression of an almost superhuman power which defies danger and fate. As Derek Traversi remarks :

"The play opens with a first passing glimpse of Caesar in his isolated and uneasy eminence. As the action proceeds... the strange alloy of grandeur and frailty in his nature will be rather more intimately revealed;"[32]

It is rarely that an unmixed sense of grandeur and greatness is revealed. When it is so, even in flashes, it is shot through by the positive vision. But generally, most statements of personal aggrandizement bear a touch of ambivalence and as we shall see, it is the negative vision of the dramatist which reveals a mask of confidence and vainglory above a sense of weakness inseparable from illusion and superstition. Thus his leaning to superstition is first seen in his desire that Calphuria should not forget to stand in Antony's way so that he can touch her. It also shows his weakness of having dynastic ambitions and indirectly confirms the apprehensions of his enemies. In the next scene, his ambivalent reaction to the offer of a crown can be connected with it. Subsequently his decision to go to the Capitol because the senate had decided to offer a crown to him and that they might change his mind, underlines the same weakness.

But all suggestions of Caesar's weakness are so inextricably connected with the suggestions of grandeur that like Brutus' idealism and fallacies, Caesar's character can always be viewed in the light of the double vision — a generally negative light subtly varied by flashes of the positive vision. A composite picture of Caesar embodying these traits is given by Cassius who is the 'iconoclast' and who finally knocks out the exalted image of Caesar from the minds of the conspirators :

"Now could I, Casca, name to thee a man
Most like this dreadful night.
That thunders, lightens, opens graves, and roars

As doth the lion in the Capitol;
A man no mightier than thyself or me
In personal action, yet prodigious grown,
And fearful, as these strange eruptions are"[33]

The comparison of Caesar with cosmic forces and with almost all those convulsions manifested in the ill-omens establishes some connection with cosmic powers and lends an authenticity to that personal power which held Rome together. But the contradiction that he is no mightier than the average man reveals the other equally authentic side. The same man whose "eye, whose bend doth awe the world", cried "as a sick girl" in fever and earlier, appealed to Cassius for help when he was drowning. And yet the likeness with "a Colossus" is maintained. This tone is the clue to the uncertain and divided responses on the part of the audience which clearly divide their reactions into two opposed categories at the time of his assassination.

We can trace it in Shakespeare's own sceptical and uncertain response to Caesar's greatness perhaps influenced by the "passionate and conflicting judgments of his time" as Derek Traversi puts it. He further says :

"The issue lay, very broadly speaking, between those who abhorred the murder of a man raised to authority, on the one hand, and those who, on the other, were ready to applaud the elimination of a tyrant."[34]

It is the first point of view which appears in the references to Caesar's superhuman power while the second, whose spokesman is Cassius and whose factional leader is Brutus, appear in the more frequent reference to the negative elements in Caesar's character.

The deftness with which these opposite traits alternate with an impression of authenticity, creates an enigmatic feeling on the part of the audience. As Schanzer puts it :

"His (Shakespeare's) enigmatic presentation of Caesar's character and motives allows responses like that of Dover Wilson (who claims a simple, undivided response) to be formed .... In fact the diversity of critical opinion on the main characters and on Shakespeare's attitude to the conspiracy bears witness to his success in making *Julius Caesar* a problem play."[35]

We have already referred to the ambivalence of Brutus' thoughts and actions with reference to Caesar's murder. We may now examine the twofold nature of Caesar's own self-consciousness which marks the scene in which he decides to go to the Capitol on the day of the assassination. One of the most outstanding technical features of this scene is, as Schanzer says, "the playwright's procedure of manipulating our response to the principal characters playing fast and loose without affections.... engaging and alienating them in turn." Schanzer applies this interpretation of Shakespeare's method to the presentation of both Caesar and Brutus but it is seen more sharply in the case of Caesar. He gives it an attractive appellation :

"The term 'dramatic coquetry' may be coined to describe this"[36]

As we shall see the method is seen most fascinatingly in the scene we are referring to.

Scene II, Act II is the turning-point in Caesar's career. In terms of character and action it shows the beginning of the downward turn in his fortunes — the 'peripeteia', if we consider him as the tragic hero. An actual waning of self-confidence accompanied by the most blatant kind of hybris which far surpasses that of any other dramatic character in Greek or Elizabethan drama, is seen here. Even Marlowe's Tamburlaine with all his rant does not surpass him. Agamemnon of Aeschylus is far more restrained even though he is guilty of hybris which mainly accounts for his murder. It is also fascinating to watch how some positive traits do appear in flashes which maintain some image of his historical greatness and make Shakespeare's presentation conform to Plutarch's.

Although the apprehension created by Calphurnia's dream is at the back of the anxiety to learn of the 'opinions of success' from the priests, Caesar maintains a pose of superb confidence when Calphurina asks him not to sit out':

> "Caesar shall forth; the things that threaten'd me
> Ne'er look'd but on my back. When they shall see
> The face of Caesar, they are vanished."[37]

This hyperbolical strain of self-aggrandizement continues throughout the scene, with touches of genuine power alternated by those of weakness displaying what Schanzer calls 'dramatic coquetry', playing fast and loose with the audiences' reactions. Derek Traversi comments on this :

"In his (Caesar's) person the grandeur of the Roman state is supremely gathered; all that we have so far seen stands in some relation to this central reality. Its human manifestation, however, is oddly and significantly faltering. Reflecting on the prevailing portents Caesar is ill at ease,..... As Calphurnia presses him to stay at home, he clings obstinately.... but with a determination which strikes him as necessary, to the pose which his situation has forced upon him. 'Caesar shall go forth' : the dangers that threaten are always *behind* him...."[38]

This is followed by a statement which combines at once a pose and a sincere reflection :

"What can be avoided
Whose end is purpos'd by the mighty gods?
Yet Caesar shall go forth;"[39]

The pose than gives way to pure courage which momentarily reveals that part of him which had made him great and has been projected by the positive vision on a plane transcending the secular one of boasts and apprehensions on which most of the action transpires :

"Cowards die many times before their deaths :
The valiant never taste of death but once.
Of all the wonders that I yet have heard,
It seems to me most strange that men should fear,
Seeing that death, a necessary end,
Will come when it will come."[40]

This balanced consciousness of death in relation to life matches that of Agamemnon just when he hesitates to walk on the crimson carpet :

"I count it dangerous, being mortal, to set foot,
On rich embriodered silks... call him fortunate,
Whom the end of life finds harboured in tranquillity."[41]

It anticipates Hamlet's "Let be" and "the readiness is all," and Cleopatra's readiness "to rush into the secret house of death".

It is just after that Caesar, like Agamemnon after his speech, lapses into hybris.

"Danger knows full well
That Caesar is more dangerous than he:
We are two lions litter'd in one day,
And I the elder and more terrible;
And Caesar shall go forth."[42]

Calphurnia's rejoinder "Alas, my lord,/ Your widsom is consum'd in confidence", pinpoints the fact that hybris results from lack of self-knowledge but it is a strange juxtaposition of the self-knowledge displayed in the earlier speech with its total lack in the latter one. This is followed by two more sudden changes-Caesar's decision to "stay at home' partly ensuing from acquiescence in superstition and partly from the subdued apprehensions, followed by a renewed lapse into that 'confidence' which consumed his wisdom. His ambition is roused by the words, "The senate have concluded /To give this day a crown to mighty Caesar."[43] As Derek Traversi says, "The appeal to vanity supports that to ambition."[44] The suggestions of Decius have only activated his hybris. It emerges in the senate-hall in the most inflated form just before the assassination :

"If I could pray to move, prayers, would move me;
But I am constant as the northern star,
Of whose true-fix'd and resting quality .
There is no fellow in the firmament.
The skies are painted with unnumb' red sparks.
They are all fire, and every one doth shine;
But there's but one in all doth hold his place.
So in the world: 'tis furnish'd well with men.
And men are flesh and blood, and apprehensive;
Yet in the number I do know but one.
That unassailable holds on his rank
Unshak'd of motion; and that I am he..."[45]

The word 'unassailable' used only a minute before he is stabbed, is steeped in irony as subsequently the blades of his assassins are steeped in blood. It discloses, as Ruth Nevo remarks, "the ironic weakness of strength" and as the same critic adds:

"Caesar's self-image of authority, his model of perfect justice, constancy, and dispassion, is 'assailed' at the very high point of its full disclosure."[46]

Traversi sees another paradox in the fall of Caesar and in his speech before it. The assassination is just going to establish his link with common humanity while Caesar "accentuates unnaturally the distance" which he thinks, separates him from other men. Like Emperor Jones of O'Neill he mentally traverses a long distance in the forest of illusions till he comes back to his starting point. As Traversi puts, "a striking contact is for the last time insinuated between the grandeur of his claim and the frailty .... which marks the individual who so precariously advances it."[47]

Caesar's final comparison of his will with Olympus is ironically followed by the peripeteia in the murder and by an anagnorisis when in the last moment he realizes the real nature of the conspirators and of Brutus and dies with the awareness of his vulnerability :

"Et tu Brute ?-
Then fall, Caesar!"[48]

The play *Agamemnon* of Aeschylus goes on after the murder of Agamemnon. Clytemnestra and Aegisthus are temporarily triumphant but after a lapse of time the spirit of Agamemnon activates Electra and through her, Orestes who destroys the murderers. This continues into the other play of the trilogy *The Choephoroe* the counterpart of which is the part of *Julius Caesar* from Act III Sc II onwards. The spirit of Caesar assists in bringing about the fall of Brutus in so far as it haunts his consciousness and further, by appearing twice, weakens his will. That is why the remaining part of the play has been called "Antony's revenge".

On the whole, however we view Caesar — as a protagonist or as a character who shares his importance with Brutus — we find that Shakespeare has taken pains to present in him a composite picture, with opposite traits in subtle combination as he has done in Brutus. This has been achieved by the use of the positive and the negative vision with quick alternations. The psychological and moral problems arising from this presentation are not incidental but a deliberate design "in the manner of Pirandello" as Schanzer has put it.

REFERENCES

1. H.B. Charlton, *Shakespearean Tragedy* (Macmillan and Co., London, 1948) pp. 70-72.
2. Ibid., p. 75.
3. Ibid., p. 75.
4. *Julius Caesar*, Act I, Sc II *ll*. 307-14.
5. ibid., *ll*. 28-29.
6. Ibid., *ll*. 39-41.
7. Ibid., Act I, Sc II *ll*. 59-62.
8. Ibid., *ll*. 84-89.
9. Ibid., Act II, Sc I, *ll*. 166-70.
10. Ibid., *ll*. 61-69.
11. Ibid., *ll*. 10-11.
12. Ibid., *ll*. 28-29.
13. H.B. Charlton, *Shakespearean Tragedy* (Macmllan, London, 1948) p. 76
14. Ibid., p. 76.
15. Ibid., p. 76.
16. Ibid., pp. 75-76.
17. *Julius Caesar*, Act II, Sc I, *ll*. 77-85.
18. H.B. Charlton, *Shakespearean Tragedy*, p. 77.
19. W.B. Yeats, *Cireus Animal's Desertion*,
20. Frank Kermode, *Introduction to Julius Caesar* (The River side Shakespeare, Houghton Mifflin Company, Boston, 1974) p. 1104.
21. Wilson Knight, *The Wheel of Fire* (Methuen and Co., London, 1930) pp. 133-34.
22. *Julius Caesar*, Act I, Sc III, *ll*. 25-28.
23. Ibid., Act II, Sc II, *ll*. 17-18; Act I, Sc III *ll*. 66-68.
24. Wilson Knight *The Wheel of Fire*, p. 134.
25. Ibid., pp. 136-37.
26. H.B. Charlton, *Shakespeaean Tragedy*, p. 77.
27. Ibid., pp. 74-75.
28. Mark Van Doren, *Shakespeare* (George Allen and Unwin, London, 1941) pp. 185-86.
29. Ernesi Schanzer, *The problem plays of Shakespeare* (Routledge and Kegan Paul, London, 1963) pp. 106-107
30. *Julius Caesar*, Act I, Sc I, *ll*. 30-53.

31. Ibid., *ll.* 72-75.
32. Derek Traversi, *Shakespeare, The Roman Plays* (Hollis and Carter, London, 1963) p. 22.
33. *Julius Caesar*, Act, I, Sc III, *ll.* 72-78.
34. Derek Traversi, *Shakespeare : The Roman Plays,* pp. 11-12.
35. Ernest Schanzer, *The Problem Plays of Shakespeare*, p. 109.
36. Ibid., p. 110.
37. *Julius Caesar*, Act II, Sc II, *ll* 9-13.
38. Derek Traversi, *Shakespeare : The Roman Plays,* pp. 40-41.
39. *Julius Caesar*, Act II, Sc II, *ll* 27-29.
40. Ibid., *ll* 32-37.
41. Aeschylus : *Agamemnon,* Trans. Philip Vellacott (Penguin Classics 1956) p. 74.
42. *Julius Caesar*, Act II, Sc II, *ll.* 44-48.
43. Ibid., 11 93-94.
44. Derek Traversi, *Shakespeare : The Roman Plays,* p. 43.
45. *Julius Caesar*, Act III, Sc I, *ll* 59-70.
46. Ruth Nevo, *Tragic Form in Shakespeare* (Princeton University Press, 1972) p. 114.
47. Derek Traversi, *Shakespeare : The Roman Plays,* p. 44.
48. *Julius Caesar*, Act III, Sc I. *l*. 76.

CHAPTER VII

The Quintessence of Dust

Before discussing the operation of the double vision in Hamlet (classing it alongside the four problem plays already discussed) it is necessary to justify its place with them while it has already an important place amongst the great tragedies. Without questioning this vital position and its attributes of a tragic masterpiece, it is relevant to state the reasons which make it, at the same time, a problem play.

In general, every tragedy poses some insoluble problems. There is also an element of ambiguity and ambivalence. For instance, *The Oresteia* presents the problem of revenge just as *Hamlet* does, and even when it is executed according to the primitive moral code of blood for blood, Aeschylus poses the problem of resolving the cyclical movement of such revenges and tries to resolve it by substituting trial by justice—the new morality of the Olympian gods—in its place. But the play still leaves the impression of a forced resolution and uses absurdities like the idea of the mother being merely the safe-keeper of the husband's trust of a son in order to justify matricide. So the solution of Aeschylus evokes more problems touching the human aspects of the play which he ignores in his concern for a cosmic reconciliation between Zeus and the Furies and the transformation of the latter into the Eumenides. Similarly, *Oedipus Tyrannus* poses the insoluble problem of how Oedipus who had fled from Corinth long back to escape the oracle's prophecy of being a parricide and thereafter destined to marry his own mother, did not try to investigate his present position earlier or the problem as to why he came with a sword to Jocasta's chamber. Again, in *Oedipus at Colonus*, we find Oedipus' anger towards his son far in excess of the cause just like Hamlet's disgust at the sin of his mother.

Thus we find that vexing problems either arising out of the situations and characters in the body of the play or thematically incorporated by the dramatist, are invariably found in tragedies. On that score, *Hamlet* with its problem of Hamlet's delay, his excessive disgust which is out of all proportion of its cause (made much of by T.S. Eliot); the constant duality in his nature with its strains of the barbaric and tender, poetic and imaginative elements; the sudden and unpredictable reactions such as seen in his various encounters in the Nunnery scene, the closet scene and the graveyard scene (with Laertes)—and many more, such as why he spares the king at prayer,—remains a veritable blind alley for the critic.

Presuming all these to be of the order of tragedy, what has made critics class Hamlet as a 'problem play' belonging with those which are usually classed as such in the Shakespeare canon? It was at the end of the nineteenth century, after Ibsen and Shaw had written their problem plays, that F.S. Boas felt it appropriate to borrow the term to classify the category of Shakespeare's plays which he described as follows:

".......certain painful studies of weakness, levity and unbridled passion of young men. This is especially the case with *All's Well that Ends Well, Measure for Measure, Troilus and Cressida* and *Hamlet*. All these dramas introduce us into highly artificial societies, whose civilization is ripe unto rottenness..abnormal conditions of brain and of emotion are generated.....We move along dim, untrodden paths....In *Troilus and Cressida* and *Hamlet* no settlement of difficulties takes place, and we are left to interpret their enigmas as best we may. Dramas so singular in theme and temper cannot be strictly called comedies or tragedies. We may therefore borrow a convenient phrase from the theatre of today and class them together as Shakespeare's problem-plays."[1]

This paved the way for ranking Hamlet as a problem-play and although W.W. Lawrence writing in 1931, excluded *Hamlet* from this group of problem plays, his indication of the dramatist's handling of the theme, characters and situations of such plays throws light on some aspects of *Hamlet*:

"........the theme is handled (in a problem play) so as to arouse not merely interest or excitement, or pity or amusement, but to probe the complicated interrelations of character and action, in a situation admitting of different ethical interpretations."[2]

The following remark of Lawrence seems to have a special application to *Hamlet*:

"The problem is......one of conduct, as to which there are no fixed and immutable laws."[3]

Thus putting all his remarks together we find that the idea of 'complicated interrelations of character and action' with reference to the conduct of the protagonist should form the ground of a very fruitful inquiry with reference to *Hamlet* as a problem play.

It was however E.M.W. Tillyard, writing on Shakespeare's problem plays in 1951, who for the first time systematically made out a case for *Hamlet* as a problem play on altogether novel premises. Trying to establish that the play is not a tragedy in the fullest sense but a problem play, Tillyard begins by adopting the idea of a "renewal...an enlightenment and...a new state of being" as essential to tragedy. After examining various hints of regeneration in Hamlet, particularly towards the end of the play, Tillyard concludes:

"If therefore this crucial passage ('Not a whit......the readiness is all......') shows nothing new, the notions of a regenerate Hamlet, and hence of play tragic in the fullest sense, are ruled out......At most Hamlet regains some of the dignity or composure....But, with no great revelation or reversal of direction or regeneration, the play cannot answer to one of our expectations from the highest tragedy."[4]

Tillyard finally makes a strong case for the other type of play which *Hamlet* uniquely is:

"Hamlet is best understood as a play less of ordinary than sheer explication or presentation, as a play presenting the utmost variety of human experience in the largest possible cosmic setting. When sheer explication, or abundance of things presented, takes first place, then we leave the realm of tragedy for that of the problem play. I have argued that *Hamlet*, though containing tragedy of sorts, and though reinforced intellectually by a noble general shape, belongs principally to this type."[5]

It is certainly absurd to deny the title of high tragedy to a play no less comprehensive in tragic scope and quality than

The Oresteia and in that play, Orestes the hero, is not regenerated but simply acquitted of a heineous crime by the interference of Athene. He leaves the stage with Apollo, still boasting that he was right in killing his mother and without the least human touch. In sheer explication and abundance of things presented. *The Oresteia* has no equal in its own way. Similarly, if *Oedipus Tyrannus* is taken singly, there is no regeneration on the part of Oedipus at the end of that play. Euripides' *Medea* is absolutely without any such quality. All of them are great tragedies. So Tillyard's argument in denying *Hamlet* the title of a tragedy has no weight.

However, we can say that *Hamlet* partakes of most of the characteristics of a problem play while being a genuine tragedy. There is, apart from the idea of regeneration, a tragic essence arising from man's encounter with circumstances and with evil-physical and spiritual. In *Hamlet* this is the most thrilling and breath-taking spectacle-manoeuvres of the hero in face of evil. Both character and circumstance acquire a compulsive form. As Charlton puts it:

"In Shakespeare, this dramatic ultimacy inheres in and also exists outside his characters. For him the stern necessity of character and the resistless compulsion of circumstance are a form or what John Morley called the modern and positive expression for the old Destiny of the Greeks."[6]

As would be evident from the foregoing discussion, the nature of *Hamlet* as a tragedy or as a problem play has been forbidding and yet fascinating to the critics. No critic touched it but with a new and often startling interpretation. T.S. Eliot abandoned the enterprise of interpreting *Hamlet* judging it to be "an artistic failure". It is certainly as instance of a critical failure to see the greatness of the play in the light of its overwhelming success on the stage in all ages. It is more so on the part of a critic who belongs with Johnson to the great classical tradition and Johnson thought the people to be the best judges of a work of art.

But Eliot's other statement in the same essay that *Hamlet* is the Mona Lisa of Literature corrects the perspective. It is as apt as any remark ever made. The mystery which for ever "teases us out of thought", revealing different meanings from different angles, is common to both works of art. This basic ambivalence is inherent in the character and actions of the protagonist which display a strain of duality most of the time. Hamlet, a paradox in himself moves in a world of paradoxes and Shakespeare has so 'gingerly' presented 'the artful balance' of these, that a member of the audience or the reader hardly sees anything uncommon in this 'impossible probability'. Even Aristotle would have permitted the validity of such a character as he had approved the equally 'impossible' (but probable) tragic experience of Oedipus. That is why Hazlitt said 'It is we who are Hamlet' and Coleridge found that he had 'a strain of Hamlet' in him.

What makes for the plausible existence of these dualities and how they make Hamlet–the character and the play–enigmatic, is the result of the dramatist's double vision. The clue to all the contradictions which have defied the attempts of all the critics to explain them or to weave them in a fabric of consistency, may ultimately be found here. If so, the line of inquiry adopted here might ultimately resolve the insoluble mystery of Hamlet.

From the very opening of the play, the negative vision presents an atmopshere charged with uneasiness, apprehension and foreboding of evil. Before the cause is disclosed, the disease is shown as having grown to the point of rottenness. It is like the opening of *Oedipus Tyrannus* when the effect of the plague is shown before the cause is known. No other play of Shakespeare opens at the dead of night with everything possible receding to a temporary non-existence, seeming to make way for the emergence of a layer of existence which lies submerged under the daylight world of reality. Two planes of existence with two contrary natures, are thus conjured—the one always lying like a substratum. From the second act, the duality becomes sharper. With chameleon-like changes into illusion and fact, appearance and reality, these two worlds continue to exist in juxtaposition to the very end of the play. What is more, their subtle combination in the main characters— Hamlet and Claudius—opens a twofold angle of vision at every step. With Hamlet these angles succeed so sharply that each seems to present a different picture, contradicting what has gone before. It is only his self-revelation in the soliloquies which gives a clue to these disparities.

In the first Act of the play (excepting scene three) the negative vision holds complete sway. The first scene sets the tone of this movement by presenting Franciso (like the Watchman in *Agamemnon*) "sick at heart" and the reference to "the graves" and "the sheeted dead" followed by the actual appearance of the ghost creates the consciousness of a power "more than man" manifesting itself. This power--that of the Ghost--is later seen to determine the frame of mind in which Hamlet continues for the rest of the play by reacting upon a consciousness already obsessed by sin and moral evil. Thus the negative vision which presents the first appearance of the Ghost under the battlements becomes intensified when Hamlet appears clad in black, brooding on his mother's sin. As Wilson Knight puts it:

"Alone in the gay glitter of the court, silhouetted against brilliance, robustness, health, and happiness, is the pale, black-robed Hamlet, mourning....the poison has started its disintegrating work. His consciousness, functioning in terms of evil and negation, sees hell but not Heaven."[7]

It is the negative vision which reveals Hell and evil to Hamlet till, in some way, they distort his vision and prevent his recognition of good which suffers under his attitude of rejection. His mother's over-hasty marriage along with her inadequate sorrow for her late husband, makes him conscious of the sin of lust and incest which, issuing from his mother, infects his own flesh and blood. This invokes a train of thought which annihilates all possibility of good anywhere:

"How weary, stale , flat and unprofitable,
Seem to me all the uses of this world !
Fieon't ! Ah, fie! tis an unweeded garden,
That grows to seed; things rank and gross in nature
Possess it merely."[8]

Allied to it, is a view of the situation from another angle—that of fickleness in love, which subsequently, he easily transfers from his mother to Ophelia, making it common to all women. The first negative conclusion ruins his own life while the other ruins an innocent person who could have brought love - a possible value to redeem him.

".. and yet, within a month -
Let me not think on't. Frailty, thy name is woman! —
A little month, or ere those shoes were old

With which she followed my poor father's body,
Like Niobe, all tears-why she, even she --
O God! a beast that wants discourse of reason
Would have mourn'd longer - married with my uncle,
My father's brother; but no more like my father
Than I to Hercules."[9]

'Good' is ruled out as the outcome. "It is not, nor it cannot come to good".

The same negative sentiment is expressed from yet another angle— that of contrast between appearance and reality. The contrast between apparent and real love shown by hanging on "As if increase of appetite had grown/By what it fed on"; is reinforced by the contrast between "Niobe, all tears" and "a beast" with the implication of Gertude being worse.

The same negative contrast between appearance and reality is seen in Hamlet's earlier reply to Gertrude which is intended to imply that the 'seeming' is all on her side and that of Claudius :

"Seems, madam! Nay, it is ; I know not seems.
'Tis not alone my inky cloak, good mother,
Nor customary suits of solemn black,
Nor windy suspiration of forc'd breath,
No, nor the fruitful river in the eye,...
That can denote me truly. These, indeed, seem;
For they are actions that a man might play;..."[10]

The image of tears is common to both the speeches, so is that of play-acting in "actions" that are played in the above speech and in "she would hang on him/As if..."[11] These negative images indicate the negative approach which Hamlet consistently makes in his first appearance till it acquires a kind of validity with the revelation of the Ghost which provides a basis for a philosophy of human nature — of 'pernicious' women and 'smiling' villains. There is a further concentration on sin an evil as manifested in the lust of Gertrude and the crime of Claudius :

"Ay, that incestuous, that adulterate beast,
With witchcraft on his wits, with traitorous gifts
... won to his shameful lust
The will of my most seeming virtuous queen.

O Hamlet, what a falling off was there,
From me, whose love was of that dignity
That it went hand in hand even with the vow
I made to her in marriage....
But virtue, as it never will be moved,
Though lewdness court it in a shape of heaven,
So lust though to a radiant angel link'd,
Will sate itself in a celestial bed
And prey on garbage."[12]

Hamlet's hysterical reaction points more to its psychic impact than to a practical spur to action in spite of his "Haste me to know't...." speech which as Kitto remarks, lacks the urgency of concrete imagery, built entirely of abstractions.

His resolve to "sweep to (his) revenge", with all his invocations of heaven and hell, finally thins down to noting in his tables,

"That one may smile, and smile, and be a villain;"[13]

He has already branded his mother "a most pernicious women". Soon the two stigmatizations include the whole human race and the personal edge which should have immediately set him on to action, is blunted by the diffusion of the sense of guilt over all humanity. It is further blunted by the passage of about two to four months during which he has only sunk into inertia, putting on an 'antic disposition' which seems to have been the only effective decision he has made at the end of the ghost's revelation :

"How strange or odd some'er I bear myself --
As I perchance hereafter shall think meet
To put an antic disposition on—"[14]

So far of the persistent continuation of the negative vision through four of the five scenes of the first Act. In between these, the third scene presents a day-scene in which three characters who are untouched by sin or crime, are presented--a loving family who ultimately perish for the only fault that they were connected with Hamlet. With reference to them and to other victims like Rosencrantz and Guildenstern, it is apt to style Hamlet, as Wilson Knight does— "the ambassador of Death". Ophelia, Polonius and Laertes constitute a direct antithesis to the 'family' of the other three— Hamlet, Claudius and Gertrude. The mutual love and innocence of the first three is presented in the light of the positive vision just as the sin, guilt and hatred (on Hamlet's part) are projected by the negative vision. But it is only, the bond of love and the freedom from sin with evil lurking at the door waiting to engulf it. There is a strange foreboding of this even though the canker is not within :

"Virtue itself scapes not calumnious strokes ;
The canker galls the infants of the spring
Too oft before their buttons be disclos'd;..
Be wary, then; best safety lies in fear:"[15]

Ophelia, to the last, keeps to "the steep and thorny way to heaven." She like Desdemona and Cordelia, continues to remind of that redeeming power of love which alone makes tragedy endurable.

The first Act thus presents through a uniform operation of the negative vision—with a short break for the positive vision in the middle — the predicament of Hamlet and the equally negative way in which he is equipped to face it. The frame of mind which, after a readiness to "sweep to his revenge", yields nothing by way of action except a school-boyish writing of his 'impression' or the situation on his 'tables', is likely to be entangled in further such impressions of life in general and would never 'take off' to effective action. His rejection of life, implicit in the first eight lines of the soliloquy coupled with his idea of death, are the two directions in which his immaturity drives him to futile thought and ineffective actions. The 'antic disposition' which was intended as a cover to plain his revenge, deteriorates into a mask under which, after his proper bent, his intellect finds infinite scope for speculations, self-accusations and even further manoeuvres—all running awry.

Thus his sudden entry into the closet of Ophelia with the dishevelled appearance of one who "had been loosed out of hell", looks like the first manifestation of that 'pose' of madness which Hamlet shows by a kind of design in relation to Ophelia. It might also be the leave-taking of a lover. Looked at from another angle the same incident appears to have a different significance. As Wilson Knight says :

"This is no mock-madness. to see it as such is to miss the power of the central theme of the play. Hamlet would not first try the practical joke of pretended madness on Ophelia whom he loved. That pallor was clearly no cosmetic... From henceforth he must walk alone within the prison of mental death."[16]

This action of Hamlet begins a series of further acts which yield two significances from two angles, particularly with reference to the three persons with whom he was emotionally involved — Ophelia, Gerturde and Claudius. If we may put it so, it was the passion of love, the passion of moral concern and the passion of revengeful hate respectively. All these, of course, run awry and Hamlet makes each pursuit worse by his rashness, lack of judgement and by a complex overlapping of these concerns and sudden bursts of frenzy which arose from the unconscious but complusive need of releasing the pent-up tension caused by the urgency to act and the inability to do so. Meanwhile the capacity for action was drained off as it were by abstract speculation.

From this point onwards Hamlet's mind begins to work and act by sharp juxtaposition which reflect the duality in his nature and his tortured vision of life. The two extremes in these juxtapositions are projected by the two visions were which was continuously active at the back of his mind.

These extremes, would not be activated, or in other words, Hamlet's consciousness would not be split (with a fission-like impact) into them, were it not for a disintegrating and corroding agent - the atmosphere of Denmark surcharged with rotteness. As Jan Kott says :

"Everything at Elsinore has been corroded.. marriage, love and friendship.. He (Hamlet) considers life to be a lost cause from the outset... there is no way out."[17]

What Jean Paul Sartre says about the effect of characters (created by the modern writer) on the reader's mind, applies uniquely to Hamlet's steeply cleaved consciousness :

"... Let him be tossed from one consciousness another as from one absolute and irremediable universe into another similarly absolute;... let him be.. invested with.. perceptions and feelings as by high insurmountable cliffs."[18]

Carrying forward the idea, Ruth Nevo, points out how the 'antic disposition', whether as a mask or as a state of sore distraction, provides a scope for the abrupt emergence of any of the two selves:

"The two selves are constantly juxtaposed in a series of

ironic reversals of each other. Public and private, or displayed and concealed, constantly interchange. From the point of view of the public self, or the desired self-image, that which is concealed is absured or contemptible, weak or wretched; from the point of view of the private self, that which is displayed is affected, bombastic, compromising, and sham. Hamlet shifts his point of view with every shift of role, so that one view of the self is constantly being undercut or subverted by the other. Thus the antic disposition multiplies the possible modes of self-reproach. Opportunities for counterpoint, for ironic reflection, for reflection and self-reflection become practically unlimited."[19]

After Hamlet's sudden entry into Ophelia's closet, the immediately following instance of extremes of self-expression occurs on the visit of Rosencrantz and Guildenstern to fish out the mystery of his distraction. He forestalls them, makes them confess their motive and then tells them of his distraction ending up on anti-climaxes. There are two distinct movements — that about the world and that about man's position in it. These are the two motifs in *Hamlet* appearing and reappearing in different garbs. The positive vision — the Apollonian—which begins with wonder and beauty, gives way to the negative vision — of destruction, disease and futility:

"I have of late—but wherefore I know not—lost all my mirth, forgone all custom of exercises; and indeed it goes so heavily with my disposition that this goodly frame, the earth, seems to me a sterile promontory; this most excellent canopy the air, look you, this brave o'erhanging firmament, this majestical roof fretted with golden fire—why, it appeareth no other thing to me than a foul and pestilent congregation of vapours."[20]

The extremes of 'goodly' and 'sterile' are driven to another set of extremes in 'excellent... brave.. majestical.. golden', and 'foul and pestilent.' They express the opposites coexiting in Hamlet's consciousness. What follows is a sharper anti-climax with opposites :

"What a piece of work is a man ! How noble in reason ! how infinite in faculties ! in form and moving, how express and admirable ! in action, how like an angel ! in apprehension, how like a god ! the beauty of the world ! the paragon of animals ! And yet, to me, what is this quintessence of dust?"[21]

The shattering close in futility has hardly been equalled in literature. For this in essence is the very theme of *Hamlet* which is the condition of man in creation in the context of overwhelming negations juxtaposed with equally exalted affirmations. The positive vision has affirmed likening man to the angels and gods but the negative vision in one stroke dashes him down to dust. A sense of futility could not be better conveyed. The statement is balanced on one side with "How weary, stale, flat and unprofitable,/Seem to me all the uses of this world!" and on the other with "What is a man/ If his chief good and market of his time / Be but to sleep and feed?" This reflection in the fifth soliloquy is followed by a similar exaltation by the positive vision followed by a negation.

> "Sure he that made us with such large discourse,
> Looking before and after, gave us not
> That capability and godlike reason
> To fust in us unus'd."[22]

The constant juxtaposition of 'god' and 'beast' and 'beast-like,' (as in 'Hyperion to a satyr'; and in the closet speech to his mother - "Hyperion's curls; the front of Jove.. / An eye like Mars... / A station like the herald Mercury... / A combination and a form... / Where every god.. / .. batten on the moor?")[23] provides a clue to the contrasted states of man in Hamlet's mind. The sharp juxtaposition of heaven and hell, health (at least implicit) and disease (which permeates the play in explicit statements and imagery) appearance and reality, and life and death are the various forms in which the negative and the positive visions are crystallized. They operate alternately and often so closely that the one 'galls' the other's 'kibe' — (to borrow a phrase of Hamlet's in another context.) to undo its effect.

Wilson Knight finds a clue to this state of mind which sharply combines opposites in the idea of the 'sick soul'. It serves to reveal the fundamental duality existing in Hamlet's make-up—the simultaneous presence of godly and beastly elements which J.M. Robertson seeks to explain equally plausibly, by his theory of transmutation of the earlier versions by Shakespeare. However, the idea of the 'sick soul' is psychologically and thematically more illuminating. Wilson Knight, referring to this idea as expounded by William James, applies it to Hamlet's condition between two worlds:

"I have tried ... to indicate this sickness which eats into Hamlet's soul. Its nature is pointed further in the chapter entitled 'The Sick Soul' in *The Varieties of Religious Experience.* Now by emphasizing these elements in the figure of Hamlet I have essayed to pluck out the heart of his mystery. And it will be clear that the elements which I have emphasized, the matter of Hamlet's madness, his patent cruelty, his coarse humour, his strange dialogue with Ophelia, his inability to avenge his father's death, are all equally related to the same sickness within. The coherence of these elements in the play must be evident. Creative action; love; passion - all these can find none but a momentary home in Hamlet's paralysed mind."[24]

Throwing more light upon the state of "the sick soul", Evelyn Underhill says,

"...the type of mind which William James called the 'sick soul'. It is the mood of the penitent... which, appalled by the sharp contrast between itself and the Perfect which it contemplates, can only cry 'out of the depths'. It comes naturally to the temperament which leans to pessimism, which sees a 'great gulf fixed' between itself and its desire, and is above all things sensitive to the elements of evil and imperfection in its own character and in the normal experience of man. Permitting these elements to dominate its field of consciousness, wholly ignoring the divine aspect of the World of Becoming, such a temperament constructs from its perceptions and prejudices the concept of a material world and a normal self which are very far from God."[25]

Miss Underhill refers to the idea of another kind of mental state which is 'at the opposite pole from this way of sketching Reality' as follows :

"... who commonly belong to James' 'healthy minded' or optimistic class... a doctrine whose teachers are drawn from amongst the souls which react more easily to the touch of the Divine than to the sense of alienation and of sin, and are naturally inclined to love rather than to awe."[26]

The conclusions of Wilson Knight and the analysis of Evelyn Underhill regarding the attributes of such a state give us many other clues to Hamlet's behaviour throughout the play leading up to a final stage like that of mystic illumination—a growth of 'wisdom through suffering' in the Greek way or as Ruysbroeck (quoted by Underhill) puts it :

"The discovery of a 'divine' essence or substance, dwelling at the apex..."[27]

The same process of spiritual evolution is seen, more comprehensively in the pattern envisaged in Dante's *Divina Commedia*, as explicated by Evelyn Underhill :

"..... the necessary life-process.. in the course of his (man's) purgation and spiritual ascent from the state of the "natural man" to that other state of harmony with the spiritual universe.. We have in the *Divina Commedia* a classic example of such a twofold vision of the inner and the outer worlds : for Dante's journey... is really an inward alchemy, an ordering and transmuting of his nature.."[28]

Hamlet's spiritual experience does not exactly correspond to this description but it can be seen to fall into three similar distinct stages — those of Inferno, Purgatory and Paradise —even if the last one is dubious or at best implied in a very slight degree in his final evolution. Such an evolution and growth under the impact of suffering which is a greater test of tragedy than that of 'regeneration' adopted by Tillyard, is most unquestionably present in the play.

Following the over-all pattern of Hamlet's growth along a complex line of movement with revelations of opposite facets of his nature (which W.B. Yeats illustrates by the image of the winding stair), we can now see it more clearly through his 'actions' in the rest of the play.

In the strict sense, these are not actions. They might he called his freakish indulgence or outbursts into some kinds of activity which carry forward the 'action' of the play which is after all a vast spectacle of inaction with reference to the main theme.

Thus Hamlet's 'sick soul' is necessarily to be seen in the context of the Inferno which Denmark is where something is already rotten as it is in the Thebes of Oedipus and requires 'cleansing' or purgation. Hamlet knows Denmark to be "an unweeded garden" before the ghost imposes his task. The consciousness of evil followed by a further crushing revelation of crime and incest create the image of Inferno. With the assumption of the antic disposition and his split consciousness begins his sojourn in the depth of hell which continues till he is seen departing to England. The Purgatorial stage seems to begin some time before this point and his consciousness of punishment and repentance coming upon him marks it more clearly since such a stage is always accompanied by remorse (as in *The Winter's Tale* when Leontes is led by Paulina to his 'sorrows') The killing of Polonius rankles in his soul:

> "For this same lord
> I do repent; but Heaven hath pleas'd it so,
> To punish me with this, and this with me."[29]

The final stage, as we have already said, is glimpsed as a fleeting vision and the latter two stages are not so pertinent to our analysis as the stage of Inferno which is, as it were, the staple 'climate' of the play and in which almost all its significant things transpire.

It is in this Inferno that the split in Hamlet's 'sick soul' is best seen. After the sarcastic encounter with Rosencrantz and Guildenstern, we find his excessive elation at the meeting with the players followed by a fit of self-accusation, depression and doubt— all in the space of half-hour of the play which would not be a few hours in actual life. We have seen the complex of positive and negative visions in the speech on man and the same interplay is seen when he is with the players and later when he is left by himself.

Hamlet's inordinate joy when he hears of the players is at the prospect of release from the state like death-in-life and of escape into the world of histrionic art. Of this he was extremely fond as appears from his avidness to direct the play within the play while inserting "a dozen or sixteen lines" of his own in this play called "The Murder of Gonzago," and his subsequent speech on play-acting.

The switch from the negative to the positive vision is abrupt as all changes with Hamlet are. As soon as Rosencrantz tells him of the players, he speaks with a joyous abandon:

> "He that plays the king shall be welcome—his Majesty shall have tribute on me; the adventurous Knight shall use his foil and target; the lover shall not sigh gratis; the humorous man shall end his part in peace; the clown shall make those laugh

whose lungs are tickle a 'th' sere; and the lady shall say her mind freely, or the blank verse shall halt for't. "[30]

After the Hecuba speech of the First Player, Hamlet's mood changes, the negative vision brings like a brain wave, self-accusation, remorse and doubt. The fit leaves him exhausted and his 'weakness and melancholy' aggravates the doubt about the authenticity of the ghost and makes him fix upon the play as a way of catching the conscience of the king.

It is in this soliloquy that the attributes of the sick soul as defined by Evelyn Underhill are most evident. Hamlet appears as the penitent—guilty not only of inaction but of apathy to the memory of his father whose ghost had commanded him to a task.

"Yet I,
A dull and muddy-mettl'd rascal, peak,
Like John-a-dreams, unpregnant of my cause,
And can say nothing; no, not for a king
Upon whose property and most dear life
A damn'd defeat was made. Am I a coward ?
Who calls me villain, breaks my pate across,
Plucks off my beard and blows it in my face,
Tweaks me by the nose, gives me the lie i 'th' throat
As deep as to the lungs ?..."[31]

There is a contrast between what he is and what he contemplates to be and there is no doubt that his remorse is deeply felt. There is a consciousness of greater evil and we see him like a 'limed soul' (as Claudius says of himself in the prayer scene) caught in the toils of inaction the more as he struggles to move towards effective action. A great gulf yawns between himself and what he desires. The only difference is that Hamlet's salvation lies in the eradication of evil-physical and spiritual—for which, as he said earlier, he did not set his life at a pin's fee.

This complex vision of a positive yearning for action glued as it were to negative foundation of inaction is seen by Ruth Nevo as a presentation of two inseparable layers in his being.

"Nowhere in drama are the involutions of self-awareness, of self-criticism which redoubles upon itself, rendered more impressively. The whole episode, players and soliloquy together, creates an inimitable impression of recession in depth, teasing the mind out of thought, as Hamlet's mind is teased, with the suggestion of layer upon layer of the undisclosed, the ulterior. In the visual arts this is exactly the effect obtained from the juxtaposition of planes of representation and the obtrusion of one upon another..."[32]

One of the auxiliary themes of the play which involves a very effective interplay of the two visions, is that of appearance and reality. Even more astutely than the presentation of Angelo in *Measure for Measure*, Shakespeare presents the two facets of Claudius—one which he displays to the world and the other which really is. When Polonius refers to the deception which may put the semblance of good by 'pious action' and 'devotion', on the devil himself, Claudius cannot help seeing its application to himself :

"O, 'tis too true!
How smart a lash that speech doth give my conscience!
The harlot's cheek, beautied with plast'ring art,
Is not more ugly to the thing that helps it
Than is my deed to my most painted word. "[33]

The pricking of conscience which is the one positive trait in Claudius and the truth of the matter—both relate to reality as against the concrete image of the painted cheek which in its turn lends a weight to the word by a transference of the quality of painting. Appearance is communicated by a concrete image while reality by an abstract one—just to emphasize that it is appearance which is paradoxically thought to be real. It anticipates the painting image in the graveyard scene where it is associated with a skull which is taken to be the final reality behind a painted face. It may be apt to refer to it to bring out this meaning :

"Now get you to my lady's chamber, and tell her, let her paint an inch thick, to this favour she must come."[34]

The negative vision glaringly brings out the final reality of death behind the mask of life. The problem of choice between this appearance of life and the reality of death is envisaged by Hamlet as a choice between the state of Becoming and the state of Being. For him only death can bring the peace and rest which is expected in the next world.

He never thinks of salvation and that is why he cannot imagine an after-state without bad dreams—the dreams which he dreaded even when he was talking to Rosencrantz and Guildenstern to put them on the wrong scent.

In the third soliloquy which expresses Hamlet's attempt to choose between death-in-life and the peace of death, we find the negative vision operating on life as well as death. If life is 'a sea of troubles,' death may have the unknown horror of dreams:

"For in that sleep of death what dreams may come, / When we have shuffled off this mortal coil,
Must give us pause".[35]

Then follows a long catalogue of ills which must be borne after this rejection of both life and death without an acceptance of life when there is no option but to live.

It is the freshness and lustre of any resolution which is inevitably 'sicklied o'er with the pale cast of thought' and Hamlet's one gift—in apprehension how like a god! —is seen to operate destructively. The tremendous power of apprehending the entire human condition while thinking of his individual problem, engulfs and obliterates all links with reality until 'nothing is but what is not'. [36]

There is a further thought-pattern of juxtaposing opposites and tossing to extremes which is the usual Hamlet-style. Taking arms counterpointed by sleep; dreams counterpointed by their alternative, the 'calamity' of living; resolution counterpointed by turning away of action. As for currents which seem to have a driving force, they prove to be only of abortive thought. The thought process is a microcosm of the play and puts what is wrong in a nutshell:

'thus conscience does make cowards of us all'.

Even here Hamlet does not speak of himself in particular. His mind escapes his problem at a tangent into the general human predicament.

Wilson Knight has an interesting comment on this thought-process which overleaps itself :

"We have (in this soliloquy) sequence of abnormal thinking holding in solution, as it were, the jarring opposites of our play. It starts from what at least seems thought of strong action ('take arms', 'oppose'), proceeds though death and suicide, and thence returns imperceptibly, yet through an increasing tilting of the balance, to a final emphasis on strong action... Suicide is the one obvious fusion... of the opposing principles of fine action and death- shadowed passivity, will and suffering, sanity and madness.. Through him life deliberately uses its own energy to contradict.... itself.. For once these extremes intershade, they are fluid and run into each other."[37]

Ruth Nevo puts the scheme of opposition thus :

"Hamlet's pale cast of thought is... that mental activity which counters every option with its opposite, every consideration with its contrary... From this cul-de-sac he sees no escape. His thought moves in clogged and wearisome circles..."[38]

Modifying a statement of Van Doren, we can say that this soliloquy "twitches remote corners of a dramatic web... we gather that the whole play is implicit here..."[39]

The immediately following encounter with Ophelia can only be expected to reveal the innocent victim caught in this dramatic web of contradictions and extremes. The negative vision throws the disintegrated psyche of Hamlet into full focus.

It is to be noted that in Hamlet's mind the two women in the play—the only two presumably whom he knew to have whatever knwoledge he had of womankind—Ophelia and Gertrude—are inextricably linked. He almost identifies one with the other and in the encounter with each—in the Nunnery scene and the Closet scene—what he says to one is with the other in mind. His extreme concern with the sin of his mother is present at the back of his mind when he speaks to Ophelia and his concern for Ophelia appears in his words to his mother. Paradoxically, he uses the opportunity in each case to find a release for the pent-up feelings he has for the other. This makes for what may be called an oblique way of communicating a sense of urgency and prevents understanding. The disgust he feels at the sin of his mother vitiates any chance of understanding with Ophelia with disastrous consequences for her when he accidentally but brutally kills Polonius.

Coupled with this identification is the suspicion or knowledge that Claudius and Polonius are evesdropping and that Ophelia is a decoy to give him away as she was giving back his gifts and this precipitates the brutality unmatched by his other such acts. Here he shows no redeeming touch, no remorse whatever except a wild display later by jumping into her grave to out-Herod Herod.

The scene is entirely conceived in an acute negative vision and the staging with its coarseness is so painful that Dover Wilson tried to account for Hamlet's brutality by suggesting that he had over-heard the scheme of "loosing" Ophelia to him while Lawrence Olivier added to the staging a sorrowful kiss on the hair.

To account for Hamlet's behaviour in this scene and in that with his mother, Gilbert Murray points out that Hamlet shares two barbaric traits with his Greek counterpart Orestes - rudeness in speech and lack of human feeling for women and the tendency "to bully any woman they are left alone with."[40]

And yet Hamlet is tender and gentle too and he does evince these traits in the closet scene after the ghost of his father reappears to him. Clearly, there are two simultaneous strains which run in two parts of his consciousness which has suffered a cleavage and one may be abruptly succeeded by the other. Even in this scene the words with which he expresses his reaction when he sees Ophelia from some distance, are gentle :

"The fair Ophelia.-Nymph, in thy orisons
Be all my sins rememb' red."[41]

followed by "I humbly thank you," when she inquires, "How does your honour;.?" We may remind ourselves that Dr. Johnson thought the earlier words to be "grave and solemn".

But Hamlet becomes excited when Ophelia returns his gifts. However, it is not so instructed to her if she is performing a role nor necessary if it is intended to bring out his love but considering Hamlet's state of mind of which she was aware from his behaviour in her closet it was as ill thought of as Cordelia's refusal to say more than 'nothing' to Lear's expectation that she would tell how much she loved him. It makes him bitter and invites sarcastic queries on honesty and beauty and a denial that he was ever capable of love. By an easy transition, he reverts to his acute consciousness of sin which was the mood of his first soliloquy.

"You should not have believ'd me, for virtue cannot so innoculate our old stock but we shall relish of it. I loved you not."[42]

It is true that Hamlet had no moral right to reproach her after he had disowned love. It is by an identification of her with his conviction that she would commit similar sins as his mother, that forces his thought that she should 'go to a nunnery'. It is wrong to read any obscene suggestion because Hamlet could be obscene in a different state of mind such as he exhibited in the play-scene.

The disparity between what Ophelia appeared to be and what she was, is added to the feeling of sin already presented and results in an overwhelming sense of revulsion from the possible marriage with her. What follows is an over-all condemnation of marriage, of the idea of having one face and 'making' oneself another, of the futility of being born or of begetting sinners, of a deliberate darkening of his character partly to repel her coupled with the desire to threaten Claudius whom he knows to be overhearing. It is like a converging of all strains in his mind—real and fallacious—which his highly tense state brings together driven to a pitch by an acute sense—again partly illusory—of her acting as a decoy and telling a lie. It is also a retaliatory flaring up at her breaking away with him and Coleridge's lines "to be wroth with one we love/Doth work like madness in the brain"[43] uniquely applies to the situation. Thus it is a complex emotion which seems to find a cathartic outburst with the only person whom he could make a butt or a scapegoat. What remains of it finds an outlet with his mother. It could be said that Ophelia is not an adequate objective correlative for this complex emotion of disgust, nausea, self-hatred, challenge and the desire for not having been born. But it is an irony of tragedy that it must have a sacrificial victim-down from Cassandra in *Agamemnon* to Ophelia, Desdemona and Cordelia. Ophelia is thus caught up in the compulsive drift to her fate with words most of which don't relate to the immediate context :

"Get there to a nunnery. Why wouldst thou be a breeder of sinners? I am myself indifferent honest, but yet I could accuse me of such things that it were better my mother had not borne me : I am very proud, revengeful, ambitious; with more offences at my beck than I have thoughts to put them in, imagination to give them shape, or time to act them in. What should such fellows as I do crawling between earth and heaven? We are arrant knaves, all; believe none of us."[44]

The lie of Ophelia that her father is at home sharpens the sense of contrast between appearance and reality which, with his mother's betrayal of her husband, and with Claudius' dissembling, becomes so acute that, at the only point in the play, he directly states it as the cause of his 'madness':

"I have heard of your paintings too, well enough; God hath given you one face, and you make yourselves another. You jig and amble, and you lisp, and nickname God's creatures, and make your wantonness your ignorance. Go to, I'll no more on't; it hath made me mad. I say we will have no more marriage : those that are married already, all but one, shall live; the rest shall keep as they are. To a nunnery, go."[45]

That Hamlet exits just after he has uttered his veiled threat to Claudius is an ample proof that this was one of the motives of his outburst. It was to lead him on the wrong scent as far as love was concerned and although this served no ostensible purpose and the threat made Claudius plan further to get rid of Hamlet, it can be said that with his intention to kill Claudius immediately after his guilt was proved in the play-scene, he could afford to threaten without upsetting his plan.

The entire scene, displaying the least agreeable side of Hamlet's character, transpires in the light of the negative vision. There is absolutely no redeeming trait so much so that we are apt to form an impression that Hamlet had an ingrained sense of cruelty and apathy–even a touch of sadism, to use an expression current much later. So far, this negative vision has brought together almost all the 'ruffled, prickly and distasteful'[46] parts of his consciousness. The desire to hurt is more than to amend and the total picture runs counter to all criteria of 'nobility' associated with the very idea of a tragic hero. Hence it seems that partly to offset this impression and partly to reveal Ophelia's reaction, Shakespeare has put the speech recalling 'the form and feature' of what Hamlet was. It is not the positive vision emphatically presenting what Hamlet was; its light is seen, as it were, from a distance illuminating a form which is no more :

"O, what a noble mind is here o'er thrown !
The courtier's solider's, scholar's, eye, tongue, sword;
Th' expectancy and rose of the fair state,
The glass of fashion and the mould of form,
Th' obsev'd of all observers - quite, quite, down!
And I, of ladies most deject and wretched,
That suck'd the honey of his music vows,
Now see that noble and most sovereign reason,
Like sweet bells jangled, out of time and harsh;
That unmatch'd form and feature of blown youth
Blasted with ecstasy."[47]

Dramatically, this speech performs an important function casting a backward glance in the stream-of-consciousness fashion and revealing the ideal form we never see in the course of the play but which nevertheless 'complements' our image of Hamlet, In Hamlet's treatment of Ophelia in this scene, the negative vision reveals a fact about Hamlet's incapacity to respond to positive feelings like love narrowing down his sensibilities which were near-paralyzed by melancholy resulting from the shock of disillusionment. Goethe's idea of a China-vase being shivered to pieces applies well to this state. As Bradley says :

"Hamlet's love .. was not only mingled with bitterness, it was also, like all his healthy feelings, weakened and deadened by his melancholy. It was far from being extinguished; probably it was *one* of the causes which drove him to force his way to Ophelia... But it was not an absorbing passion;.. and when he declared that it was such a love as forty thousand brothers could not equal, he spoke sincerely indeed but not truly. What he said was true... of the inner healthy self... but it was only partly true of the Hamlet whom we see in the play... And psychologically it is quite sound, for a frequent symptom of such melancholy is a more or less complete paralysis, or even perversion, of the emotion of love."[48]

Abandoning love and spurning the only girl whose love could have redeemed him is tragic enough and yet an equally frenzied scene with his mother was shortly to be enacted. What emerges from these encounters is that Hamlet is "passion's slave" and wherever he displays his passion it is in the light of the negative vision. It is not that he doesn't possess reason; he has a fair share of man's god-like reason and thoughts that wonder through eternity—only that this "passion" and "reason" are not held in a balance—or to apply his own words to himself, "blood" and "judgement" in him are not "comeddled."

That is why Hamlet longs for being like his anti-type or to use Yeats' concept his "mask" — and to unite with it. It is the only way to secure wholeness. He sees this type in Horatio and for the first time in the play, and characteristically just after his hopes in Ophelia are lost, he confesses to Horatio his desire to have a man who embodies balance, restraint and moderation :

"..... Dost thou hear ?
Since my dear soul was mistress of her choice
And could of men distinguish, her election,
Sh' hath seal'd thee for herself; for thou hast been
As one, in suff'ring all, that suffers nothing :
A man that Fortune's buffets and rewards
Hast ta'en with equal thanks; and blest are those
Whose blood and judgment are so well comeddled
That they are not a pipe for Fortune's finger
To sound what stop she please. Give me that man
That is not passion's slave, and I will wear him
In my heart's core, ay, in my heart of heart, As I do thee."[49]

This urge for wholeness is due to the double vision which Shakespeare has endowed Hamlet with, although he is not able to possess what belongs to his anti-type. He is able to see clearly two types of men—his type and that represented by Horatio—see the difference and desire a synthesis. This is also expressed by the notion of "complementarity" which Oppenheimer applies to two opposite manifestations of the same object. One part, divided and incomplete by itself complements its opposite. In this case, the oppoite embodies a maturer and more balanced state.

In a different terminology and using mythical and archetypal notions, Hamlet's mental make-up can be seen as a tension between the primitive Dionysian energy and the Apollonian rationality. Hamlet as a man of reason and as a sometime combination of the courtier, scholar and soldier, is constantly trying to adhere to a norm of balance and serentity which could be termed Apollonian but he is, in spite of himself, drawn by the wild, primitive strain in his nature which always gets the better of the rational part of him. This clash between the two aspects of the personality of the tragic hero is seen in Nietzcohe's idea of tragedy and it is the Dionysian element which is responsible for his undoing :

"The vision of Apollo builds up before us a heroic world, sublime, magnificent, rejoicing in its splendid individuality. But with this Apollonian vision is combined the wild, self-annihilating rapture of the music of Dionysus. From that tragedy sprung, and in that each tragedy dies away, while the power and the glory and the glamour of this heroic world dissolve in the end ecstatically back to airy nothing. The individual, whom Apollo had bidden, above all, to know himself, here loses himself once more and rejoices to be lost, in the vast onward Dionysian sweep of life."[50]

Tragedy occurs because the positive elements in the protagonist are overpowered and nullified by the negative elements and this movement to a decline and to catastrophe is presented in the light of the negative vision. Thus the entire movement of Hamlet's tragedy with reference to his character and actions, can be viewed as the 'clash' between the Apollonian and the Dionysian parts of his being. His soliloquies reveal how he wants to be a man of reason and his concept of man - 'in action how like an angel, in apprehension how like a god', coupled with Ophelia's reference to what he himself was, 'The courtier's, soldier's, scholar's, eye, tongue, sword; The expectancy and rose of the fair state, / The glass of fashion and the mould of form,' reveals the Apollonian ideal which he cherished and had actually attained. But the 'passion' which overcame him from time to time, such as in the scene which followed the revelation by the Ghost, in the scene with the players, in the nunnery scene, in the wild abandon after the play-scene, in the closet scene and in the grave-yard scene in his grappling with Laertes—shows that the Dionysian part of him was always waiting below the conscious self to 'possess' him and overwhelm his being.

Ironically, it is in his Dionysian temper that he kills the king and achieves his end in spite of all his ratiocination, The fact was that the Apollonian man who could be like an angel in action had become corroded and near-paralyzed by•the shock he received at the contradiction of those very virtues he cherished in the conduct of his mother and by the enormity of the evil—individual and universal — which he saw around him. This rendered the Apollonian element ineffectual and released the Dionysian which could have been kept in restraint by the Apollonian. As Nietzsche says, 'the individual whom Apollo (the rational part) had bidden, above all, to know himself, here loses himself once more.. in the vast onward Dionysian sweep of life'. Hamlet has never truly known himself and his tragic progress can be seen as a movement to self-knowledge through the alternations of thought and 'wild and whirling' acts until he is 'chastened and subdued' as we see him near the end of the play.

So it is that at the end of his tragic pilgrimage, Hamlet evinces a note of acceptance. The real growth or education through suffering on his part has been a movement from negation to affirmation. When Horatio says "If your mind dislike anything, obey it," Hamlet replies :

"Not a whit, we defy augury : there is a special providence in the fall of a sparrow. If it be now, 'tis not to come, if it be not to come, it will be now; if it be not now, yet it will come - the readiness is all. Since no man owes of aught he leaves, what is't to leave betimes ? Let be."[51]

It is the point of consummation which the positive vision highlights and the stages in the growth of this 'perturbed' spirit which the negative vision had continuously focused have reached a point when it is technically no longer necessary. It is 'calm of mind, all passion spent' - the proper end of a tragedy according to the classical ideal.

If we rightly understand Hamlet's spiritual evolution up to this stage we can see the straight, undeviating movement till the end. Even Charlton's negative point of view makes allowance for this movement under a positive vision.

".. if Hamle's duty is to be done, Providence will occasion its doing, as indeed Providence does in the heat of the fencing match..."[52]

The conclusion of the play is thus a working out of

Providence or shaping by a Divinity and by an identification of his will with the will of God, Hamlet had discovered the true way to action as Thomas Becket in *Murder in the Cathedral* had done in a different context. But it is true that the old hybris has left him. So it emerges as a paradoxical truth in the light of all we have been saying about Hamlet's evolving make-up, that finally he gets over the duality which had marked his thoughts and actions. The negative part of his nature which made these thoughts and actions ineffective has been purged. The Dionysian element becomes synthesized with the Apollonian. In this connection what Joseph Calarco says applies uniquely to *Hamlet :*

"Tragedy involves a paradoxical union of opposed illusions whose purpose is to place man beyond, unmediated suffering and beyond the despair which he feels when suffering can neither be intelligible in some context larger than the individual experience of pain... Nietzsche sees tragedy as the wedding of the Apollonian and the Dionysiac."[53]

That Hamlet has passed beyond suffering and despair and that his personal pain is no longer important to him, can be clearly seen in his words to Horatio :

"But thou wouldst not think how ill all's here about my heart; but it is no matter."[54]

We can see how wrong it is to interpret this as merely "the courage of despair."[55]

When subsequently, he displays complete equllibrium in the fencing - match and shows faith in allowing Laertes to choose his foil, he has risen above the level of the desire to win. He accepts his punishment by 'a sore distraction' and disclaims 'evil'. These words in his apology to Laertes have a wider symbolic sense. The final execution of his task is just as he wished, killing the king when he was 'about an act that hath no relish of salvation in it'[56]. And though it was in a Dionysian temper that he stabs the king and makes him drink the remaining poison, we can see that it is also an act of justice on the testimony of two victims for whose death he was responsible while Hamlet himself was the third. So in this combination of justice, the Oresteian theme is incorporated, with the role of Apollo who wanted justice to acquit Orestes. Hamlet would certainly have been similarly acquitted by public opinion had he lived, since the guilt of Claudius was publicly proved.

Another plane on which the synthesis of the Apollonian and the Dionysian element is effected is in Hamlet's choice of Fortinbras to succeed him. After the death of Claudius, Hamlet is for a few moments in possession of the title to the throne and having been for long (excluding the earlier self Ophelia knew and the latter brief part) predominantly Dionysian in make—up, he chooses the man of action who is not "passion's slave" as his successor. In other words, he had always been longing for the Apollonian man and in his desire to have Horatio in his heart's core he gave expression to this longing. But he could not have Horatio as his successor. So this man of royal blood who appears at the appropriate time, is immediately accepted as the one who would be his 'complement' and in this idea the dramatist has presented Hamlet's final vision of what he would have longed to be.

Calarco says that "Lear's final vision combines both realms (of Apollo and Dionysus). In this vision *King Lear* displays its affinity with Greek tragedy."[57] We can say the same of *Hamlet*, because Hamlet's final vision is also of a such a synthesis — his attributes being complemented by those of Fortinbras. It matters little that Hamlet was dying— the vision as it existed when he named Fortinbras his successor, included a synthesis of the two elements.

REFERENCES

1. Frederick S. Boas, *Shakespeare and His Predecessors* (John Murray, London, 1896) p. 288.
2. W.W. Lawrence, *Shakespeare's Problem Comedies* (Frederick Ungar Publishing Co. New York, 1931) p. 4.
3. Ibid., p. 4.
4. E.M.W. Tillyard, *Shakespeare's Problem Plays* (Chatto and Windus, London 1950) p. 24 and 32.
5. Ibid., pp. 34 and 36.
6. H.B. Charlton, *Shakespearean Tragedy* (Macmillan, London, 1950) p. 21.

7. G. Wilson Knight, *The Wheel of Fire* (Methuen and Co. London, 1930) pp. 17, 28, 29.
8. *Hamlet*. Act I, Sc II, *ll*. 133-37.
9. Ibid., *ll*. 145-53.
10. Ibid., *ll*. 76-84.
11. Ibid., *l*. 143.
12. Ibid., Act I, Sc V, *ll*. 41-57.
13. Ibid., *l*. 108.
14. Ibid., *ll*. 170-2.
15. Ibid., Act I, Sc III, *ll*. 38-43.
16. G. Wilson Knight, *The Wheel of Fire*, p. 21.
17. Jan Kott, *Shakespeare our Contemporary* (Methuen and Co., London, 1965) p. 49.
18. Jean Paul Sartre, *What is Literature ?* (Bernard Frenchman, Paris and London, 1950) p. 167.
19. Ruth Nevo, *Tragic Form in Shakespeare* (Princeton University Press, 1972) pp. 140-41.
20. *Hamlet*, Act II, Sc II, *ll*.. 292-300.
21. Ibid., *ll*. 331-309.
22. Act IV, Sc IV, *ll*. 36-39
23. Ibid., Act III, Sc IV, *ll*. 56.
24. G. Wilson Knight, *The Wheel of Fire*, p. 29.
25. Evelyn Underhill, *Mysticism* (Methuen, London, 1910) pp. 98-99.
26. Ibid., p. 99.
27. Ibid., p. 100.
28. Ibid., p. 102.
29. *Hamlet*, Act III, Sc IV, *ll*. 172-74.
30. Ibid., *ll*. 317-22.
31. Ibid., Act II, Sc II, *ll*. 560-69.
32. Ruth Nevo, *Tragic Form in Shakespeare* (Princeton University Press, 1972) p. 149.
33. *Hamlet*. Act III, Sc I, *ll*. 49-53.
34. Ibid., Act V. Sc I, *ll*. 187-89.
35. Ibid., Act III, Sc I, *ll*. 66-68.
36. *Macbeth*. Act I, Sc III, *l*. 141.
37. G. Wilson Knight, *The Wheel of Fire* (Methuen and Co., London 1930) pp. 306-7.

38. Ruth Nevo, *Tragic Form in Shakespeare* (Princeton University Press, 1972) pp. 154-55.
39. Mark Van Doron, *Shakespeare* (George Allen and Unwin, London, 1941) p. 192.
40. Gilbert Murray, *Hamlet and Orestes* ("Five Approaches of Literary Criticism", Collier Books, 1962) p. 262.
41. *Hamlet*, Act III, Sc I, *ll.* 89-90.
42. Ibid., *ll.* 117-19.
43. S.T. Coleridge, *Christabel*, Part II.
44. *Hamlet*, Act III, Sc I, *ll.* 121-29.
45. Ibid., *ll*, 142-49.
46. Gilbert Murray, *Hamlet and Orestes* ("Five Approaches of Literary Criticism", Collier Books, 1962) p. 262.
47. Hamlet, Act III, Sc I, *ll.* 150-60
48. A.C. Bradley, *Shakespearean Tragedy* (Macmillan and Co., London, 1904) pp. 157-58.
49. Ibid., *ll.* 61-72.
50. F.L. Lucas, *Tragedy* (Collier Books, New York, 1965) p. 62.
51. *Hamlet*, Act V, Sc II, *ll*, 211-18.
52. H.B. Charlton, *Shakespearean Tragedy* (Macmillan, London, 1950) p. 104.
53. Joseph Calarco, *Tragic Being : Apollo and Dionysus in Western Drama* (University of Minnesota Press, Minneapolis, 1968)
54. *Hamlet*, Act V, Sc II, *ll.* 203-5.
55. H.B. Charlton, *Shakespearean Tragedy*, p. 103.
56. *Hamlet*, Act III, Sc III, *l.* 92.
57. Joseph Calarco, *Tragic Being : Apollo and Dionysus in Western Drama*, p. 143.

CHAPTER VIII

The Serpent of The Nile

Antony and Cleopatra is the most mature tragedy of Shakespeare. It stands at the climactic point of Shakespeare's evolution as a tragic artist. It is not his greatest tragedy but one in which he most fully reveals his poetic and dramatic powers. The compulsion of the historical plot and perhaps his own choice precluded that intense concentration on a single character which we find in the four great tragedies usually classed as superior to it. But as a work of dramatic art the play is unique. It shows no falling off in Shakespeare's powers as can be slightly seen in *Coriolanus* and conspicuously in *Timon*.

Apart from what Coleridge called the "happy valiancy" of the style of *Antony and Cleopatra* which characterizes the play, lending it a sweep and dynamism from beginning to end, the play is sustained by a powerful vision which in its double manifestation, knits up the most contradictory matter into a meaningful whole. Moreover, the intensity of vision lends power to everything mean and noble alike. That is how Coleridge perceived it :

"There are few plays in which he impresses the notion of angelic strength so much..... This is greatly owing to the manner in which the fiery force is sustained throughout."[1]

Bradley tries to probe deeper into this quality, marking it as an intense activity :

"One may notice that in calling *Antony and Cleopatra* wonderful or astonishing, we appear to be thinking first of the artist and his activity, while in the case of the four famous tragedies it is the product of this activity, the thing presented, that first engrosses us."[2]

By emphasizing the artistic activity rather than its product, Bradley is underlining the deft manipulation and presentation of character and action irrespective of the tragic content. What is more, Shakespeare presents these with an intriguing complexity and ambivalence so that there are two aspects seen alternately or at the same time as we view the main characters and their actions. Ernest Schanzer, in the conclusion to his book, speaks of this double effect, giving an Elizabethan example :

"The image which these presentations suggest is not the web woven of a mingled yarn, good and ill together, but rather the toy which the Elizabethans called a 'perspective', presenting two quite different pictures, according to our angle of vision."[3]

From this arises the two-fold significance and meaning from the same action or situation and the same trait in the character can be interpreted in two ways. This quality is most conspicuous in *Antony and Cleopatra*. As we have seen with reference to the characters and their actions in the plays already considered, it is due to the fact that there is a continuous highlighting of contradictory facets of the character as the action proceeds. This process can be most easily seen in Cleopatra than in any other character although Helena, Angelo, Cressida, Brutus and Hamlet have their double facets which make them problematic. Other characters in all these plays also display contradictions. This is seen in their thoughts and actions and consists essentially in the mode of their presentation.

By now it is clear that it is Shakespeare's double vision which is invariably active in this dramatic mode of exhibiting the thoughts, emotions and reactions of the characters. As Schanzer puts it with reference to *Antony and Cleopatra* (but applicable to others of these plays as well) :

"... it is done simply and emphatically through the constant juxtaposition of opposed evaluations of the same actions and events."[4]

This is what accounts for the enigmatic nature of many of the actions of Cleopatra and even of Antony in the course of the play resulting in "uncertain and divided responses" on the part of the audience. And a constant repetition of them makes *Antony and Cleopatra* a problem play.

It was Ernest Schanzer who included *Antony and Cleopatra* among the problem plays of Shakespeare in 1963 although the Circe-like inconsistent quality of Cleopatra and the inexplicable transformation of Antony into "a strumpet's fool" on the one hand and the "immortal longings" and intimations of Heaven, on the other, had always been its baffling points.

L.C. Knights has hinted at a very significant point in the presentation of the tragic experience in the play :

"In *Macbeth* we are never in any doubt of our moral bearings. *Antony and Cleopatra* on the other hand, embodies different and apparently irreconcilable evaluations of the central experience."[5]

Schanzer elaborates this point further,

"Throughout the play, and to an extent far exceeding anything found in *Julius Caesar* and *Measure for Measure*, we are confronted with these opposed evaluations, and in such a way as to exclude—at least in those open to the play's full imaginative impact—a simple and consistent response."[6]

Philip Edwards approaches the problematic nature of the play selecting a typical feature in Shakespeare's dramatic teachnique-that of contrary valuations of what the characters and their actions stand for. He remarks :

"*Antony and Cleopatra* is a positive demonstration of the 'contrary valuations;' it is the play Shaw recognized, 'a faithful picture of the soldier broken down by debauchery, and the typical wanton in whose arms such men perish', and it is also the more generally recognized tragedy of supersession, of the ousting of the old richness and generosity by the colourless efficiency of youth, a 'faithful picture' indeed of a decline which makes the hero's partner, blessed even in her riggishness, rise to a nobler quality of being."[7]

Edwards concludes, "The play is equally these two pictures : not one first and then the other. It is an Egyptian obelisk testifying to the impossibility of single vision.."

From this conclusion it is but one step to the idea we have been postulating — that it is only a double vision with positive and negative strains which can alternately, or sometimes simultaneously, so focus the character and their actions and reactions that it results in a two-fold impression on the audience and one is intrigued and ultimately prone to accept either or both of the contrary impressions so received.

Let us see how Shakespeare uses this technique in *Antony and Cleopatra*, the most typical of his plays from this point of view.

The very first scene of the play opens by presenting two contrary views of Antony. It also begins the polarities between the secular and the spiritual, between reason and passion and between duty and love — all three symbolized by the opposition between Rome and Egypt. There is an ambivalence in the presentation — the same emotion is morally condemned and immediately later, presented with a spiritual significance.

As Antony, Cleopatra and their train enter, Philo says to Demetrius :

"Look where they come !
Take but good note, and you shall see in him
The triple pillar of the world transform'd
Into a Strumpet's fool."[8]

Just after these lines, as if to correct the balance, the contrary view is given. Cleopatra asks Antony, how much he loves her. Then she insists.

"I'll set a bourn how far to be belov'd." Antony answers in words which dwarf all secular criteria :"Then must thou needs find out new heaven, new earth."

Commenting on these two perspectives on Antony's love, Derek Traversi says this of the first :

"Nothing in the coming tragedy, no poetic exaltation of the passion that animates the main protagonists, can make this first estimate irrelevant;"[9]

Then of the second, he says :

"The sense of a superhuman content apprehended though love is one that the play will repeat and develop, in relation to a superb emotional expansiveness, even in the process of passing judgement upon it."[10]

Ruth Nevo calls it a "grand abolition of reckoning."[11]

Thus begins "the synchronization of two differing velocities within the contest of the tragic progress" and from the point of view of dramatic technique, what Schanzer calls "dramatic coquetry, consisting in an alternatre enlisting and repelling of the audience's affections for a character",[12] which will continue for the rest of the play.

At the very source of the dramatic imagination it is the light of the shaping vision which is projected, in turn, positively or negatively upon these two characters. Characteristically, it is the negative vision which precedes and is followed so surely and closely by the positive vision that Shakespeare the artist seems keen to make up for the historical truth of the negative vision by the poetic truth which he sought to project by the positive vision. Sometimes, in a very complex manner, the one is shot through with the other. This effect like that of shotsilk, particular to Cleopatra, is found only in one other character—Falstaff—in the whole canon of Shakespeare.

What follows is Cleopatra's ironical charge of Antony's being "Caesar's homager" and in reply Antony's sweeping dismissal of all secular greatness and identification of the earth itself with dung. All earthly notions of size are ruled out in "Here is my space". This sharp juxtaposition also brings out Antony's "choice" which is at the heart of his tragedy :

> Let Rome in Tiber melt, and the wide arch
> Of the rang'd empire fall ! Here's my space.
> Kingdoms are clay : our dungy earth alike
> Feeds beast as man. The nobleness of life
> Is to do thus."[13]

Even the standard of 'nobility' corresponding to the common quality in Shakespeare's tragic heroes, is newly defined and paradoxically it joins with nobility in the absolute sense later on as seen in his treatment of Enobarbus after he deserts him and of other soldiers.

New horizons of meaning are for even opening up and two contradictory notions are ultimately reconciled just like the idea of sensuous and spiritual love.

Cleopatra's development shows two broad curves, the first spanning the first four Acts and the second the fifth Act and within each, we find juxtapositions of the negative and positive visions. The development of Antony discloses a single curve and within it can be discerned two distinct stages — a major part extending up to scene III of the fourth Act and a brief part of the remaining two scenes of this Act. The first part discloses a uniformly negative movement sparsely touched by the positive vision. The remaining part shows the positive vision at work redeeming the character from those negative traits which had made him lose the empire of the world. Shakespeare does not stop here. There is a third stage of the mythical development of Antony after his death in the dream of Cleopatra in scene two of the fifth Act. And, as if to offset everything, there is an extraordinary positive development of Cleopatra's character in the whole of the fifth Act. It is clear that up to the middle of the fourth Act, Shakespeare dramatizes the negative side of both characters till 'this world' is completely lost to them and does it as it were, as an historical necessity. Then he handles the theme to bring out the poetic and imaginative significances which engaged him more deeply. But the character of Cleopatra engrosses him so much that even during the negative development with her freaks and tantrums, in many of such situations, he charges her person with a 'fiery force' that in a trice, we see the positive vision engrafting a magic to everything that is negative till paradoxes emerge and "the priests bless her when she is most riggish."

The 'dramatic coquetry' of Shakespeare was never seen to better advantage than in his delineation of Cleopatra. And this is at the heart of its quality as a problem play.

Shakespeare seems to have created Enobarbus (who has no historical authenticity in Plutarch) solely in order to have a chorus—like character to be present on the stage, to watch and to comment on the character and actions of both Antony and Cleopatra so as to bring out their paradoxical traits. Often, the negative and the positive visions are projected through him.

We can take the instance when he describes the changing moods of Cleopatra which she mostly 'affects' to keep Antony in her power but which also reveal an inexplicable combination of falsehood and truth. When Antony announces his decision to go to Rome, Enobarbus says :

"Cleopatra, catching but the least noise of this, dies instantly; I have seen her die twenty times upon far poorer moment. I do think there is mettle in death, which commits some loving act upon her, she hath such a celerity in dying."[14]

It is a statement made in a lighter vein intended to be a comment upon Cleopatra's power of feigning and her changing moods but it is also, as a part of dramatic vision, an anticipation of Cleopatra's 'intimacy' with death which is revealed in the last Act. She can make a 'calculated' use of this power but also reveal it in earnest. Derek Traversi puts the relationship between art and reality with reference to this statement as follows :

"....the power which sees death in terms of the 'loving act', and confers a touch of beauty even upon the cynicism of 'such a celerity in dying', is one in which life and its opposite are strangely blended in a fusion of tenderness and moral realism. This is, indeed, a first faint anticipation of the mingled failure and triumph of Cleopatra's end."[15]

It is an illustration of how certain basic images like those of love and death knit the whole play into a visionary unity. Similarly the image of 'a new heaven, new earth' is carried forward in the suggestion of something like a divine power in her 'passions'.

When Antony says, "She is cunning past man's thought," Enobarbus replies :

"Alack, sir, no! Her passions are made of nothing but the finest part of pure love. We cannot call her winds and waters sighs and tears; they are greater storms and tempests than almanacs can report. This cannot be cunning in her, if it be, she makes a show'r of rain as well as Jove."[16]

Even though there is a touch of irony in these words, the subsequent drift of the imagery leaves little doubt that the dramatic vision is seeking to project a picture of Cleopatra which has two sides — that of a woman who feigns and can use her powers like 'toils' to hold Antony but the power of whose emotions is like that of the elements so that it can match that of the gods. This movement of imagery re-appears in the scene with Antony when he comes "to give breathing to his purpose" of going to Rome. Cleopatra again uses her art and genuine emotion to recall his earlier love for her;

"When you sued staying,
Then was the time for words. No going then!
Eternity was in our lips and eyes,
Bliss in our brows' bent, none our parts so poor
But was a race of heaven. they are so still.."[17]

Thus it is a bilateral development of character and the

two aspects — the scheming and the divine — appear constantly in contradiction which seems to make her enigmatic. Yet the human quality is not diminished and it only enhances her infinite variety. In contrast to this, Antony's character is developed unilaterally: there is nothing of the schemer in him; he doesn't feign and the image of the strumpet's fool betokens only a decline of his heroic figure which is still subject to a welling-up of the old spirit and a desire to break away from the bondage of passion :

"O, then we bring forth weeds When our quick minds lie still, and our ills told us/ Is as our earing."

He adds :

"These strong Egyptain fetters I must break
Or lose myself in dotage."[18]

It is a conflict between love and duty but it is not so acute as to be presented internally. There are acute phases but they are temporary. For example, when Antony learns about Fulvia's death, there is again an upsurge of the desire to be free.

"I must from this enchanting queen break off.."[19] It can be said to be working out of the nature of excess : there is a reaction marked by a shock. The shock of the death of Fulvia makes him conscious of the dotage and excess of idleness, as later, the defeat at Actium and Cleopatra's apparent betrayal make him again conscious — too late of his 'viciousness' which 'seeled' his eyes and deprived him of his judgement.

In this light, what Antony says further in the consciousness of his duty, has a terrible application to his subsequent fate :

"Much is breeding
Which, like the courser's hair hath yet but life
And not a serpent's poison."[20]

So is his 'passion' for Cleopatra. In due course, the 'serpent of old Nile' is to infuse her poison in his life so that he loses that world, lives in deception and dies in deception too. But this is only one angle. The other angle reveals that the world is well lost for a heaven where "Dido and her Aeneas shall want troops" when this "peerless" pair goes there.

This reveals another aspect of the play which we must take into account when we consider the suggestions of heaven and immortality which offset the negative effect. While the negative vision often hints at evil in the wiles of Cleopatra as the frequent identification with serpents and poison shows us, the poetry redeems it with imagery which lifts the situation above the murkiness with wings of heaven. The positive vision irradiates from it and the divinity of the spell which Cleopatra had for Antony becomes plausible. This shift in the angle of vision is invariably accompained by high poetry.

Between these two polarities of contrary valuations Antony (and often the audience as well) is swayed and even though his choice is unequivocal, these oscillations determine the rhythm and inner moral structure of the play. The outward concrete polarities of Rome and Egypt which embody symbolic values, reinforce this rhythm. Needless to say, the negative and the positive visions continually and in turn illuminate this movement — a process more complex than in any other play of Shakespeare.

Ruth Nevo takes these oscillations as determining the structure of the play :

"But what in fact happens is that the impossible choice from which tragedy springs is reproduced, upon a higher level of generality and in the imagination of the audience, by the expressive structure of oscillation with its dialectic of contraries."[21]

This structure is, as already suggested, reinforced by the oscillation of the play between its two settings—Rome and Egypt — which provide a shift of values against which the characters and their actions are most meaningfully displayed.

Thus the shift of scene from Egypt to Rome with Antony shown as "oscillating" on to the secular pole, emobodies the seeds of his swing back. But it also reveals what he could be, once he was away from his 'spell' and also the true nature of the "temporal' Cleopatra once the spiritualizing influence was away. Eliminating all differences of time or space, Shakespeare presents the two states simultaneously.

The other side of Antony as soldier emerges in Rome from three angles — one, in the reference by Caesar who evokes Antony's past greatness in the positive vision; the other, in the reference by Sextus Pompey giving a measure of his present greatness, and the third by Enobarbus viewing him in comparison with Caesar. They together give a composite picture of a perfect soldier who is ultimately compared to Mars. Caesar says of his past thus :

"Thou didst drink
The stale of horses and the gilded puddle
Which beasts would cough at. Thy palate then did deign
The roughest berry on the rudest hedge;
Yea, like the stag when snow the pasture sheets,
The barks of trees thou brows'd. On the Alps
It is reported thou didst eat strange flesh,
Which some did die to look on."[22]

Sextus Pompey pays a compliment to his soldiership :

"... his soldiership
Is twice the other twain."[23]

Enobarbus positively thinks Caesar no match for him :

"If Caesar move him,
Let Antony look over Caesar's head
And speak loud as Mars."[24]

In Egypt, Cleopatra seems to reveal her fuller nature on the evil side. In speech which is like a self-revelation she identifies herself in an image which vibrates through the play joining other such images of serpents and poison. It reminds of Coleridge's concept of Geraldine. The paradox is that such images too enthral the imagination by a kind of supernatural appeal. The image of herself is preceded by a contradictory image of Antony with its metallic brightness. Light is juxtaposed with darkness; an Atlas-like colossal figure juxtaposed with the worm of the Nile and what is more, within the second image dazzling brightness of the sun is fused with blackness whereas endless time denotes 'eternity' of another sort than referred to by Enobarbus in his famous speech. The whole speech can be said to embody a rare network or architectonics of imagery :

"The demi-Atlas of this earth, the arm
And burgonet of men. He's speaking now,
Or murmuring, 'Where's my serpent of old Nile ?'

For so he calls me - Now I feed myself
With most delicious poison. Think on me,
That am with Phoebus' amorous pinches black,
And wrinkled deep in time ?"[25]

This brings the negative side of Cleopatra's intrinsic nature into focus and the image of blackness associated with serpents and of poison which annihilates life begin to be associated with her and this explication of her nature begins to take possession of our minds. In contrast, Antony is associated with brightness and light. Further, Antony's prospective marriage with Octavia seems to be the end of his Egyptian affair. The inevitable outcome of this drift of events is expressed in the words of Maecenas, "Now Antony must leave her utterly."[26] At this low ebb, by an unparallelled stroke of dramaturgy which is typical of this play of double vision, Shakespeare puts the positive side of Cleopatra through the richest and most picturesque poetry. Even before these words are uttered, the positive vision irradiates the mental horizon by the halo cast around the appearance of Cleopatra on the Cydnus and the first meeting of Antony with her. We are reminded of the angelic strength and the fiery force referred to by Coleridge. The images of blackness, serpents and poison are more than offset and, without any action whatever, sheer poetic evocation of the past sways the balance in favour of Cleopatra. The alternation of contraries by the poetic vision was never more marked. Flashback operates so naturally that we are oblivious of what is happening in the present and take the image flashed from the past as the only reality. The present becomes only "a fly by an eagle." In reply to the words of Maecenas, "She's a most triumphant lady." Enobarbus tells how "she purs'd up" Antony's heart, when she first met him upon the Cydnus :

"I will tell you.
The barge she sat in, like a burnish'd throne,
Burn'd on the water. The poop was beaten gold;
Purple the sails, and so perfumed that
The winds were love-sick with them; the oars were silver,
Which to the tune of flutes kept stroke, and made
The water which they beat to follow faster,
As amorous of their strokes. for her own person,

It beggar'd all description. She did lie
In her pavilion, cloth—of—gold, of tissue,
O'erpicturing that Venus where we see
The fancy out-work nature. On each side her
Stood pretty dimpled boys, like smiling Cupids,
With drivers—colour'd fans, whose wind did seem
To glow the delicate cheeks which they did cool,
And what they undid did."[27]

The positive vision builds up this picture combining concrete and ethereal elements which account for the secret of its appeal. The barge shone to the extent that it emitted light like an exhalation - combining the two elements. Solid gold of the poop, coupled with silver oars is combined with perfume which makes the winds love-sick—a synthesis of the sensuous and the ethereal. Then the music of flutes making the water amorous is again followed by a combination of concrete and etheral images in the cloth-of-gold, fans and the wind from them cooling and flushing the cheeks of Cleopatra. In between, there is a suggestion of an infinity of skill needed to describe her person which the poet's powers fall short of. It reminds of Marlowe describing Helen's face only with a question.

The same technique of synthesizing the concrete and the abstract and endowing a sensuous quality to the ethereal, is seen in the following passage. The wharfs feel the perfume with their 'sense' and the air itself is so enamoured of Cleopatra that it is restrained from going to gaze on Cleopatra only by the fact that it could not leave a gap in nature.

It is to be presumed that Keats, the only other poet who effects such synthesis of the concrete and the ethereal derived his inspiration from *Antony and Cleopatra* which was the most 'underlined' of the plays in his copy of Shakespeare's plays.

Before we proceed to note the supermost expression of this quality in the most famous of all lines in the play, we must take cognizance of another positive quality in Cleopatra which has mythical parallels. It also combines the positive and negative paradoxes in symbolic form. Cleopatra, it is well-known, often appeared in the habiliments of the Egyptian goddess Isis—the goddess of fertility and of the moon.

Isis is shown as a woman with a cow's horns with a solar disk between them. She was the wife of Osiris — the Egyptian deity of agriculture.

Now the references to Isis are too abundant in the play not to reveal an identity between Cleopatra and the goddess — direct and oblique. The suggestion of fertility which appears at many places also reinforces the identity. In Agrippa's speech which follows the description by Enobarbus, the words, "she cropped" is an indication of what may be called subterranean imagery. Cleopatra's association with the moon is equally repetitive. The image of the moon in Antony's words for her "our terrene moon / Is now eclips'd;"[28] in her own words, "there is nothing left remarkable / Beneath the visiting moon",[29] which explicate her own desolate state after the death of Antony; in "A sun and moon" which she uses to describe the dream-image of Antony and above all the words spoken before her suicide :

"now the fleeting moon
No planet is of mine."[30]

show this identification, conscious and unconscious. The two horns of Isis, with the image of the sun, when identified symbolically with Cleopatra, alongwith the changefulness associated with the moon, symbolize the two changing aspects of her character. The inclusion of the sun-image connects with her own image "with Phoebus' amorous pinches black" and we can also identify Antony with the sun in view of the numerous references in the play. His identification with Osiris is also implicit. What emerges from this is the method of multiple suggestions through imagery adopted by the dramatist to focus the aspects of changefulness, fertility and above all, of contradictions in Cleopatra's character. She is both goddess and serpent, changeful like the moon and 'marble-constant'; flees like 'a cow in June'[31] and yet remains "commanded / By such poor passion as the maid that milks";[32] delights in catching Antony like a fish and tricks him so that he dies as a result of her lie and yet dies with the words "Husband, I come". The divine and the baser elements are so fused in her as to be indistinguishable. That this was Shakespeare's deliberate concept is proved by her words at the end : "I am fire and air; my other elements /

I give to baser life."[33] At each of these points in the play where the antithetical aspects of Cleopatra's character reveal themselves, we can see the working of the positive and negative visions.

Thus the speech of Enobarbus in which Shakespeare fuses the two visions is meant to validate the concept that the divine and 'riggish' elements were inseparable and together they made the spell which was cast not only on Antony but even on the "holy priests". The reference to her agelessness effectively counters and co-exists with "wrinkled deep in time." When Maecenas remarks that Anotny "must leave her utterly" after his marriage with Octavia, Enobarbus says :

Never ! He will not.
Age cannot wither her, nor custom stale
Her infinite variety. Other women cloy
The appetites they feed, but she makes hungry
Where most she satisfies; for vilest things
Become themselves in her, that the holy priests
Bless her when she is riggish."[34]

From the point of the presentation of Cleopatra's view on the Cydnus, Shakespeare's imagination can be seen to be rapidly moving (as Antony's temporal fortunes move to a decline) to a mythical concept of both Antony and Cleopatra and the poetry becomes charged with a power to keep pace with this 'apotheosis', shifting the balance from the secular to the spiritual. It is also intended to offset the dramatic effect of the losses on the secular plane which Antony suffers during the subsequent part of the play.

It may be relevant to quote what Kermode says in this connection, although he does not connect the idea to the two fold strain in Cleopatra's character.

"... there are other patterns of theme and image which ... should certainly not be omitted from any consideration of its total effect. These elements might for convenience be labelled hints of apotheosis and divine fertility. I mentioned that Antony is insistently associated with Hercules, and Cleopatra with Venus, but it is not less important that they have also association with Egyptian divinities. Cleopatra appears in the habiliments of the goddess Isis, and accepts (up to the last moment) the affinity with the moon which this identification with its goddess suggests : She is the "terrene moon" reigning over the sphere of Antony's mutability. And Antony plays Osiris to her Isis. The union of these divinities assures the fertility of Egypt : in Plutarch's study of the myth (well-known in Shakespeare's time) Orisis is the Nile which floods and makes fertile the land : he is form, the seminal principle, and Isis is matter. From their union are bred not only the crops but animals, such as the serpents of the Nile... The presence of this myth in Shakespeare's imagination is suggested by the numerous reference to the Nile, its floods, and its serpents. Cleopatra is Antony's "serpent of old Nile", and she herself speaks twice in II, V, of the serpents and "scaled snakes" that breed from the melting of Egypt into Nile."[35]

Kermode concludes, "There is obviously in the play a strong sense of the goodness of this fertility.. and of the godlike status of its agents."[36]

The assimilation of this fertility myth can be seen in the final suggestions of regeneration on the spiritual plane to which it transposes the stuff of the play.

This is also the reason why the subsequent negative movement of the play which would be anything but entertaining to the audience, becomes acceptable to their imagination. Suggestions that the total undoing on the secular plane was being compensated by some inexplicable power in the being of each of these characters, are maintained because of this elevation in myth and symbol and the poetry takes its cue from them.

The following two Acts, tracing the downward curve of Antony's career, lead to the peripeteia, half-way through in the defeat at Actium. It is followed by self-knowledge—the anagnorisis—which, coming too late and in flashes, gives way to a kind of transfiguration. Finally a supreme conviction that the world was well lost for love coupled with a perception of the melting of appearances, close his career. This later growth is interspersed with positive and negative response to Cleopatra as if a swift movement through contradictions would purge their love of grossness and lift it above contradictions. From the end of Act IV, Sc XIV, all contradictions in character and action are over and the negative vision is hardly seen to operate. Thus from Act II, Sc.

III to this point, the play is that of Antony's movement to his catastrophe and it mostly transpires in the light of the negative vision.

One of the reasons why Antony's love for Cleopatra is not always suffused with the positive vision is that in spite of his exaltation, he is moving in the midst of appearances and his love can be seen adjusting itself to changing selves of Cleopatra as his sense of duty fails to adjust itself to the changing demands laid upon it. That is his tragedy and it lay in his 'choice' which McCollom considers as the central fact in tragedy.

In contrast to this presentation of Cleopatra's whims, vanities and convulsions, which are all presented in the negative vision with sudden flashing of the positive, the subsequent view of the rift between Antony and Octavius is steeped in the starkest negative vision. It is only a cosmic image of eating and grinding which can convey it, and Enobarbus, who as chorus is often the spokesman of the extremes of contrary visions, inspires awe as he expresses it;

"Then, world, thou hast a pair of chaps - no more;
And throw between them all the food thou hast,
They'll grind the one the other."[37]

For the rest of the play up to the death of Enobarbus the negative vision finds its chief spokesman in him. With the landscape of ruin fully revealed and its secular causes laid bare, Enobarbus is no longer necessary to the scheme of the play.

In the steep downward movement of Antony's fortunes, the antithesis between Antony and Octavius is evident at all points but it is obvious that due to his enslavement to the passion for Cleopatra it is he alone who undoes himself. The responsibility is later fully accepted by him. Shakespeare has made this aspect far more important to accord with his categorical choice. This choice also leads to the fatal choice of fighting by sea when all other considerations argued for a land-battle. This choice dictated by Cleopatra led to the shameful 'choice' of following her in the thick of battle and leaving his fleet without a general. It is like Forster's image of a huge serpent with smaller serpents coiling within it. The larger evil of the choice is made up of smaller choices — all equally momentous — which together determine its magnitude.

Thus the greatest turning point in the history of the ancient world is represented as a quick series of fatal steps taken by Antony in the hard, unextenuating light of the negative vision. We see everything connected with his infatuation. It is the greatest peripety that ever occurred but the anagnorisis when it comes, is clouded by his passion and these clouds 'dislimn' only before his suicide.

It begins with his decision to fight Octavius by sea which is reinforced by Cleopatra's 'By sea ! What else ?' When Enobarbus reminds him,

"Most worthy sir, you therein throw away
The absolute soldiership you have by land;
Distract your army, which doth most consist
Of war—mark'd footmen; Kleave unexecuted
Your own renowned knowledge; quite forgo
The way which promises assurance;..."[38]

Antony is firm and he does not listen when the veteran soldier tells him not to "trust to rotten planks". Canidius knows that Antony's judgment has been warped by his passion. He tells the well-meaning soldier :

"Soldier, thou art; but his whole action grows
Not the power no't. so our leader's led.
And we are women's men."[39]

This part impulse, part insinuation of Cleopatra which makes him fight by sea is joined with the other fatal impulse to abandon the fight at its height and follow Cleopatra. This point — the actual crisis of the play and its peripety — marks the spiritual nadir of Antony and being determined by his will, detracts so much from tragic quality that to raise the drama to a tragic height, Shakespeare had to use the utmost resources of poetry. Subsequently he had to follow the same method — of making Cleopatra a positive character and by using his poetic resources in order to make her end tragic.

Thus there is no feeling of pity or terror at Antony's fall as we feel at the fall of Coriolanus or Othello. That comes later when the positive side of his nature is revealed. Till this point, he had chosen with full awareness. As Scarus says with a devastating implication that the greater part of the world was lost for a wanton's 'kiss' :

"The greater cantle of the world is lost
With very ignorance; we have kiss'd away
Kingdoms and provinces,"[40]

Two words are fine instances of a double meaning. We have already noted one, the other, 'ignorance' suggests the want of self-knowledge in Antony.

When Enobarbus asks about the state of the fight, Scarus says:

"On our side like the token'd pestilence,
Where death is sure. You ribaudred nag of Egypt —
Whom leprosy o'ertake !— i'th'; midst o'th' fight,
When vantage like a pair of twins appear'd,
Both as the same, or rather ours the elder —
The breese upon her, like a cow in June —
Hoists sails and flies."

Scarus continues the description of what was an anti-climactic act of cowardice or dotage :

"She once being loof'd
The noble ruin of her magic, Antony,
Claps on his sea - wing, and like a doting mallard,
Leaving the fight in height, flies after her.
I never saw an action of such shame;
Experience, manhood, honour, ne'er before
Did violate so itself."[41]

Caesar's triumph is complete with the decision of Canidius to submit his legions and horsemen to Caesar. It was Caesar's genius which ultimately won and virtually pursued Antony's and the crowning irony of the play — of dramatic as well as historical events--was that Atnony was doubly caught in the toils of Cleopatra as it is recognized but also in the imperialistic ones of Octavius. The 'toils' of Cleopatra had sapped him of the power with which he could meet the designs of Caesar. As Miss M.C. Bradbrook says,

"In *Antony and Cleopatra*, although Antony is descended from the god Hercules and Cleopatra is the incarnation of Isis, mutability rules.."[42] We could say that Octavius and Cleopatra were both the agents of this mutability till the death of Antony and then Cleopatra herself becomes its victim. The later speeches of Antony and the final speeches of Cleopatra are the evidence of this power.

At this point Cleopatra's power is more obviously visible. But neither Octavius' 'genius' or Cleopatra's toils could have proved decisive unless Antony himself proved devoid of all wisdom, self-knowledge and judgement. When Cleopatra asks Enobarbus :

"Is Antony or we in fault for this ?"
Ebobarbus replies :
"Antony only, that would make his will
Lord of his reason. What though you fled
From that great face of war, whose several ranges
Frighted each other ? Why should he follow ?
The itch of his affection should not then
Have nick'd his captainship.."[43]

Thus the negative vision is focused from three angles making for divided and uncertain responses on the part of the audience : the enslavement of Antony to the love of Cleopatra; his own act of making his passion overcome reason and what the soothsayer had told Antony asking him to "make space enough" between himself and Caesar, because "thy, spirit/Is all afraid to govern thee near him."[44] If Enobarbus' statement is taken into account alongside the soothsayer's, the reason for Antony's deserting the scene of battle can be better appreciated. Then this point can be seen to be so presented as to become one of the problems of the play. If we take into consideration the historical account of the battle as given by Harmsworth, Antony's flaw would appear to be more responsible than Cleopatra's defection while the soothsayer's prophecy remains a subterranean factor :

"On September 2nd a great sea battle was fought off the promontory of Actium. Antony was defeated, as Cleopatra made for the open sea during the fight, and Antony, in his infatuation, hastened after her. A few days after, the land army, left without a leader, surrendered.."[45]

The fact that the army was "left without a leader" was responsible for the final defeat and it waited for a few days for Antony. In the play the surrender is immediate, but it makes no difference to the conclusion.

After this defeat, Antony is tossed between the instinct to attribute the blame to Cleopatra and the acceptance of responsibility for himself. Both were true but which was the truth of the moment ? Here again a problem is posed and it is only the viewpoint of tragedy which can finally resolve it. But we can also judge from the text.

Just after the defeat we find Antony dejected and desolate in a state of self-loathing, urging his followers to take the ship laden with gold and divide it amongst themselves and live by making their peace with Ceasar, while he had resolv'd upon another course, presumably of death.

"I am so lated in the world that I
Have lost my way for ever....
I follow'd that I blush to look upon.
My very hairs do mutiny; for the white
Reprove the brown for rashness, and they them
For fear and doting."[46]

"Rashness", "fear" and "doting" stand for the three factors for Antony's defeat which we have already pointed out but Antony has still not accepted full responsibility because rashness doesn't convey his flaw. Traversi sees the attempt to evade the present sense of shame and to seek compensation (what may be called "cheering himself up" in the words T.S. Eliot uses for Othello) in the recalling of past glories.

"He at Philippi kept
His sword e'en like a dancer, while I struck
The lean and wrinkled Cassius and 'twas I
That the mad Brutus ended; he alone
Dealt on lieutenantry, and no practice had
In the brave squares of war. Yet now— no matter."[47]

Next comes the desire to shift the blame to Cleopatra :

"O, whither hast thou led me, Egypt ? See
How I convey my shame out of thine eyes
By looking back what I have left behind
'Stroy'd in dishonour."

Antony then tries to pitch the exaltation and immensity of this love which made him think of a "new heaven" and "space" against all powers human and a divine, and unconsciously seeks to justify his act in following her :

"Egypt, thou knew'st too well
My heart was to thy rudder tied by th'strings,
And thou shouldst tow me after. O'er my spirit
Thy full supremacy thou knew'st, and that
Thy beck might from the bidding of the gods
Command me."[48]

Traversi finds in these lines what may be called the 'objective correlative' of the tragedy :

"The last phrase is very close to the central experience of this many-sided tragedy. The infatuation that has called the former "pillar of the world' from 'the bidding of the gods' is finally a renunciation of the hero's full stature; but that it could have this effect, that Cleopatra could establish over him her 'supremacy', is a sign of the force which it exercises... over its victim."[49]

Shakespeare was indeed faced with the difficult problem of presenting Antony's 'inglorious' choice and that is one cf the reasons of the uniform poetic evocation of the charm of Cleopatra to make the choice plausible. What was implicit in 'Here's my space' and 'Let Rome in Tiber melt' and in Enobarbus' numerous evocations of her spell was to prepare the way for this justification.

The attempt to create this magnitude reaches almost absured extremes when Antony says :

"Fall not a tear, I say; one of them rates
All that is won and lost. Give me a kiss;
Even this repays me."[50]

Of this Ruth Nevo remarks :

"What we perceive is that, despite the grand assertion that one tear "rates/All that is won and lost," the dialectic of contraries which the play has presented has entered corrosively and destructively into Antony's own experience..."[51]

Antony loved his soldiers and it shows the state of extreme despair to know that he must part from them. Enobarbus had been his alter ego and his leaving him betokened Antony's end. He stood "at the still centre of the perturbations and oscillation" which racked the world of *Antony and Cleopatra* — Shakespeare's "most complex and independent reflector."[52] He is both involved and detached as an observer and above all he was the only one from whom the audience got the most important information about Antony and his relationship with Cleopatra. His desertion meant that this function was no longer necessary and that Antony's career was near its end.

The desertion of the spirit of Hercules betokens the end of the heroic career of Antony. After that he was only a shell without the possibility or recovering his old heroism. In Plutarch, it is the spirit of the god Bacchus or Dionysus, the god of wine, with different implications. Shakespeare, with a desire to emphasize Antony's heroism, effected the change.

All three were negative occurrences and all of them signal the approaching end of Antony. The following scene is like a last flicker just before the flame goes out and it serves to rehabilitate Antony in the high esteem of the audience which would make death, when it comes, tragic. If this brief scene of pure heroism had not been inserted, the whole plan of the play would have gone awry. The positive vision of the dramatist redeems Antony and, in a way, resuscitates him from death-in-life even for a brief spell.

Cleopatra has hereself buckled Antony's armour and when she asks "Is not this buckled well?" Antony who had called her "the armourer of my heart", says:

> "Rarely, rarely !
> He that unbuckles this, till we do please
> To daff't for our repose, shall hear a storm.
> Thou fumblest, Eros, and my queen's a squire
> More tight at this than thou Dispatch. O love,
> That thou couldst see my wars to-day, and knew'st
> The royal occupation ! Thou shouldst see
> A workman in't."[53]

Antony goes to battle 'like a man of steel' without waiting for 'more mechanic compliment'. Cleopatra's 'he goes forth gallantly' concisely shows his transformed self. Of this, Ruth Nevo says : "The tenderness, the elation, the marriage harmony of this scene and of the scene of their greeting after the triumph of the second day's battle recalls the joy of Othello greeting his fair warrior at Cyprus."[54]

The other positive turn given to Antony's character to raise him in the opinion of the audience is his treatment of Enobarbus after his desertion. Without any blame or anger, he calmly orders to send his treasure after him :

"Go Eros, send his treasure after; do it;
Detain no jot, I charge thee. Write to him —
I will subscribe — gentle adieus and greetings,
Say that I wish he never find more cause
To change a master."[55]

This gesture shows that Antony is above malice even for one who has deserted him. All the above 'actions' express Antony's character and the ground for the final positive dream—picture given by Cleopatra, is prepared.

Six short scenes present the swiftly moving action culminating in Antony's final defeat for which he thinks Cleopatra's betrayal responsible. Whereas Antony had reconciled himself to the earlier and more crucial defeat without any violent reproach to Cleopatra, he cannot do so now. It is an oscillation to violent hate from ardent love and no art of Cleopatra can restore understanding :

"All is lost !
This foul Egyptian hath betrayed me.
My fleet hath yielded to the foe, and yonder
They cast their caps up and carouse together
Like friends long lost. Triple—turn'd whore! 'tis thou
Hast sold me to this novice; and my heart
Makes only wars on thee. Bid them all fly;
For when I am reveng'd upon my charm,
I have done all."[56]

The image of 'melting' which is most integral to the play, is now used with the greatest thematic significance. It is used for annihilation and dissolution of secular greatness and glory.

"All come to this ? The hearts
That spaniel'd me at heels, to whom I gave
Their wishes, do discandy, melt their sweets
On blossoming Caesar; and this pine is bark'd
That overtopp'd them all..."[57]

The images of 'discandy' and 'melt' subsequently appear as 'dislimn' in the final speech of Antony about the unreality of experience. Since Antony had rejected Rome and its values and left them to melt in the Tiber so far as he was concerned, he had also experienced the gradual melting away of appearances. The above speech marks a point when everything including Cleopatra had proved to be deceptive—reality behind appearance had begun to emerge. Hence the words he speaks to Eros just before his suicide are a kind of summing up of his life—experience and of the 'wisdom' which he has attained. Ironically, it is after this speech that he learned of the supposed death of Cleopatra which was actually a lie communicated by her to calm his anger. It was the last display of appearance by Cleopatra which became the immediate cause of his suicide. Antony who had so far been inextricably caught in the web of appearances now sees them as a part of himself :

"Sometime we see a cloud that's dragonish;
A vapour sometime, like a bear or lion,
A tower'd citadal' a pendent rock'
A forked mountain, or blue pormontory
With trees upon't that nod unto the world
And mock our eyes with air. Thou hast seen these signs,
They are black vesper's pageants".[58]

This is the 'pageantry' of human life which is seen in evening —light in the evening of life which now Antony has before him. The 'melting' of appearances which have deluded him all his life, is like the unfolding of a secret of existence. He thinks that his own body, being subject to dissolution, is such on appearance, and the appearance of Cleopatra whose reality appeared but now, is a confirmation. What he thought tangible and concrete, has become indistinct :

"That which is now a horse, even with a thought
The rack dislimns, and makes it indistinct,
As water is in water.
My good knave Eros, now thy captain is
Even such a body. Here I am Antony
Yet cannot hold this visible shape, my knave..."[59]

Miss M.C.Bradbrook says of this. "In this magnificent stormy sunset, there is conveyed without full unfolding, the imaginative form of this play."[60]

All values of Antony have proved fallacious but this 'anagnorisis' is not final. When the false news of Cleopatra's death — which again was an appearance of which he was not aware—is brought, Antony gives way to a burst of sentiment which contradicts his 'awareness' of reality, and falls upon his sword. An unprecedented situation of ironies is created which is partly the reason why Antony's death does not evoke the emotions of pity and fear. There is tragic irony in the fact which the audience knows and Antony does not know when he talks of "overtaking" Cleopatra in the next world and visualizes how all the spirits in the haunt where "souls do couch on flowers," would flock to them. The most evocative poetry lends a validity to this vision which we know to be based on an essential irony :

"All length is torture. Since the torch is out,
Lie down, and stray no farther. Now all labour
Mars what is does; yea, very force entangles,
Itself with strength. Seal then and all is done...
Where souls do couch on flowers, we'll hand in hand
And with our sprightly port make the ghosts gaze.
Dido and her Aeneas shall want troops,
And all the haunt be ours."[61]

As Gratiano says at the end of Othello's dying speech "All that is spoke is mar'd" so we can say that Antony's highly positive poetic speeches are all marred by the basic irony. Cleopatra is still alive and for all his divine flights, Antony would not find her in Elysium and that behind all this other-worldly sentiment Cleopatra's trick which costs him his life, rankles in the mind of the audience. If the end were not tragic, here was one more comic incongruity in this play abounding in them. Antony falls on his sword with these words :

"My queen and Eros
Have, by their brave instruction, got upon me
A nobleness in record. But I will be
A bridegroom in my death, and run into't
As to a lover's bed."[62]

This marks the emergence of the positive vision and the extravagance of emotion which marked the earlier speech on meeting Cleopatra in Elysium has given way to a quiet acceptance of death. The irony which detracted from the tragic effect of the earlier speech is also absent because the speech is more an absolute affirmation than a wishful thought. It is the very contrary of Hamlet's negative approach to death and it reminds of Claudio's "if I must die,/ I will encounter darkness as a bride/ And hug it in mine arms"[63] from which he retracted. But Antony speaking these words while he is actually dying, leaves no doubt about his final acceptance of death.

From this point onward, the short period which passes till Antony's death, is irradiated with poetry which rises to increasing power and afterwards, the positive vision further activates the poetry which now fully approaches what Coleridge calls "fiery force" with reference to the play as whole. The poetry is like a conjuration in word and image, adequate to Cleopatra's transformation which it presents. Mythical suggestions too multiply as the theme of the play leaves the secular plane lower and lower in its movement towards a new evaluation of existence. Accordingly, what was merely wished for in the beginning — 'a new heaven, a new earth' — is actually being realized. In such a heaven and earth, a heroic figure can be as great as other cosmic bodies. Hence, right before Antony's death, this mythical stature is imposed on him and to Cleopatra's imagination, his death betokens the annihilation of the sun itself :

"O sun,
Burn the great sphere thou mov'st in ! Darkling stand
The varying shore o'th' world. O Antony,
Antony, Antony !"[64]

In this swing to a positive evaluation of Antony's character, Cleopatra's 'action' of communicating a lie, however, negative, plays a crucial part. According to Ruth Nevo, it is this which leads to a different conclusion than would inevitably have been in the total failure of his career :

"Defeated, humiliated, and betrayed, his suicide at this point could only have registered that total failure of a life and the recognition that Philo's words at the beginning of the play were strictly true and his love for Cleopatra a snare and a delusion. What saves Antony from this consummation of his story is Cleopatra's lie. For the fact (as he believes it to be) that she has killed herself reverses the situation entirely. His faith in her and in himself is restored, and with it his resolution to kill himself, not in a despairing apathy, but in the saving anguish of grief... the dream of harmony, of reconciliation between love and martial dedication, is retrospectively validated."[65]

It is a striking example of how by a single stroke of the positive vision, the drift to an ignominious conclusion (as it historically was) can be changed into a splendid affirmation. Derek Traversi notes it as a movement of the play towards "a metaphysical balance of love and death in an enriching combination of contraries."[66]

To manage the end of tragedy is the most difficult part of its dramaturgy. We have the example of most of the tragedies of Euripides and even of Sophocles in which, having carried the complication consistently in character and action, it was impossible to effect the desired conclusion without introducing deus ex machina - a god or goddess who by his or her interference, restored the desired balance. In *Hippolytus, Ion* and *Iphigenia in Tauris* of Euripides, Artemis in the former and Athena in the latter two appear to wind up the plays consistently with their concepts. Similarly, in *Philoctetes* of Sophocles, without the appearance of the god Heracles, Neoptolemus could not have been shown living upto his values while at the same time performing his task. Otherwise, inconsistency in the conception of the character would have been inevitable.

Shakespeare was able to preserve the consistency which he envisioned in the character of Antony by a deft use of the two visions. Thus Cleopatra's lie was put to a dramatic use which provides the opportunity for resuscitating the image of Antony and giving a positive turn to the play. Thus love and death are put in a positive relationship and the contraries of a total loss on the secular plane and an equivalent gain on the spiritual plane are plausibly brought together. What is more, this positive movement continues till the end. Shakespeare uses poetry as the medium of this operation of the positive vision. Derek Traversi says of this :

"The poetry which expresses the exaltation of the lovers tends, by its unique magnificence, to impose acceptance.. we see in the end of the tragic process not merely a certain affirmation of life, even in the acceptance of death, but ... the logical conclusion of an entanglement sought after and accepted; the end of a course which has been from the beginning both perverse and life—destroying."[67]

Both the aspects — perverse as well as positive, annihilating life and affirming it — are ultimately reconciled by the positive vision. In other words, what would have been destructive of life has been transformed into something creative. This is also a clue to the regenerative quality which is attributed to *Antony and Cleopatra* and which it shares in common with the last plays. There is also a peculiar feeling of something happening — or some transformation going on — leading to a consciousness of a higher plane of existence when Antony dies. It is something like evolving superhuman dimensions of an aspiration however illusory while he was alive. If art transfixes moments of the highest illumination or transcedence in its medium and eternalizes them, then the aspiration with which Antony dies is also validated and given an existence on the eternal plane. The dream-image later cherished by Cleopatra is an identification of Antony with his transcendental aspiration in equivalent cosmic imagery. From this point of view his dying words acquire their proper significance :

"I am dying, Egypt, dying; only
I here importune death awhile, until
Of many thousand kisses the poor last
I lay upon thy lips."[68]

The moment clearly passes beyond the temporal plane. The process of enlargement of his stature to match the image behind this exalted aspiration has begun :

"Noblest of men, woo't die ?....
O, see, my women,
The crown o'th' earth doth melt. My lord !
O, wither'd is the garland of the war,
The soldier's pole is fall'n ! young boys and girls
Are level now with men. The odds is gone,
And there is nothing left remarkable
Beneath the visisting moon."[69]

The transformation in Cleopatra begins to come too. With words that clearly mark her descent from her infinite 'becomings' with her self-conscious poses ranging from majesty to riggishness, she comes to identify herself with 'the maid that milks' as Lear does with the 'poor bare, forked animal' — the 'unaccommodated man.' And she uniformly rises to true majesty as well as to this elemental femininity.

"No more but e'en a woman, and commanded
By such poor passion as the maid that milks
And does the meanest chares. It were for me
To throw my sceptre at the injurious gods;
To tell them that this world did equal theirs
Till they had stol'n our jewel. All's but nought :
Patience is sottish, and impatience does
Become a dog that's mad. Then is it sin
To rush into the secret house of death
Ere death dare come to us ?"[70]

The positive vision settles upon Cleopatra too, once she has renounced her 'becomings'; and transcended, or is in the process of transcending, 'baser life'. That the characterisation of Cleopatra deeply engaged Shakespeare's imagination and involved all his creative power is proved by the fact that he has devoted the whole of the fifth Act to her.

The premonitions of a 'better' life and the positive, unambiguous acceptance of death marks her very first speech when we see Cleopatra next, in Act V, Sc II — the last scene of the play.

"My desolation does begin to make
A better life. 'Tis paltry to be Caesar :
Not being Fortune, he's but Fortune's knave
A minister of her will; and it is great
To do that thing that ends all other deeds,
Which shackles accidents and bolts up change,
Which sleeps, and never palates more the dug,
The begger's nurse and Caesar's."[71]

Cleopatra's longing for death as a sleep is positive with homely concrete imagery in contrast to Hamlet's which was speculative and depended on what kind of sleep it would be. It would appear at the end of the play in an over-all synthesis.

This longing for death is absolute and does not depend on any negotiations with Caesar. Derek Traversi says of the significance of this speech as part of a cumulative movement :

".... the last great scene leads to the final resolution. It opens, significantly, with her assertion that the very completeness of her 'desolation' may be the prelude to what she calls — though, in point of fact, death is her only conceivable goal - a 'better life'... The act she envisages is 'great precisely in that it ends her slavery to the world of contingencies... She does so, moreover, by an act which she conceives to be as gentle as 'sleep'."[72]

It is this thought of death which lends a validity to Cleopatra's dream of Antony which, as already pointed out, enlarges his image to cosmic proportions because the secular and temporal considerations which would interfere with this idealization cease to apply after his death. There could be no better instance of what Oppenheimer calls 'complementarity' which stands for the perception of what is an equally significant manifestation of an object seen through the individual subjective consciousness and which, though different, helps to integrate the object. Antony's original self is integrated by the union of this dream-image :

"His face was as the heav'ns and therein stuck
A sun and moon, which kept their course and lighted
The little O, the earth....
His legs bestrid the ocean ; his rear'd arm
Crested the world. His voice was propertied
As all the tuned spheres,...."[73]

The meeting with Caesar and the Seleucus episode don't detract from the unity of the scene or from its progressive movement to the climactic point—Cleopatra's suicide. Even the suggestion that Cleopatra wanted to negotiate with Caesar and the conjecture that if Caesar had not intended to deceive her and take her to Rome in his triumph, she might have lived, don't detract from this sustained drift. As a matter of fact Cleopatra wanted to outwit Caesar from the very beginning and her words to Antony show this. When Antony tells her,

"Of Caesar seek your honour, with your safety",

She replies, "They do not go together"[74] and all her subsequent 'actions' are more for her honour that for her safety. Moreover, she has known of Caesar's intentions from Dolabella before her meeting with him and what follows is clearly to prove Ceasar "ass unpolicied". Thus it is only to fool his preparation by making him think that she is interested in living while resolution to die is 'placed' :

"My resolution's plac'd, and I have nothing
Of woman in me. Now from head to foot
I am marble-constant; now the fleeting moon
No planet is of mine."[75]

The final "act" of Cleopatra is again 'complementary' to her earlier career and integrates her image — as Antony's image is integrated by her dream—vision. The cumulative oscillating movement — the complex web of a mingled yarn — now gives way to an adamantine will to purge herself by death — to become 'fire and air' leaving other elements below :

"Give me my robe, put on my crown; I have
Immortal longings in me.. Methinks I hear
Antony call ... Husband I come.
Now to that name my courage prove my title !
I am fire and air; my other elements
I give to baser life."[76]

In Cleopatra's death, all the paradoxes which were associated with her being are resolved. Derek Traversi speaks of this :

"The immortality to which she now aspires stands at the opposite pole to the 'dungy earth' from which her love sprang. In the light of this association of love and immortality, death assumes - for the duration of this incident a fresh poetic function. It becomes a dissolution, imposes a purging of all the grosser elements upon which love itself has been based and which are now in the process of returning to the earth from which they sprang. 'I am fire and air; my other elements/ I give to baser life."[77]

With this resolution of the paradox which was Cleopatra, love as a redeeming power and as an absolute value is validated. The baser elements which are abandoned have also contributed to it. Even the poison which she was so familiar with as to say "now I feed myself/With most delicious poison"[78] and the serpent which "with Phoebus' amorous pinches black", was symbolically herself play a positive role in realizing her 'immortal longings'. The symbolic serpent becomes an asp— "my baby at my breast/that sucks the nurse asleep"[79] and its poison is "as sweet as balm, as soft as air". Finally, her life which by its paradoxes and inconsistencies had defied the wits of her lovers and enemies alike, now allows its 'intrinsicate' nature to be parted and resolved plainly into divine and earthly elements through death.

Mark van Doren puts the transformation thus : "The strength of Cleopatra has never appeared more clearly than in the charm with which she yields herself to death. Her greatness cannot be distinguished from her littleness, as water may not be defined in water."

This synthesis is clearly effected in the light of the positive vision which does not so irradiate the death of a protagonist in the whole range of Shakespeare's works. It is also seen from another angle by the coolest and most critical of her observers :

"... she looks like sleep,
As she would catch another Antony
In her strong toil of grace.:[80]

Here is a final union (most valid because objective in the extreme) of those elements which had existed in Cleopatra without being reconciled — the evil and the good, something entrapping in its toils like a snake and yet with a power comparable to divine grace. The two opposites are finally reconciled in her death.

REFERENCES

1. A.C. Bradley, *Oxford Lectures on Poetry* (Macmillan, London, 1962 ed.) p. 279.
2. Ibid., p. 279.
3. Ernest Schanzer, *The Problem Plays of Shakespeare* (Routledge and Kegan Paul, London, 1963) p. 226.
4. Ibid., p. 196.
5. L.C. Knights, *Some Shakespearean themes* (Chatto and Windows, London, 1969) p. 134.

6. Ernest Schanzer, *The Problem Plays of Shakespeare*, p. 194.
7. Philip Edwards, *Shakespeare and the Confines of Art* (Methuen and Co., London, 1968) p. 121.
8. *Antony and Cleopatra*, Act I, Sc, I, *ll* 10-13.
9. Derek Traversi, *Shakespeare, The Roman Plays* (Hollis and Carter, London, 1963) p. 80.
10. Ibid., p. 81.
11. Ruth Nevo, *Tragic Form in Shakespeare* (Princeton University Press, 1972) p. 307.
12. Ernest Schanzer, *The Problem Plays of Shakespeare*, p. 195.
13. *Antony and Cleopatra*, Act I, Sc I *ll*. 33-36
14. Ibid., Act I, Sc II *ll*. 137-140.
15. Derek Traversi, *Shakespeare, The Roman Plays*, p. 89.
16. *Antony and Cleopatra*, Act I, Sc II, *ll*. 142-46.
17. Ibid., Act I, Sc III, *ll*. 33-38.
18. Ibid., Act I, Sc II 11 106-7 and 11 113-14.
19. Ibid., *1*. 125.
20. Ibid., *ll*. 186-88.
21. Ruth Nevo, *Tragic Form in Shakespeare*, pp. 311-12.
22. *Antony and Cleopatra*, Act I, Sc IV, *ll*. 61-68.
23. Ibid., Act II, Sc I, *ll*. 34-35.
24. Ibid., Act II, Sc II, *ll*. 4-6.
25. Ibid., Act I, Sc V, *ll*. 23-29.
26. Ibid., Act II, Sc *ll*. 1.237.
27. Ibid., *ll*. 194-209.
28. Ibid., Act III, Sc XIII, *ll*. 153-54.
29. Ibid., Act IV, Sc XV, *ll*. 67-68.
30. Ibid., Act V, Sc II, *ll*. 238-39.
31. Ibid., Act III, Sc X, *1*. 14.
32. Ibid., Act IV, Sc XV, *ll*. 74-75.
33. Ibid., Act V, Sc II, *ll*. 287-88.
34. Ibid., Act II, Sc II, *ll*. 238-44.
35. Frank Kermode, *Introduction to Antony and Cleopatra* in 'The Riverside Shakespeare' (Houghton Mifflin Company, Boston, 1974) p. 1345.
36. Ibid., p. 1346.
37. Ibid., Act III, Sc V, *ll*. 13-15.
38. Ibid., Act III, Sc V, *ll*. 41-46.

39. Ibid., *ll* 68-70.
40. Ibid., Act III, Sc X, *ll*. 6-8.
41. Ibid., Act III, Sc X, *ll*. 15-24
42. M.C. Bradbrook, *Shakespeare The Craftsman* (Chatto and Windus, London, 1969) p. 117.
43. *Antony and Cleopatra*, Act III, Sc XIII, *ll*., 3-8
44. Ibid., Act II, Sc III, *ll*. 29-30.
45. Harmsworth, *History of the World*, p. 2805. (Harmsworth, London, 1905.
46. *Antony and Cleopatra*, Act III, Sc XI, *ll*. 3-4 and 12-15.
47. Ibid., *ll*. 34-40.
48. Ibid., *ll*. 51-61.
49. Derek Traversi, *Shakesperare. The Roman Plays*, p. 142.
50. *Antony and Cleopatra*. Act III, Sc XI, *ll*. 69-71.
51. Ruth Nevo, *Tragie Form in Shakespeare*, p. 329.
52. Ibid., p. 331
53. *Antony and Cleopatra*. Act IV, Sc IV, *ll*. 11-18.
54. Ruth Nevo, *Tragic Form in Shakespeare*, p. 335.
55. *Antony and Cleopatra*, Act IV, Sc V, *ll*. 12-16.
56. Ibid., Act IV, Sc XII, *ll*. 9-17.
57. Ibid., *ll*. 20-24.
58. Ibid., Act IV, Sc. XIV, *ll*. 2-8.
59. Ibid., *ll*. 9-14.
60. M.C. Bradbrook, *Shakespeare the Craftman*. p. 119.
61. Ibid., Act IV, Sc XIV, *ll*. 46-54
62. *Ibid*., *ll*. 97-101.
63. *Measure for Measure*. Act III Sc, I *ll*. 84-86.
64. *Antony and Cleopatra*, Act IV, Sc XV, *ll*, 9-12.
65. Ruth Nevo, *Tragic Form in Shakespeare*, p. 337.
66. Derek Traversi, *Shakespeare. The Roman Plays*, p. 184.
67. Ibid., p. 178.
68. *Antony and Cleopatra*, Act IV, Sc XV, *ll*. 18-21.
69. Ibid., *ll*. 59-68.
70. Ibid., *ll*. 72-82.
71. Ibid., Act V, Sc II, *ll*. 1-8.
72. Derek Traversi, *Shakespeare. The Roman Plays*, pp. 190-91.
73. *Antony and Cleopatra*, Act, V, Sc II, *ll*. 79-84.
74. Ibid., Act IV, Sc XV, *l*. 46 and *l*. 47.

75. Ibid., Act V, Sc II, *ll.* 237-40.
76. Ibid., *ll.* 276-88.
77. Derek Traversi, *Shakespeare, The Roman Plays.* p. 199.
78. *Antony and Cleopatra*, Act I, Sc V, *ll.* 26-27.
79. Ibid., Act V, Sc II, *ll.* 307-8.
80. Ibid., *ll.* 343-45.

Tillyard E.M.W., *Shakespeare's Last Plays* (Chatto and Windus, London, 1938).

Tindall, William York, *The Literary Symbol* (Indiana University Press, 1955).

Traversi, Derek, *Shakespeare, The Roman Plays* (Hollis and Carter, London, 1963).

Underhill, Evelyn, *Mysticism* (Methuen and Co., London, 1911).

Mark, Van Doren, *Shakespeare* (George Allen and Unwin, London, 1914).

CHAPTER IX

A Comparative View of the Problem Plays with Reference to Their Common Qualities

(A) Contrary fecets and the Double Vision

We have so far considered six plays of Shakespeare, three of them usually acknowledged as problem plays while the other three are tragedies of the first order in their own right but at the same time, display several qualities of problem plays. Thus *All's Well, Measure for Measure* and *Troilus and Cressida* are of the genre proper which is that of the dark comedies or problem comedies while *Julius Caesar, Hamlet* and *Antony and Cleopatra* could be called problem tragedies. In a way every tragedy embodies some problem but the response to that problem is not divided or ambiguous — everyone feels almost alike about the ironies, the sufferings and the presentation of the basic problem of existence. But the problem play—whether tragedy, comedy or a play partaking of the qualities of both, like *Troilus and Cressida*—evokes ambiguous or divided responses with regard to the characters and their actions. As already pointed out in the course of the discussion of each of these plays, these divided responses, or two-fold impressions received with a change in the angle of vision, are due to the operation of the dramatist's double vision which presents alternately or at the same time, two incompatible facets of the characters and their actions. This happens most frequently in all these six plays and apart from divided responses, there are contradictory and apparently irreconcilable views of the same character and action.

Philip Edwards styles this dramatic use of the double vision as a scheme of "contrary valuations". He says "We all have the same double valuation of everything we live through... Our views of art, whether of art as a whole, or of individual poems and paintings, share this unstable focus."[1] He calls these opposed valuations of every experience as the epic and burlesque visions — the one is serious and elevated while the other is scoffing and annihilating. As shown in O'Neill's play *The Great God Brown*, the Dionysian view is scoffing and destructive which is very near what is meant by Edwards. By presenting these opposed views, Shakespeare finally evolves an integrated view presenting the reality of experience. This is the secret of his counterpointing in characterization, situations and actions of the characters.

R.A. Foakes communicates a similar idea of taking into account 'contrary valuations' when he makes a case for judging a play by "the pattern.. established by the sum of relations existing between the parts of the action"[2] in the play. Tillyard, while investigating the quality which makes *All's Well* and *Measure for Measure* problematic, says that "there is something radically schizophrenic about them".[3] Psychological truth and conventions of fairy-tale often seem to pull apart the characters and the plot. It is because both these contrary elements — reality and illusion—were equally necessary to evolve the version of experience Shakespeare was aiming at through them. *Hamlet* and *Troilus and Cressida* are 'full of interest and complexity but divided within themselves only in the eyes of those who have misjudged them'.[4] Again the complexities are not there for their own sake but due to the visionary mode through which Shakespeare was evolving a view of the wholeness of experience by presenting the progress of the characters through 'contraries'. These contradictions and paradoxes give an impression of incongruity and sometimes make the character enigmatic but also make it more attractive and life-like. It's because there are submerged Jekylls and Hydes in all of us and when they arise to take possession of a person more frequently and suddenly, we find his behaviour abnormal because ordinarily, one part—in all civilized men the worse part—remains restrained and controlled by reason and judgment. But when these guards weaken, the baser nature asserts itself, whether as mere excess of passion or as violence of primitive nature. Often 'blood' and 'judgment' are commingled and reason keeps passion so much subdued that the person appears to have transcended it completely. Such persons are not "passion's slaves" as Shakespeare's tragic heroes are. But like Horatio and Fortinbras, they exist only as colourless contrasts to the heroes pointing at the norm from which the protagonist has diverted.

This contrast between the men of passion and those of reason can also be presented as one between the Dionysian and the Apollonian types. As already pointed out earlier in the discussion, the idea was first stated in this form by Nietzsche. Categorizing the human types into Apollonian and Dionysian, he applied the idea to tragedy:

"The vision of Apollo builds up before us a heroic world, sublime, magnificent, rejoicing in its splendid individuality. But with this Apollonian vision is combined the wild, self-annihilating rapture of the music of Dionysus. From that tragedy sprung,....."[5]

The cause of tragedy is that the protagonist who was initially gifted both with Apollonian and Dionysian attributes, fails to strike a balance and allows himself to be lost in the "Dionysian sweep of life". The 'Psychic background' of all Shakespeare's tragedies is this clash of the primitive Dionysian energy with the Apollonian rationality. We can see it in Hamlet, Antony, Othello, Macbeth and even in King Lear. The contraries of reason and passion manifested in other forms can be seen in Brutus, Troilus, Angelo, Claudio and even in Coriolanus.

In the problem plays proper, we find a remarkable operation of the double vision which accounts for their being equivocal in their total effect and for the two-fold impact of their characters and their actions. Jonathan Dollimore suggests that a play incorporates these contradictions because it explores a reality which can be perceived only through them.[6] Thus all problem plays—whether tragic or comic in tone—explore a reality beyond the reach of other, particularly earlier plays of Shakespeare which incorporate the double vision to an extent which varies with the complexity of the theme and characters. But in the problem plays, the interplay of the double vision is the very stuff which lends them a meaning and significance.

In short, it was a more massive undertaking in these plays from the technical point of view. Throughout, the plots and characters move unpredictably and even though contrary facets emerge, they all finally appear consistent with the version of life which evolves at the end. We could call it a consistent inconsistency. Otherwise we shall be compelled to dismiss these plays as artistic failures which they are not.

These contradictions were called "abnormal conditions of brain and of emotion" which leave us "excited, fascinated, perplexed" and we were "left to interpret their enigmas as best as we may".[7] This was the view of Boas who did not push his inquiry further enough to see them as parts of a larger design. A much later critic, Ernest Schanzer, also evolved a definition of a problem play which took into account the ambivalent aspects of presentation of character and action and analyzed the plays spotting out most of them but still not going far enough to see that it was Shakespeare's double vision which had so focused them to a specific end. With Schanzer we reach nearest to understanding the 'effect' of such presentation and adopting it as the test of a problem play:

"The definition of the Shakespearean problem play which I therefore suggest is: "A play in which we find a concern with a moral problem which is central to it, presented in such a manner that we are unsure of our moral bearings, so that uncertain and divided responses to it in the minds of the audience are possible and even probable."[8]

The object of this book was to discuss the problem plays of Shakespeare with a view to bring out all these characteristics adopting the operation of the double vision as our 'wayfinder' as it were, and following up this illumination further to see the intention of the dramatist behind it—in other words, to explore what Shakespeare was upto in these plays. Sometimes, our conclusions are implicit in the discussion of these plays and the evolving pattern is always emphasized. It now remains to take a retrospective view of these discussions and to put together, from a comparative point of view, the conclusions about 'what Shakespeare was about' which emerge from them. Identities between these plays which help to reinforce general conclusions, will also be taken into account.

(B) Towards a common ground

After a discussion of the nature of the problem play in general and of the problem plays Shakespeare in particular, the introducing chapters of this book had traced the evolution of Shakespeare's technique in handling the problem plays from *Julius Caesar* to *Antony and Cleopatra*. In actual treatment we considered the plays in two groups: the problem comedies and the problem tragedies. These two groups also show how Shakespeare's double vision went in greater consonance with the tragic form than with the comic form.

Before we discuss this important conclusion, it would be well to review the treatment of each of these plays so as to evolve a common ground and to arrive at other points of identities which may disclose themselves during this examination.

Our discussion of *All's Well* opened by stressing the role of the double vision in presenting the main characters. It is evident in the progress of Helena through the play that the contradictory nature of her make-up and behaviour is determined by the positive and the negative vision. The complexity of characterization appears to grow in our knowledge as we watch the focusing of the two visions and Helena ceases to be enigmatic for us. She becomes a convincing product of antitheses like Cleopatra and we never doubt the reality of both facets of her personality— the clever wench and the girl who could be the instrument of divine power— 'a most weak and debile minister; great power, great transcendence.'[9]

Thus two opposite facets of the same character, apparently irreconcilable, are seen in this play. This marks the most important common feature in all the other plays discussed in this category. In *Measure for Measure* we find the same duality with reference to Angelo; in *Troilus and Cressida*, in the case of Cressida; in *Hamlet* from Hamlet's point of view in Claudius and Gertrude and from the point of view of other characters in Hamlet; and in *Antony and Cleopatra* in Cleopatra. In *Julius Caesar* this duality manifests itself in Brutus in a slightly different way. This common theme of a dual strain is inextricably connected with that of Appearance and Reality and moral ambivalence which includes the question of virtue and vice and finally, of good and evil.

(a) Duality

Thus duality which is mostly unresolved, appears as the most important common theme in the problem plays and since it is by the use of the double vision that this effect is achieved, it becomes the central point in our conclusions. Other common themes—almost all of them—are connected with it like the spokes of a wheel and can be most conveniently accounted for in relation to it. The example of Helena with which we introduced this point of identity is the most typical because in her character two elements of duality—the two strains in her character—are seen further apart without an apparent link.

What makes this theme even more important is the fact that so far, critics have tried to explain this element of duality in various ways except by pointing out the operation of the double vision of the dramatist as being responsible for it. Their conclusions are unsatisfactory and have either left the characters like Hamlet and Cleopatra as enigmas or dismissed the character of Helena as an incongruous combination of realism and folk-lore. Without having a peep into the artist's "rag-and-bone shop" they have even attributed it to his imaginative failure. "The heart of the mystery" of Cleopatra and Hamlet remains still 'unplucked' and the understanding of the readers and spectators is reconciled to their being eternal enigmas.

It is the contention of this book that these dualities are there due to the conscious design of the dramatist as a part of his artistic vision in which the positive and the negative visions played an 'essemplastic' role. An artist like Shakespeare would not have conceived characters like Hamlet, Cleopatra, or Helena as made of incompatible elements or left them unresolved unless he so intended and he used his double vision with consummate skill in each of the plays to create the desired effect.

Hence in this comparative summing-up, it will be desirable to reiterate the main points of this conscious workmanship and to see with reference to each of these plays the connection of the common theme of duality and of the subsidiary themes of appearance and reality and moral ambivalence with the double vision.

(i) Duality in 'All's Well' : To begin with *All's Well*, we find that the two strains in Helena—of realism and folk-lore are actually a combination of the qualities of the head and the heart and Helena embodies them in a sharp and intensified form which enables her to achieve her object. It was only consistent with the need of her task to have the intense convictions which released her own potential powers. Moreover, Shakespeare had to present her as human and yet to make her work miracles. So he used the positive vision to show her enhanced spiritual powers and the negative vision to keep her down to earth. In all such cases, characteristically, Shakespeare begins with the negative vision to keep the human element firmly impressed on the minds of the audience and not let it be blurred by the spiritual dimensions which unfold themselves later.

Thus the striking incident which makes Helena an intriguing figure right in the beginning—shedding tears for Bertram while others mistake them for her father—is presented in the light of the negative vision. This trait, in the light of the soliloquy which follows, is almost that of feigning sorrow. So Shakespeare meant to emphasize it. This is a quality of the head—of simulation and policy—which continues to show itself consistently in her subsequent pursuit of Bertram. It does not leave her at any time even in the course of her supernatural performance in curing the King. Her power, which is now seen to incorporate the spiritual and the supernatural, is presented in the light of the positive vision. Her character acquires wholeness and plausibility because her extraordinary power can be easily connected with her exaltation in love. The two facets are thus interconnected and the dramatist has used the two modes of presentation in order to make her 'adequate' to the theme. The two visions are used to achieve this 'complementarity.' Shakespeare has given Helena more such speeches than have been referred to in the earlier discussion, which prove that the contriving and the loving selves were quite integral to each other. Talking to Parolles, Helena confesses that she wished Bertram well in the court of France but,

"That wishing well had not a body in't
which might be felt...."[10]

That she was determined to follow her love is further expressed by the line in the following soliloquy:

"Who ever strove
To show her merit that did miss her love?"[11]

While she is already making her plan to win Bertram for husband, she says to the Countess who corners her to make a confession:

"Then I confess,
Here on my knee, before high heaven and you.....
I love your son....
Nor would I have him till I do deserve him......
Thus, Indian-like,
Religious in mine error, I adore
The sun that looks upon his worshipper..."[12]

Later, she can point Bertram to the King as if she was claiming an object as a prize:

"This is the man",[13] which is anything but the way to win the object of her love. He is treated no better that a 'commodity' and the sympathy of the audience is with him. But when leaving her, Bertram goes to Florence, her love is affirmed in poetry which leaves no doubt about its selflessness:

"O you leaden messengers,
That ride upon the violent speed of fire
Fly with false aim....do not touch my lord....
I am the caitiff that do hold him to't....better' twere
I met the ravin lion when he roar'd
With sharp constraint of hunger....."[14]

This is followed by stratagems which ultimately make her the rightful wife, and she again claims Bertram with the words, "Will you be mine now you are doubly won?"[15]

In spite of the fact that she did love him, it is a business-like claim of one who has paid the price. To use the words of the French king spoken in another context, we can see "a sunshine and a hail"[16] in her at once.

But there is no doubt that Shakespeare intended to present Helena and her pursuit of love with the bed-trick (that he used the device twice shows that he didn't disapprove it) sympathetically and it does make her character more plausible and attractive as a type of woman who can have a real existence. It is the use of the two visions which makes all contradictions credible as in the case of Cleopatra. There is no sign of an imaginative failure if the play is read in this light.

(ii) An evolutionary view : On the other hand, *All's Well* is considered to be the first play presenting the spiritual transformation of a sinner through the virtue of love. However sketchy and indirect this process may be, the play is well on way to *The Winter's Tale* where virtue and grace are the means to conversion and the concept of the discarded virtuous woman develops from Helena to Hermione. The process can be seen through *Measure for Measure* where the bed-trick is given the sanction of betrothal till in *Cymbeline* it is refined to disguise and the only strategem is to follow the lover faithfully. In *The Winter's Tale* it is further refined to Paulina's strategem to keep Hermione in secret for sixteen years and bring her back to 'life' in the statue-scene. So we can see that the process which *All's Well* began by transforming Bertram through Helena is continued by the transformation of Angelo through Isaballa, of Posthumus through Imogen and of Leontes through Hermione. The role of younger girls like that of Marina in *Pericles*, of Perdita in *The Winter's Tale* and of Miranda in *The Tempest* is added in the course of evolution of the dramatic form.

Further, in its inclusion of a greater sense of evil in the scope of comedy, juxtaposing it with good, and presenting their interaction, *All's Well* stands immediately before *Measure for Measure* and anticipates the Last Plays. In short, both the negative and the positive vision find a greater display in it in character and action, than in any previous comedy.

(iii) Duality in Measure for Measure—from grimness to grace : Both the above trends increase with *Measure for Measure*. Commenting on the thematic affinity of *All's Well* with this play, Philip Edwards comments:

"*All's Well that Ends Well* and *Measure for Measure* are twin plays... There seems no doubt that the two plays... are Shakespeare's attempt to recreate comedy. The fables are as bizarre and 'unlikely' as ever they were, with their incidents from folk-lore, like the healing of the king and the substitution of the bride, and the complicated contrivances which give to the happy endings an air of prestidigitation. These wonder-working matters are, however, accompained by a deep plunge into very serious moral problems."[17]

Apart from underlining this fact which we can attribute to the technical use of the positive and negative visions in the field of comedy which begins with *All's Well*, Edwards goes on to point out a far-reaching process similar to the one already noticed by us:

"Modern criticism has established beyond disproof that there is in these plays, interwining with the far-fetched plots of comedy, a Christian or near-Christian pattern of providence and redemption... and shows quite clearly that the movement from disaffection... to a state of harmony can certainly be an emblem of achieving grace... there is now a sense of sinners being saved; and it is certainly not too much to say that... there is the hint in the wooing of Bertram by Helena, and of Isabella by the Duke, of the betrothal of heaven and earth....Comedy expands to include more of the grimness of this world and more of the mystery of the next."[18]

The view of 'grimness' is clearly that of the negative vision, while the mystery of the next world is an extension of spiritual exploration by the positive vision which continues up to *The Tempest*. Providence, redemption and grace are all in the process of being progressively highlighted by the positive vision. But the exploration of the grimness of evil by the negative vision also continues and Caliban, Antonio and Sebastian are its latest manifestations.

Measure for Measure is seen to be paving the way, more than *All's Well*, for this movement from an initial state of evil to its final purgation through grace which culminates in its perfect form in *The Tempest*. More than anything, it incorporates the theme of forgiveness which makes it rise above the inflexible retributive code of the tragedies where 'black vengeance' is invoked 'from the hollow hell';[18(a)] where 'most foul, strange, and unnatural' murder begets further 'bloody and unnatural acts'; [18(b)] and characters are 'anatomized' to find if there is 'any cause in nature that make these hard hearts'.[18(c)] Even the rigid chastity of Isabella, so criticized by the critics, seems to be integral to this movement. As John Lawlor puts it:

"Shakespeare therefore made Isabella utterly inflexible in her chastity—that characterization which is the starting-point of all recognition of the play's peculiar nature—and put it beyond question by making her a novice, so that a willed resolution, which must include the will to forgive, becomes the essential theme".[19] As Professor Muir soundly observes, forgiveness in this play is

'not the forgiveness prompted by sexual passion as in Whetstone, nor even the magnanimity suggested in some of Giraldi's stories, but Christian forgiveness—that is, the forgiveness of enemies.'[20] Lawlor adds: "Shakespeare has in this play implicitly rejected the matter of revenge as intractable, alien to his characteristic insight and method."[20(a)]

It is as if Aeschylus had made Electra forgive Aegisthus or O'Neill had made Lavinia forgive Brant.

Thus we see that *Measure for Measure* is unique among the plays in the Shakespeare canon in the period 1600 to 1608 when we have *Timon of Athens* — a play which embodies an unforgiving nature in Timon. Moreover, 'grace' and 'grimness' are so juxtaposed that evil and its means of transformation are seen close together and we don't see the design of the dramatist till the very end. Larry S. Champion puts it thus:

"Angelo is presumably Shakespeare's second comic vision of character (after Bertram) developed on the level of transformation. From a position of Angelo's initial innocence.. to the disastrous revelation of the inadequacy of his moral determination when put to the practical test, to the spiritual quagmire in which publicly his tyrannical misuse of power and privately his ignominious lust for Isabella involves him, to the shock which humbles his pride and leads to his contrite repentance, to the dispensation of mercy through which his evil deeds are abrogated and his life spared, the playwright attempts comically to trace the destruction and regeneration of a character and his moral values."[21]

Four stages in this transformation of Angelo can be distinctly pointed out. They make a complete curve which will be repeated in the case of Posthumous and Leontes—

innocence, onslaught of evil with the resulting conflict, conversion to evil, and final penitence and transformation.

The Duke's affirmation of Angelo's virtues has no touch of their 'seeming' as yet, and it can be taken as a fair measure of his 'innocence':

"There is a kind of character in thy life
That to th' observer doth thy history
Fully unfold. Thyself and thy belongings
Are not thine own so proper as to waste
Thyself upon thy virtues....."[22]

The second stage of the onslaught of evil and conflict, can be seen in the soliloquy spoken after Isabella's departure:

"Is this her fault or mine?
The tempter or the tempted, who sins most?
Ha!
Not she; nor doth she tempt; but it is I
That, lying by the violet in the sun,
Do as the carrion does, not as the flow'r,
Corrupt with virtuous season.......
O cunning enemy, that, to catch a saint,
With saints dost bait thy hook!"[23]

The following soliloquy shows the conversion to evil which culminates in his perfidity in ordering the execution of Claudio in Act IV Sc II. The closing lines mark the paradox:

"Blood, thou art blood,
Let's write 'good angel' on the devil's horn;
Tis not the devil's crest."[24]

His penitence and transformation lose something of their quality by their being forced by exposure and not spontaneously ensuing as in the case of Leontes or Posthumus. But so is the penitence of Antonio and Sebastian in *The Tempest* or for that matter, of Caliban. The words, however, do have a ring of genuine feeling:

"I am sorry that such sorrow I procure;
And so deep sticks it in my penitent heart
That I crave death more willingly than mercy;
'Tis my deserving, and I do entreat 'it."[25]

(iv) Duality in other problem plays : This theme though

comparatively less emphatic from this point of view in the remaining four of the problem plays, arises from the duality in the characters and the play of the double vision in relation to two contrary aspects, real and apparent, in their characters. In *Hamlet* and *Antony and Cleopatra*, duality manifests itself not as an evolutionary process but as a paradoxical combination of good and evil in the same character after the manner of *All's Well*. Cleopatra is more akin to Helena than to any other character of tragedy or comedy in the combination of opposites and so is Hamlet if we think of the effect of evil in relation to good in his nature. There is no other character in Shakespeare except Falstaff who displays the same contrariety, although duality can be seen in Brutus and almost all other tragic heroes.

This leads us to different aspects of contrariety which are common to all the problem plays.

(b) Appearance and Reality

The theme of contradiction between appearance and reality is the most important element common to all the problem plays and it has been adequately stressed in the discussion of relevant situations and characters in these plays in relation to the double vision. It is actually a manifestation of duality and wherever there is an opposition between what a person is and what he or she appears to be, this divergence between the two facets of the character may create the effect of irony or paradox. *Hamlet, Troilus and Cressida, Measure for Measure* and *Antony and Cleopatra* are replete with this contradiction. In fact it is one of their basic themes. It may underline the tragedy or constitute the tragic element as it does in the first two of these plays. In *Measure for Measure* it is the very soul of the plot while in *Antony and Cleopatra* it is connected with 'becoming' and 'being' which are the two phases of the evolution of the main characters. In *Julius Caesar* and *All's Well* this theme is not exploited for determining the tenor of the plot or characterization.

In *Hamlet* the theme is, in a sense, more intrinsic to character and action. In asserts itself right in the beginning and continues till the unexpressed meaning implicit in the last utterance of Hamlet, 'the rest is silence'. Hence an analysis of the dichotomy may serve to throw greater light on its problems.

When the Queen asks Hamlet, "Why seems it so particular with theea",[26] he uses it to express what is wrong with the situation and not with himself. Everything in the play resolves into this antithesis between appearance and reality. Hamlet has "that within which passeth show"[27] while it is only "the trappings" which are noticed by others.

Gertrude's appearance was that of a woman "who would hang on" her husband "As if increase of appetite had grown / by what it fed on;"[28] while the reality was that of a woman who married her husband's brother who was like a satyr. "Within a month" is an example of a subjective distortion of reality typical of Hamlet.

With the revelation by the Ghost, the contradiction between the two facets becomes more acute. Claudius had "won to his shameful lust", the will of his "most 'seeming' virtuous queen." This appearance of Gertrude is juxtaposed with the creature who would "sate itself in a celestial bed / And prey on garbage."[29] The radiant angel was actually an animal and Hamlet exactly echoes the idea in his question to his mother in the closet scene :

"Could you on this fair mountain leave to feed,
And batten on this moor ? "[30]

The food imagery used to indicate lust and physical appetite reappears more forcefully in *Troilus and Cressida* and in the reproach of Antony to Cleopatra.[31]

The crushing force of the two-fold revelation that his mother and Caludius were not what they appeared tilts the balance from action to thought, from the intensity to act in "Haste me to know it", to the avidity to ruminate on the paradox in human nature which had riven deep into his mind. The split has occurred.

The actual cleavage which leads to the 'antic disposition' began with the shock at the contradiction between appearance and reality at the behaviour of his mother before the revelation by the Ghost; it is driven to a climactic point by the revelation and continues at that pitch through similar 'experiences'. Action has no place in this movement which continues till the graveyard scene. It begins to constitute the very fabric of his mind and conditions his thoughts and acts. It is characteristic that all such thoughts and acts are marked by the negative vision.

Among these experiences which aggravate his sense of divergence between appearance and reality, that of encounter with Ophelia in the so-called nunnery scene is characteristic because it is here that Hamlet makes a statement which brings us to the heart of the matter— the reason why his mind has become distracted to the point of madness. It is the only clue he provides in the play :

"I have heard of your paintings too, well enough; God hath given you one face, and you make yourselves another. You jig and amble, and you lisp, and nickname God's creatures, and make your wantonness your ignorance. Go to, I'll no more on't, it hath made me mad."[32]

It is obvious that Hamlet is referring to women in general and treating Ophelia as a butt. The charges he bring against the wantonness of women show that he had noted these in other women. It seems to be wrong to say as some critics have made out, that his experience of women was limited to his mother and Ophelia. Nor was his experience of men limited to those in the play. As Shakespeare has presented him, Hamlet was a man who had seen and thought more of human beings than appears at first sight and if we take his age to be nearly thirty as hinted in the reference to Yorik in the graveyard scene, the above comment on the "two faces" of women was based on wider experience. If we couple with this the other statement of Hamlet, "there is nothing either good or bad, but thinking makes it so,"[33] we feel that he had seen more of good and evil before he encountered them—particularly evil—in the play. The conclusion which emerges is that Hamlet's perception of the dichotomy between appearance and reality revealing the apparently good and really evil aspects of the same person (however inapplicable to Ophelia) was based on a firm foundation and constitutes the very stuff of his consciousness.

The world and everything in it including man, is also subject to the same two-fold vision with one taking a sublime view and resolving all into a wonderful work of creation and the other dashing the glassy essence into pieces disclosing foulness and dust.

"I have of late—but wherefore I know not—lost all my mirth,... this goodly rame, the earth, seems to me a sterile promontory : this majestical roof fretted with golden fire it appeareth no other thing to me than a foul and pestilent congregation of vapours. What a piece of work is a man! How noble in reason ! How infinite in faculties ! in form and moving how express and admirable ! in action how like an angel! in apprehension how like a god ! the beauty of the world ! the paragon of animals ! And yet, to me, what is this quintessence of dust ?"[34]

There are three movements, each of them juxtaposing appearance and reality in a rising crescendo of rhetoric suffused with strong feeling. But the interrelation of the two versions of experience is different from what is generally noticed. Which of them is appearance and which is reality? What Hamlet first speaks of, he posits as the reality; the other he qualifies with 'appears' 'seems' and 'to me' and conveys the idea of their being appearances which are also subjective. In the closet scene again it is the contrast between appearance and reality which he wants to bring out to his mother and release her from the deceptive 'appearance' of her present husband.

"Here is you husband, like a mildew'd ear
Blasting his wholesome brother. Have you eyes ?...
Ha! have you eyes ?
..... What devil was't
That thus hath cozen'd you at hoodman-blind ?[35]

The repetition of the idea of being unable to use her eyes shows that she is led only by appearance in her opinion of Claudius and has not yet seen the reality. That, in fact, is the accomplishment of a task he has imposed upon himself.

Another statement of the contrast between appearance and reality is towards the end of the play-scene. It is as important as the one he makes to Ophelia. Both concern himself — the madness and the mystery — and both are equally baffling. Incidentally, 'appearing' to be mad and being really sane was to create a contradiction about oneself to the point of making the two inseparable.

It is remarkable that Hamlet directly speaks truth when he is most excited; when he thinks, he goes to truth in a winding way. He is now excited and tells Rosencrantz and Guildenstern that they would never get beyond seeing his appearance just as a man who does not know how to play on a pipe, will at the most 'fret' it :

"Why, look you now, how unworthy a thing you make of me! You would play upon me; you would seem to know my stops; you would pluck out the heart of my mystery;... 'Sblood, do you think I am easier to be play'd on then a pipe ? Call me what instrument you will, though you can fret me, yet you cannot play upon me".[36]

The expression 'seem to know' points to the basic contradiction between the appearance of understanding him and the reality regarding its impossibility. Just afterwards, there is further play on the appearance of a cloud which may be either like a camel or like a weasel or a whale according to the viewpoint of the observer, with the implication that it was neither.

Another outstanding instance of this dichotomy refers to the character and action of Claudius. It is also more explicitly stated. Polonius after instructing Ophelia to walk in the lobby and read the prayer-book, remarks :

"We are oft to blame in this :
'Tis too much prov'd, that with devotion's visage
And pious action we do sugar o'er
The devil himself."[37]

The king, who is a villain with a conscience, feels its prick and he draws a contrast between the appearance of his word and the reality of his deed behind it :

"O, 'tis too true !
How smart a lash that speech doth give my conscience !
The harlot's cheek, beautied with plast'ring art,
Is not more ugly to the thing that helps it
Than is my deed to my most painted word,"[38]

The speech is direct without any use of 'appears' or 'seems' ; There is no anticlimactic or paradoxical effect. The discrepancy between what appears and what actually is, gets a vivid expression through concrete images. It is interesting to note that in both the above speeches one abstract image is fused with one concrete image — 'devotion's visage' combined with 'the devil' (sugared over) and 'painted word' combined with 'harlot's cheek'. The inner balancing of the abstract for appearance against the concrete for reality is an example of the imaginative workmanship which accounts for the effectiveness of the imagery.

The final words of Hamlet spoken just on the point of death, again juxtapose the visible events which he calls "th' occurrents, more and less, which have solicited"[39] against the untold reality which he only suggests by the words "the rest is silence." The events were the appearance which, as Horatio narrates at length, were "carnal, bloody and unnatural acts"[40] but no one could tell the reality which Hamlet leaves unsaid in "silence" and which could not be narrated or explained. It was his mystery and in spite its infinite versions, it so remains.

John Lawlor says."A drama of appearance and reality is a drama of purpose largely gone awry."[41] The statement is true of Hamlet and it is because the world of appearance so agonizes his inner world of reality that there is a constant spectacle of suffering which is aggravated as he fails to adopt the one to the other. Van Doren rightly says "Within these two frames the spectacle of Hamlet is forever suspended."[42]

The play which evinces the greatest intellectual affinity with *Hamlet* is *Troilus and Cressida* and the theme of appearance and reality along with the situations and reflections in each play establishes this identity more than any other. There is a spirit of scepticism, bitterness and disillusionment which can also be connected with this theme in both plays. The problem of value which stands at the heart of *Troilus and Cressida* also hinges on the contradictory attitudes and angles of vision related in turn to appearance and reality.

As Anne Barton says, "Among Shakespeare's own plays, *Hamlet* seems closely associated with *Troilius and Cressida*.... These two plays.... radically different in tone and structure, are alike in exploring the hiatus between a character's words and actions.... In *Troilus and Cressida* they (words) exist only to be broken." She adds, ".... verbal descriptions through which value is established prove to be false visions without substance in reality."[43]

Tillyard has pointed out that "multiplication of planes of reality beyond anything similar elsewhere.... threatens to destroy the play's internal harmony....."[44] He says that Triolus "does in fact for a brief time inhabit two incompatible worlds".[45] The idea that living in his earlier world which was cherished as one of reality he found another world of a different reality come down on his consciousness with an impact which thwarted not only his balance but prevented a dynamic growth of his character. It is partly true of Hamlet and it was only the plot which made him move out of the quagmire of irresolution caused by the hiatus between the two worlds of appearance and reality. This hiatus corrodes Troilus' mind as it does Hamlet's.

In both plays, words are uttered to create an effect of appearance and they are contradicted by actions in some way or other. Daniel Seltzer speaks of Shakespeare's attempt to solve certain ethical equations in dramatic form in *Triolus and Cressida*. Most of these ethical values don't equate and the point where most of these equations go wrong is the point of divergence between what a person or subject seems to be and what it actually is.

In the discussion in the relevant chapter on *Troilus and Cressida* we have already traced the evolution of Troilus through the vicissitudes of his experiences. They broadly reveal a rising and falling curve — the rise and fall corresponding to his movement through appearances and reality respectively. There is a combination of his idealistic and illusory evaluations of two women from two points of view— of Helen as a theme of honour and of Cressida as an object of love.

Troilus' argument begins with the subjective assertion, "What's aught but as 'tis valued ?[46] and continues extolling Helen's 'apparent' worth :

"Is she worth keeping ? Why, she is a pearl
Whose price hath launch'd above a thousand ships,
And turn'd crown'd kings to merchants ...."[47]
He continues in the same key :
"She is a theme of honour and renown,
A spur to valiant and magnanimous deeds,

Whose present courage may beat down our foes,
And fame in time to come canonize us;"[48]

The love for the other woman, is idealized beyond all proportions only to prepare for the final disillusionment.

"This is the monstrosity in love, lady, that the will is infinite, and the execution confin'd; that the desire is boundless, and the act a salve to limit."[49]

The utmost reach of Helen's power to launch ships and to inspire brave deeds is seen to be destructive leading to the ruin of Troy and to Hector's death within the scope of the play. So 'honour and renown' was only in appearance; the reality was that she was the object of "mad idolatry" whose "service" (based on apparent worth) was greater than "the god" (her real worth).

Cressida's real worth is shown in the light of her 'monstrous' change so that ultimately Troilus thinks of two Cressidas - one apparent and the other real. When Troilus says, "The bonds of heaven are slipp'd dissolv'd and loos'd' And with another knot, five-finger tied"[50], it is implied that the divine appearance has dissolved and the real person (authenticated by the concrete food imagery) has appeared with faster knots of her new love. The bonds of heaven were intangible whereas the bonds of reality are tied by five fingers so that love and faith are brought within their grasp through the concrete "fragments, scraps, the bits, and greasy relics."[51] The other play which reveals such a startling gap between the world of appearance and that of reality is *Antony and Cleopatra*.

Apart from what has been already pointed out in the relevant chapter, we may notice the continuous strain of this contradiction in relation to the theme of the play—love and passion as against power and material greatness of the secular world. Apart from their symbolic manifestation in Egypt and Rome, we find an inter-relation between them—the power of passion increases in importance as the secular power becomes more threatening while it was subject to fluctuations when secular power was subsidiary to it. In other words, it was subject to appearances against the backdrop of secular power which threw it into relief; but when this backdrop became an active, threatening force, passion was transformed into love to oppose and transcend it. The appearances or 'becomings' of passion were transformed into a state of being which was the final reality emerging from the play. This is wholly true of Cleopatra while it can be shown that Antony's love entered a state of being after his perception of the dissolution of appearances before his death in spite of all his earlier talk of a new heaven and new earth.

We shall here draw a line between passion and love. As the play begins, the 'love' of Antony and Cleopatra is not free from the suspicion of appearance. The object of the introduction of Philo and Demetrius is to make the audience see it from their angle. So two angles of vision — that of these persons and the other of the lovers—are put forth. The lovers in their talk of presenting it as too great to be 'reckoned' in earthly terms are unconscious of its being 'passion'. There is a cleavage between intention and act, between 'becoming' and 'being'. While it is valid to treat these divine promptings as genuine and even the passion cannot be fully accounted for by treating it as purely sensual, we cannot but admit that it is more 'appearance' than reality and permits fluctuations which are seen on the part of both these characters. Antony wants to 'break off' from the 'enchanting' queen and feels the love for her to be only strong 'fetters'.

If we examine these two expressions along with a few more occurring in Antony's other speeches, we can form a composite picture of his attitude to this love. These other expressions are so near each other and near those pointing to an ethereal concept of love that an impression of duality is inescapable. The dramatist continues to create this impression of duality till the middle of the fourth Act when the world of appearances recedes like the "unpurged images of the day" in Yeats' *Byzantium*.

"O, then we bring forth weeds / When our quick minds lie still",[52] "the present pleasure by revolution low'ring";[53] and finally, "She is cunning past man's thought"[54] (including the sense of 'artful' to appear in different moods as it suits her) and the remarks of Enobarbus following it, with the idea of enchantment and fetters, show that both of these lovers are aware of some other element in their relationship - Cleopatra of using powers which make her love a game of appearances —her 'becomings'—and Antony finding his joy swelling and ebbing but like a 'limned soul' caught in her toils.

These fluctuations, notwithstanding his compulsive attachment to Cleopatra, underline the Dionysiac element alternating in agonies and ecstasies—the very instability showing the presence of another element which impedes understanding. It is never made clear but is always implicit as a shadowy part of her nature which may be lightly referred to as a part of her becomings but is actually a policy to preserve her interest and identity which she keeps masked by these becomings. When the veil is lifted thrice : in her flight in the battle of Actium, in her permission to allow Thyreus to kiss her hand and in the final betrayal of her army in the second fight, Antony sees her real self behind the appearance. After the last climactic point, the appearances give way completely. It is also because Cleopatra, with the death of Antony and the knowledge given by Dolabella finally realizes that she does not stand to gain any more by appearances.

This is what may be called an unsympathetic view in face of equally plausible arguments which can be made out to prove that underneath these appearances there was an invisible reality of love which was 'intrinsicate' like her life. But her repeated avowals in the fifth Act that "*Now* from head to foot/I am marble-constant; *Now* the fleeting moon/No planet is of mine",[55] and other statements show that there is a considerable justification for the other view and Shakespeare was at pains to make both of them valid by his double vision.

The image of 'melting' is very frequent and vital to the theme of the play. It is applicable in a significant way to the melting of appearances. The process is seen to reach a culmination in the melting of one appearance into another in the last speech of Antony:

> "Sometime we see a cloud that's dragonish
> A vapour sometime like a bear or lion,
> A tower'd citadel, a pendent rock,
> A forked mountain, or blue promontory
> With trees upon't....
> That which is now a horse, even with a thought

The rack dislimns, and makes it indistinct,
As water is in water... now thy captain is
Even such a body."[56]

It is but one step to the disclosure of reality. From this point the play presents the dissolution of appearances and the characters present only one facet — that of reality.

Antony had not been a man of appearances; he was only caught in them. The process envisioned in his speech applies to the play's quality. The real change occurs in Cleopatra. But in Antony, the flamboyance in his nature gives way to a solidity and economy; the passion which made him sound the heights of exaltation and depths of despair now gives way to a classical calmness and the Roman becomes a Roman again. That was his reality and now he ends with it :

"...I liv'd the greatest prince o'th' world,
The noblest; and do now not basely die,
Not cowardly put off my helmet to
My countryman—a Roman by a Roman
Valiantly vanquish'd."[57]

Cleopatra's appearances—her becomings—had come to an end with Antony's death and through situations which confirm her single-mindedness, such as her unequivocal acceptance of the idea of death, she arrives at her final reality. It is the reality which has emerged from infinite variety and ironically, she becomes a 'woman' like 'the maid that milks' when she says 'I have nothing / Of woman in me:'[58]

Obviously, the play's duality had come to an end once the person who provided that quality had abandoned it. That she does just near the end which comes like a burnt-out fire which has gone out by itself before the curtain falls. That is why Cleopatra's emergence in her real self is immediately followed by her death.

It now remains to consider this dichotomy of appearance and reality in the only other play in our group of problem plays in which it is manifested—*Measure for Measure*. Here it is avowedly a theme just like justice and mercy since it is explicitly stated by the Duke with reference to Angelo.

"Hence we shall see
If power change purpose, what our seemers be."[59]

He already knows that Angelo has more of the appearance of the "kind of character" he had credited him with and of the many purposes he wanted to serve by making him his deputy, one was to expose him. Thus the argument of critics that the Duke takes over the control of the plot after Isabella has rejected Claudio's plea for life, is based on false premises. He controls the plot and devises ways to work his ends from the very beginning. It is not in minute details but in the broad drift and without planning his encounter with Isabella he had paved the way for a situation when Angelo would expose himself.

If Angelo is saintly in appearance only and wears it like a mask from the time of his meeting with Isabella, she becomes the medium of the expression of the reality in him. It is an interesting process of unmasking.

When Angelo is informed that "the sister of the man condemn'd"[60] desired access to him, his curiosity, which marks the first weak point in him, leads him to a dialogue which proves to be disastrous to his 'saintliness'. He permits her to talk and it is obvious that unconsciously, he allows himself to be influenced by the kind of arguments which would gradually strip his pose and appeal to the human self which lay repressed under it. Meanwhile, the imagery used by Isabella is constantly battering at the mask to reach the heart of the inner man. We can consider the degrees by which she succeeds.

The entire dialogue between the two on the first meeting is so complex in its movement that on different levels, conscious and unconscious, it is possible to trace the effect of Isabella's talk on Angelo which ultimately wears out the mask.

The beginning with the words, "There is a vice that most I do abhor/And most desire should meet the blow of justice," meets Angelo's unrelenting mind with the right poise and establishes an unconscious identity between their moral attitude. The following statement of Isabella,

> "For which I would not plead, but that I must;
> For which I must not plead, but that I am
> At war 'twixt will and will not."[61]

shows that she had moved into a neutral zone where she doesn't wish to plead for something she is actually pleading and is sharply divided within herself on the moral issue. The division and vacillation are real and not in appearance and although Isabella seems to give up the issue by preparing to go, and Angelo is almost monosyllabic (he has one short line four times as against two to ten of Isabella), there is no doubt that by now he is less indifferent and wants to convince her. This creates a moral concern which was not there to begin with. It is not only to be fair but to appear so. It is here that the tone of Isabella's argument and its imagery changes from secular to the religious and continues so for five speeches. This change in imagery is very relevant to the effect produced. We may juxtapose the two speeches which mark this turning point :

"No ceremony that to great ones longs,
Not the king's crown, nor the deputed sword,
The marshal's truncheon, nor the judge's robe,
Become them with one half so good a grace
As mercy does."[62]

The imagery is secular. It is followed by :

"Also, alas,
Why, all the souls that were, were forfeited once,
And He that might the vantage best have took
Found out the remedy. How would you be
If He, which is the top of judgment, should
But judge you as you are ?O, think on that;
And mercy then will breathe within your lips
Like man new made."[63]

In the first speech the secular authority which Angelo had used against her brother is shown to be of a lower order than spiritual grace manifested in mercy. The crown, the sword, the truncheon and the robe are all concrete symbols of this less effective power. By this, Isabella reduces the secular barrier which was only the appearance of power while the real power was mercy which constituted the power of God. This was also His remedy which corrected man and saved his soul. It could make Angelo a new man while he saved both the body and soul of Claudio and acted like God.

With this image of secular power as mere appearance, Angelo is brought on the same level as other human beings in relation to divine power. Now he could be shown as misusing it unlike God. Having thus stripped the illusion of human authority, it is but a step to show that he is going contrary to God's will—his show of justice is a 'fantasic trick' while his authority is only a 'glassy essence'.

The imagery thus serves to remove one layer after another in this authority of Angelo and reducing his status to that of a plain human being, places him on the same level as another sinner who needs the mercy of God.

"Go to your bosom,
Knock there, and ask your heart what it doth know
That's like my brother's fault. If it confess
A natural guiltiness, such as is his,
Let it not sound a thought upon your tongue
Against my brother's life."[64]

On the mental and spiritual plane Isabella has removed all the layers of appearance in Angelo and now the last layer—that of 'saintliness'—is attacked by a subtle psychological suggestion that he could be guilty of a similar fault as her brother. The establishment of a common ground of austerity with which their encounter began, followed by the reduction of Angelo from his high impeccable state to that of a frail mortal, and ending in suggestion of his own possible susceptibility and culpability, - this intricate psychological movement serves to drop Angelo's mask. His 'appearance' of saintliness is stripped and the 'reality' of 'the devil's horn' is about to emerge. Angelo only holds on his falling mask till he makes his proposal to Isabella.

The unmasking begins with "She speaks, and 'tis such sense/ That my sense breeds with it."[65] The thought-suggestion in the possibility of weakness like Claudio's being present in him is brought to a head by Isabella's words "Hark, how I'll bribe you"[66] to which momentarily a wrong interpretation could be attached. Even when Isabella enlarges upon it as 'prayers', the insinuation has unconsciously worked. It is a deliberate device of the dramatist to put it as the last straw on his mind in this process of transformation.

How the unmasking had occurred while the reality was always there, is put by Angelo in his following soliloquy :

"From thee : even from thy virtue !
What's this ? what's this ? Is this her fault, or mine ?
The tempter, or the tempted, who sins most,
Ha !
Not she ; nor doth she tempt; but it is I
That, ling by the violet in the sun,
Do as the carrion does, not as the flow'r,
Corrupt with virtuous season."[67]

This echoes Isabella's, "Even for our kitchens / We kill the fowl of season", showing how the epithet which was used in connection with Claudio to condone his fault is now used by himself to affirm his own fault.

The psychological aspect which as we noticed, established a common ground between Isabella and Angelo and was unconsciously present in every exchange between them, is finally emphasized by Angelo's words :

"O cunning enemy, that, to catch a saint,
With saints dost bait thy hook!"[68]

Finally, the divergence between the appearance which he had maintained so long and the reality which emerged under the influence of Isabella is put effectively by Angelo in his second soliloquy :

"The state whereon I studied
Is, like a good thing being often read,
Grown sere and tedious; yea, my gravity,
Wherein—let no man hear me — I take pride
Could I with boot change for an idle plume
Which the air beats for vain. O place, O form,
How often dost thou with thy case, thy habit,
Wrench awe from fools, and tie the wiser souls
To thy false seeming![69]

Thus the theme of appearance and reality seems so to engross Shakespeare's mind during the period he wrote the problem plays that it is a major aspect not only of these plays but also emerges as a prominent element in *Othello* and partly in *King Lear* and *Macbeth*.

(c) The Theme of Death

Although death is not the main but a co-related theme, it emerges with such emphasis and with such opposed attitudes in at least three of the problem plays, that no discussion of them can be complete without referring to it. In *Hamlet*, *Measure for Measure* and *Antony and Cleopatra* the theme appears as inseparable from the characters and their actions. The double vision also conditions its relationship with the general theme of the plays. The attitudes to death can also be seen to be complementary and in a vital relationship to this life and the next.

In *Hamlet*, as has been observed in the discussion in the relevant chapter, Hamlet's attitude to death evolves from a completely negative to a positive one. This evolution spans the whole of the play and marks the growth of Hamlet illustrating the diction of Aeschylus — "Man shall learn wisdom by affliction school'd."[70]

The very first appearance shows him dressed in black, mourning the death of his father and shortly after, contemplating suicide. He wants his flesh to melt out of the contamination it has caught from his mother's sin. Only the commandment of God seems to deter him. There is no doubt that he wants to expiate for this sin by his own death although as we know later, his rejection of death proceeds not from God's command but from the same attitude of negation which makes him reject life and everything that goes with it and live a life no better than death. It is the typical attitude of an inhabitant of the Waste Land.

This later revelation of his attitude to death comes with the third soliloquy which is wholly preoccupied with the idea. The question which has so long 'possessed' him, now comes to a point of decision but as we know once again, decision and execution are beyond him. Again an unconscious pretext serves him :

"To die, to sleep;
To sleep, perchance to dream. Ay, there's the rub;
For in that sleep of death what dreams may come,
When we have shuffled off this mortal coil,
Must give as pause."[71]

Unconsciously, Hamlet has again implied his preference for a death-in-life—'calamity' in his own words. It is however little noticed that 'dreams' however unknown or horrible, which had deterred him from suicide, were no worse than his 'dreams' in real life. As he said to Rosencrantz and Guildenstern, Denmark to him was a prison because of 'bad dreams' :

"O God, I could be bounded in a nutshell and count myself a king of infinite space, were it not that I have bad dreams."[72]

If Hamlet had bad dreams in life, due to which he was ill-at-ease, what worse could happen in death! It was a baseless fear and in due course he gets over it.

However, the fear of death at this point becomes a distinguishing mark of Hamlet's character. C.S. Lewis remarks of this :

"If I wanted to make one more addition to the gallery of Hamlet's portraits, I should trace his hesitation to the fear of death; not to the fear of dying but a fear of being dead."[73]

At the same time Hamlet is obsessed with another feeling — that it were better if he had not been born. When his disgust with life reaches a pitch he says to Ophelia (assuming the situation to apply to all women) :

"Get thee to a nunnery. Who wouldst thou be a breeder of sinners ? I am myself indifferent honest, but yet I could accuse me of such things that it were better my mother had not borne me".[74]

The reference to the idea of not being born is an alternative to suicide as the most desirable state of avoiding all the ills of life. It is a wishful thought — impossible to realize *after* one is born but it has a long philosophical tradition and in drama it first appears in Sophocles. The chorus in *Oedipus at Colonus* says :

"In the accumulation of many years
Pain is in plenty, and joy not anywhere
When life is over-spent ;
And at the last there is the same release
When death appears,
Unheralded by music, dance, or song,
To give us peace.

Say what you will the greatest boon is not to be;
But, life begun, soonest to end is best,
And to that bourn from which our way began
Swiftly return."[75]

This anticipates both the alternatives thought of as a release by Hamlet. The same idea is found in *the Eudemus*, one of the early ethical writings of Aristotle. Eudemus says, "Best of all not to be born",[76] which is a desire to maintain the purely spiritual nature undefiled by the association of the body. It is noteworthy that Hamlet wants to attain it by purging the defilement of the body, if necessary, by suicide.

There is an interesting connection of this outlook with Dionysus, the god who prompted human beings to be swept by the primitive urges of their nature and who often led them to annihilation. Hence death is more directly connected with the Dionysian way of life. Mythically, the maxim of not to be born as the highest good was attributed to Silenus, the foster-father and companion of Dionysus. Eugene O'Neill quotes Silenus telling human beings, "the best good is never to be born,"[77] and he also quotes Heine who elaborated this idea of a pre-natal freedom in his poem to Morphine :

"Lo, sleep is good; better is death; in sooth
The best of all were never to be born."[78]

So Hamlet incoporates a long tradition of philosophic thought about Death in relation to the ills of life when he makes his statement.

The attitude towards death which Hamlet adopts, though for the most part negative, is not static. As far as thought is concerned, Hamlet's thoughts go beyond death to the contemplation of a life of peace putting an end to the "heart-ache and the thousand natural shocks / That flesh is heir to."[79] Only, he cannot put it in action as he cannot his other cherished designs. That finally he undergoes a seachange and accepts Death without speculations is a measure of the evolution in his character. The following words uttered to Horatio just before the fencing-match, can be compared with the words of Gloucester in *King Lear*.

"Not a whit, we defy augury : there is a special providence in the fall of a sparrow. If it be now, 'tis not to come; if it be not to come, it will be now if it be not now, yet it will come—

the readiness is all. Since no man owes of aught he leaves, what is't to leave betimes. Let be."[80]

This is an affirmation of death as 'a necessary end' and its acceptance. Negation has given way to a positive faith in providence and death.

There is however, nothing like Keats' "Now more than ever seems it rich to die."[81] For this we have to wait till *Antony and Cleopatra*. Meanwhile, the play which juxtaposes both attitudes in an artistic counterpointing so that the evocations linger and haunt the mind with an urgency and a passion absent in *Hamlet* is that veritable mine of problems — *Measure for Measure*.

The death-theme—as an urgent proccupation with the experience of death (not merely the 'idea' of it as in *Hamlet*) — appears with the Duke, in disguise as a Friar, preparing Claudio for death. The rhythms are incantatory and the ideas translate themselves into experience as he goes on :

> "Be absolute for death : either death or life
> Shall thereby be the sweeter...
> Merely, thou art Death's fool;
> For him thou labour'st by thy flight to shun,
> And yet run'st toward him still...
> Thou'rt by no means valiant;
> For thou dost fear the soft and tender fork
> Of a poor worm. Thy best of rest is sleep;
> Thou hast nor youth, nor age,
> But, as it were, an after-dinner's sleep
> Dreaming on both;... What's yet in this
> That bears the name of life ? Yet in this life
> Lie hid moe thousand deaths;"[82]

Claudio apprehends this mentally as well as sensuously. He feels the spell of death as a welcome alternative to life and his mind is at once made up.

> "To sue to live, I find I seek to die,
> And seeking death, find life. Let it come on."[83]

There is nothing equivocal, sceptical or insincere about it. There is no cerebration, as in the case of Hamlet. Claudio's animal instincts have felt the appeal of the imagery which is most sensuous. There is no feeling of anything invisible or pertaining to a spiritual existence after life.

The appeal of Isabella for an acceptance of death is also rendered in terms of the senses :

"Dar'st thou die ?
The sense of death is most in apprehension;
And the poor beetle that we tread upon
In corporeal sufferance finds a pang as great
As when a giant dies."[84]

The acceptance of Claudio is absolute. His attitude is as positive as Antony's who wished to join Cleopatra in the next world —an illusory feeling. Claudio prepares to die in full awareness of death being 'darkness'. Hence his acceptance is more positive. The fact that he changes for a moment does not affect the moral quality. Antony's "I will be / A bridegroom in my death, and run into't / As to a lover's bed,"[85] is not so spontaneous as Claudio's :

"If I must die,
I will encounter darkness as a bride
And hug it in mine arms."[86]

Whereas Antony's image creates an impression that death is a *means* of union and death as such doesn't come to mind with any impact, Claudio's image personifies death in the form of darkness and when he speaks of the act of hugging it, disbelief is entirely suspended and we do actually *feel* the experience as anyone could have it. It is likely that no other writer's imagination could show a man 'embracing' darkness as a bride, gathering it in his arms ! It is an example of the positive vision working with rare creativeness as against the negative association of sleep and dreams in Hamlet's soliloquy.

Claudio's decision is based on a sensuous apprehension of his destiny and he has no fear. But as soon as cerebration comes with the idea of Angelo's risking this soul for the same kind of immorality of which he was accused, Claudio's imagination sets to work connecting the immorality of which Isabella would be guilty if she saved him with the damnation Angelo is willing to incur for a trivial thing without any justification. Isabella *could* have a justification in saving him and so he concludes that her act would become a virtue rather than a sin.

This is one of the most intriguing problems of the play and critics are so divided over it that the concepts of morality would have to be explored before deciding what could have been right on Isabella's part. We should better decide the matter by saying that whatever is required by the plot is right—whatever is, is right because otherwise we shall have a different kind of play. And it is justified because what Claudio says is quite consistent with the kind of animal instincts he is given. Moreover, the least cerebration on the part of such temperaments would bring about sudden and decisive changes. So weighing Isabella's sin against Angelo's damnation, he finds it too light. He even concludes that if a man like Angelo, with all his wisdom, commits it then it is not a sin of such magnitude :

"If it were damnable, he being so wise,
Why would he for the momentary trick
Be perdurably fin'd ? - O Isabel !"[87]

We have dealt with the implication of the situation only to explore the changes in Caludio's attitude towards death. With this possibility of escape he is suddenly affected by the fear of death which is always in proportion as one desires to live. This fear is again rendered in purely sensuous terms as against the abstract way in which Hamlet thinks of the fear of death which for him, becomes a fear of dreams. Claudio's fear is concrete :

"Ay, but to die, and go we know not where ;
To lie in cold obstruction, and to rot;
This sensible warm motion to become
A kneaded clod; and the delighted spirit
To bathe in fiery floods, or to reside
In thrilling region of thick-ribbed ice;
To be imprison'd in the viewless winds,
And blown with restless violence round about
The pendent world: or to be worse than worst
Of those that lawless and incertain thought
Imagine howling, - 'its too horrible.
The weariest and most loathed worldly life
That age, ache, penury and imprisonment
Can lay on nature, is a paradise
To what we fear of death."[88]

The epithet 'we' suggests that Claudio incorporates the fear of all human beings with his own fear and hence it multiplies out of all proportion as the love of life increases.

This is expressed in his appeal :

"Sweet sister, let me live.
What sin you do to save a brother's life,
Nature dispenses with the deed so far
That it becomes a virtue."[89]

After Isabella spurns his request, and the Duke intervenes, Claudio immediately comes back to his initial position because the effect of cerebration is countered by her violent outburst and by the Duke's revelation (even if it is a psychological ruse) : "Let me ask my sister pardon; I am so out of love with life that I will sue to be rid of it."[90]

It may be relevant to glance at Antigone's willing sacrifice for the sake of the proper burial of her brother which, in a similar situation, Isabella would also have done since she says :

"O, were it but my life !
I'd throw it down for your deliverance
As frankly as a pin."[91]

The word "deliverance" establishes an identity in the attitude towards death between Isabella and Sophocles heroine.

Claudio's attitude to death anticipates that of Antony and to some extent of Cleopatra so far as the positive side is concerned. The fear of death completely disappears in *Antony and Cleopatra*. Whether physically or spiritually, death is viewed as a welcome prospect—not as an escape from life but as its consummation. Here lies the uniqueness of Shakespeare's vision in this play. Antony thinks of death only towards the end of his life, but Cleopatra, in her intimate association with poison and serpents, seems to have established a kinship with death in her mastery of its means. As Caesar says at the end :

"her physician tells me
She hath pursu'd conclusions infinite
Of easy ways to die."[92]

Secondly, there are occasions in the play when both Antony and Cleopatra seem to transcend death in the exaltation of their love. In case of Cleopatra, a further device has been used by what may be called a figurative method to present death as a part of the 'viles' to which she was accustomed. Finally, in the fifth Act there are more positive references to death in the speeches of Cleopatra than in those of any other character in Shakespeare, culminating in her actual death which is the most elaborate presentation of the kind in the whole canon.

We shall examine these conclusions in detail.

Both Antony and Cleopatra evince sufficient proof that for them, death is part of their venture in love. Intensity is the bargain. It is the dramatist's own vision, like that of a painter who makes a rough sketch on the canvas, to shape these characters, particularly that of Cleopatra as temporal and timeless, living on two planes. It is his own concept independent of history which he uses to lend a spiritual dimension to an affair of earthly passion and evolve a genuine tragedy out of it. Hence we see a part of them dolphin-like above the sea of the senses and there is a corresponding counterpointing in a musical sense to keep this balance in the minds of the audience all the time. The character of Enobarbus—entirely Shakespeare's creation—is elaborated like a chorus to keep it like a burning flame before our eyes and even Charmian and Eros have a similar function. The death-theme also gets its affirmation from Antony and Cleopatra themselves in their constant pull to 'immortal longings' in the realization of which death has a necessary role. In their mental world it becomes a friendly figure and in contrast to Hamlet or Claudio, fear of any sort does not exist. The turn of the perspective is noticeable from the very beginning. Enobarbus says :

"I do think there is mettle in death, which commits some loving act upon her, she hath such a celerity in dying."[93]

The subsequent reference by Cleopatra identifying herself with serpent and poison — the agents of death — confirms this 'love' :

'Where's my serpent of old Nile ?'
For so he calls me. Now I feed myself

With most delicious poison. Think on me
That am with Phoebus' amorous pinches black,
And wrinkled deep in time?"[94]

The other love confirms yet another—identify that with the sun whose heat has made her dark and wrinkled (with the suggestion of serpent and Nile-mud) suggesting infinite age and immunity to death. The earlier suggestion that death loves her creates an image of timelessness by living in time and mastering the agents of death.

Hence the paradox. The processes in time which make others decay and deprive them of power, strengthen Cleopatra even when she seems to be panting for breath. Enobarbus the 'Tiresias' of the play, says :

"I saw her once
Hop forty paces through the public street ;
And, having lost her breath, she spoke, and panted,
That she did make defect perfection,
And, breathless, pow'r breathe forth."[95]

The idea of death as the price of love continues to move like an undercurrent in the plot since Antony suggested "a new heaven, a new earth" to reckon this love. This idea, not static in its context continues to spread out like the river from its source broadening and finally disclosing a wide sea-like stretch before it really breaks the bounds of this world and flows in to the next. A new heaven, a new earth are actually realized when Antony speaks of "Where souls do couch on flowers, we'll hand in hand, And with our sprightly port make the ghosts gaze..."[96]

The infinite reach of his love is not contradicted by the fact that Cleopatra whom he hopes to meet there is still alive in the monument. Similarly his speech just before his death is an affirmation and stands in a direct contrast to Hamlet's negative attitude. Claudio's speech, as already pointed out, excels it in apprehension through the senses but the quality of affirmation is the same :

"But I will be
A bridegroom in my death, and run ino't
As to a lover's bed."[97]

It is however, Cleopatra's attitude towards death which is the highest point of affirmation in this respect ever attained by any character in Shakespeare. Shakespeare's creative imagination was deeply stirred by the idea. What is noteworthy is that Cleopatra's transformation goes along with her resolution to die. As she says after the death of Antony :

"All's but nought;
Patience is sottish, and impatience does
Become a dog that's mad. Then is it sin
To rush into the secret house of death
Ere death dare come to us?"[98]

Her second speech reveals the germ of a new life in this resolution. It is still of this earth and marks the completeness of transformation :

"My desolation does begin to make
A better life. 'Tis paltry to be Caesar :
Not being Fortune, he's but Fortune's knave,
A minister of her will; and it is great
To do that thing that ends all other deeds,
Which shackles accidents and bolts up change.."[99]

The third speech marks the final stage of Cleopatra's transformation so that she becomes just the contrary of what she had been:

"My resolution is plac'd and I have nothing
Of woman in me. Now from head to foot
I am marble-constant; now the fleeting moon
No planet is of mine."[100]

There is a greater affirmation of death not only because there is no touch of a negative element by way of fear or hesitation but also due to a positive *experience* of the instruments of death. It will be clear if we compare a few lines from *Measure for Measure* with two in this play. The Duke in his memorable speech to Claudio says:

"Thou'rt by no means valiant ;
For thou dost fear the soft and tender fork
Of a poor worm".[101]

Cleopatra, while applying the asp—the worm with 'the soft and tender fork' says :

"Dost thou not see my baby at my breast/ That sucks the nurse asleep ?"[102]

It is certainly as far as loving death could go when one can love its 'instrument' usually feared.

Finally, we can perceive this love in a rhythm which re-appears like a final chord of music at the end. We have already referred to the comment of Enobarbus, "I do think there is mettle in death, which commits some loving act upon her". We now find the same idea uttered by Cleopatra. A most remarkable appearance of an earlier statement comparable to the words of Richard II re-appearing in Henry IV ('The time shall not be many hours of age...') :[103]

"The stroke of death is as a lover's pinch,
Which hurts and is desir'd."[104]

G. Wilson Knight says almost to the same effect :".. these two, love and death, are synchronized in *Antony and Cleopatra*. In (this play), death is the consummation of life, itself "a better life", in truth no death at all, but life. Here life conquers death".[105]

On the point of concluding this discussion, our attention is caught by a curious recurrence of the death-and-sleep motif which marks the two earlier plays *Hamlet* and *Measure for Measure*. In *Hamlet*, as we have seen, death as sleep is desired and then rejected. In the other play, the Duke calls death, "Thy best of rest". In *Antony and Cleopatra*, Cleopatra *becomes* sleep—the ne plus ultra in this line of evolution. And yet in this sleep of death, the quality of life doesn't desert her. As Octavius says :

"She looks like sleep
As she would catch another Antony
In her strong toil of grace."[106]

(d) Two categories with common visionary modes :

The problem plays discussed in this book can also be divided into two categories in each of which there is a common visionary mode. In the first and the earlier group there is a predominantly negative visionary mode, with the negative vision dominating for the most part of the plays. In the second and later group there is a predominantly positive mode, with the positive vision irradiating the atmosphere of the play and moulding the characters and conditioning their actions. The other vision—the positive in the first group and the negative in the second group — also appears contrasting and juxtaposing the contrary element but it is not allowed to determine the tone of the play.

It is illuminating to make this division because it throws light upon the way the dramatist's mind was moving towards a more positive exploration of human existence in the last plays. There is more of 'grimness' of the vision of evil in the first group and more of the intimations of divine grace which redeems, in the other.

In the first group we can place the plays chronologically written earlier—*Julius Caesar, Hamlet* and *Troius and Cressida* ; while in the second group come those written later, *All's Well, Measure for Measure* and *Antony and Cleopatra*. This is a valid grouping which also takes account of the thematic affinity in the plays. It has not been noticed so far that this broad categorization would enable us to call the first three as plays of negation and the latter three as plays of affirmation. It may be worthwhile to develop this view.

Julius Caesar, Hamlet and *Troilus and Cressida* mark an earlier period in Shakespeare's career. The latter two are distinctly sceptical and bitter in tone-faith and love seem to be corroded and the protagonist is disillusioned and disgusted with life and human beings as such. Virtue seems to be a mask and the reality behind appearance seems to be elusive and the disparity when revealed upsets the mind of the protagonist. In *Julius Caesar* too the protagonist is drawn to an illusory ideal which he ill-achieves and his failure underlines an inability to direct his faith and love in a wholly constructive channel. So in the facet which Brutus presents earlier to the world. He is bitter at the lot of Roman people mutely suffering the yoke of dictatorship which might result in tyranny with the crowning of Caesar. As far as Caesar is concerned, his judgement is flawed due to hybris and he is dreadfully illusioned about his invulnerability. Brutus too wears a mask as far as Caesar is concerned. So no moral value has its proper functioning or recognition. The apparently positive virtue—Brutus' love for Rome and the Roman people—is fraught with a delusion as is implied in the subsequent events. The inception of the design of assassination is in a starkly negative atmosphere darkened by ill omens. The mind of Brutus is figuratively in a state of insurrection. Later the suddenness and ease with which Antony is able to demolish his arguments show that his ideal was not built on firm foundation. The ghost of Caesar is a projection of the guilty conscience of Brutus. That is why it reveals itself to Brutus as his "evil spirit".

In addition to this, all these three plays end on a note of futility of the cause which was the central motif of the play and the main drive for action on the part of the protagonist. Both the character and its actions seem to have defeated the purpose of their existence. It is due to their flaw and to the irony of circumstances, and this accounts for the deeper note of tragedy in the two (*Hamlet* and *Julius Caesar*) and near-tragedy in the other (*Troilus* and *Cressida*). The flaw, in a direct or indirect way, is related to their choices. Brutus explicitly makes a choice between love and duty and his flaw makes his pursuit go awry. Troilus makes his choice with all the sanctity of the heart's emotions but his choice goes awry due to the unworthiness of the object which applies with a more devastating irony to his plea for the choice of honour against expendiency with regard to Helen. In both cases he made 'the worship more than the god' The one accounted for the fate of Troy and the other for his disillusionment. Both Brutus and Troilus illustrate the idealist's tragedy. Hamlet too is an idealist's tragedy of a 'choice' which ran counter to his task-of taking upon himself the much more difficult task of 'setting right' the 'cursed spite' which was the larger evil infecting Denmark and of reforming his mother—to make her 'throw away the worser part' of her heart and 'live the purer with the other half'. The problems of these plays arise from these preoccupations with which the protagonist is intensely involved. It is due to them that the course of their progress through the play is determined leading to a note of futility.

As against these, the plays of the second group could be called those of affirmation in which the values for which the main characters have lived, ultimately triumph on the secular or the spiritual plane. Their characters and actions are ultimately vindicated by the positive vision.

Enough has already been said to show how Helena, striving by the sheer force of her love, succeeds in marrying Bertram and during her quest to fulfill her impossible task, her entire movement from the healing of the king to the bed-trick and the final winning of Bertram would be utterly petty and despicable were it not for the positive vision which projects her love most of the time. What is more, all her exploits become credible and from a clever wench, she becomes a 'debile minister', with 'great power, great transcendence'.

In *Measure for Measure* it is the positive vision which makes Isabella a naturally virtuous and redeeming character who, in its absence, would appear a moral prig. Similarly, no one thinks that Lucio's description of the Duke as "the old fantastical Duke of dark corners"[107] fits him because most of the time whatever he says or does, is presented in a positive light. His assumption of the role of providence which, in a less virtuous character, would be deemed hybris, makes him emerge without presumption and his habit of a friar which demanded humility, accounts for it to a great extent. He is the very opposite of what Lucio describes him to be on his very face, and he does not lose temper even when he reveals himself to him which is a measure of the self-mastery he has acquired. His concern for his subjects' welfare and for the salvation of the souls of those with whom he is intimately associated in his role as friar shows that he deserves to wield the power he assigns to himself:

"He who the sword of heaven will bear
should be as holy as severe;
Pattern in himself to know,
Grace to stand, and virtue go;[108]

His final gesture of forgiving all sinners, defaulters and calumniators, shows that he lacks nothing in extending a God-like mercy which is the strongest vindication of his role—of "one that, above all other strifes" had "contended especially to know himself ".[109] He makes others too know themselves, particularly Angelo.

Hence it is not to understand the absolute fitness of the Duke's role to his character, which inclines critics to find fault with the scheme of the play and to split it into two halves after Act III Sc. I. It argues a complete lack of understanding of the dramatist's over-all vision which shapes the play into an organic whole. It is certainly due to a lack of understanding of Shakespeare's dramatic technique of consistently illuminating aspects of character by the positive or the negative vision according as it was necessary for his dramatic purpose.

Thus Mary Lascelles seems not to have appreciated the organic relationship of the Duke with the total design of the play with reference to his character and action when she says:

"The duke himself does not engage our concern by what he does, or suffers. How, we may fairly ask, does he—or should he—engage it? Criticism has for some while inclined towards the opinion that here is one of those persons in Shakespearean drama who should be regarded as important in respect rather of function than of character."[110]

Now it is precisely this equivalence of character and function which is maintained by the positive vision and those who overlook its role, would certainly find the Duke's character unengaging and his function out of proportion to its importance.

The third play which can be called a play of the positive vision is *Antony and Cleopatra*. Implying that Shakespeare has taken special pains to present Cleopatra so as to eclipse all temporal values. William Rosen says,

"Shakespeare lavishes his imaginative splendours not upon military values and the ideals which Antony must attain, but upon Cleopatra, love, and the Egyptian attractions he is called upon to renounce."[111] Elaborating on the nature of her compulsive appeal, he adds:

"Cleopatra generates enormous excitement and this accounts for her great appeal. Never passive, her energy is as boundless in grief as in love. Mistress of infinite variety, she commands a tremendous repertoire of emotions and moods to suit all occasions."[112]

Add to it what Coleridge says of the "angelic strength" and "fiery force" of the play and we get a clue to the way how at every step when secular power in one form or the other, has challenged her power and her identity, the dramatist has at once restored the balance and swayed it in her favour by virtue of poetry which dwarfs everything temporal.

The irradiating power of this poetry issues from the heart of the positive vision and the play is thickly interspersed with its effects. In flashbacks, comments and present moments they create an illusion and an impression that these "illusions are real and the real enactments of the play are but shadows."[113] As a matter of fact these "illusions are the only reality of the play so far as the main theme is concerned, because they alone seem to connect with a higher reality.

The role of the positive vision in highlighting such moments is one of the triumphs of Shakespeare's art. Such moments are also presented in the tragic progress of Antony but they originate in one way or another, in his love-relationship with Cleopatra, and in the last analysis can be traced to her influence. This view would supplement what has already been said about the shaping effect of the positive vision which puts *Antony and Cleopatra* foremost in the second category of problem plays.

(C) Imagery in the Problem Plays

No discussion of any category of Shakespeare's plays can be complete without a discussion of their imagery and it is all the more necessary in such an exploration as the present which is directed at discovering a common ground.

Let us first see which kind of imagery can be considered as thematic in each of these plays and what other kinds are used as a subsidiary means of explication.

The first of these, plays (chronologically considering), *Julius Caesar* has comparatively fewer thematic images compared to *Hamlet* or *Antony and Cleopatra*. But two kinds of imagery—disorder and blood can be considered seminal to the play and appearing early enough, they continue till the end. The other tragedy—*Macbeth*— has them in a more developed form and since there is an affinity between Brutus and Macbeth, the use of this imagery in the two plays in not without thematic import.

The imagery of disorder explicates in a two-fold way—externally, with reference to external nature and internally, with reference to Brutus' mental landscape. The first reference in the play is to the disorder in the mind of Brutus which is as yet in the germ, and it sets the tone pointing to what may follow:

"Vexed I am
Of late with passions of some difference,
Conceptions only proper to myself,"[114]

It is followed by numerous images of disorder in external nature, "a tempest dropping fire,"[115] the flaming hand of a slave burning like twenty torches, yet unscorched, men in fire walking up and down, the owl at noonday—all indicating reversal of nature's normal order. This culminates in the image connecting all these with the state of Rome, which as Clemen points out, establishes an identity between the situation, the atmosphere and the person who is supposed to be the cause of this disorder. As Cassius says:

Now could I, Casca, name to thee a man
Most like this deadful night
That thunders, lightens, opens graves, and roars
As doth the lion in the Capitol;
A man no mightier than thyself or me
In personal action, yet prodigious grown,
And fearful, as these strange eruptions are."[116]

Clemen says, "By means of the imagery, the night and the thunderstorm are made very vivid, being also a suitable background for the dark conspiracy. The mood and situation naturally suggest the likening of Caesar to this fearful night."[117]

The next explication through imagery is of the growing disorder in the mental landscape of Brutus which is a progression of its earlier manifestations and constitutes a movement of the theme of the tragedy:

"I have not slept.
Between the acting of a dreadful thing
And the first motion, all the interim is
Like a phantasma or a hideous dream.
The Genius and the mortal instruments
Are then in council; and the state of man
Like to a little kingdom, suffers then
The nature of an insurrection."[118]

This internal disorder which began with 'passions of some difference' has already found another expression in the soliloquy which ratiocinates on its cause, trying to evolve a way which leads to the other kind of imagery—the shedding of blood. It was evolved as a solution but ironically aggravates the disorder.

"So Caesar may.
Then, lest he may, prevent.....
And therefore think him as a serpent's egg....
And kill him in the shell."[119]

As this is being uttered, the disorder in external nature reinforces the internal disorder (which follows in the 'insurrection' image) and exhalations are seen whizzing in the air. Just after, the imagery of blood gets a more explicit statement even though it is given a ritualistic air:

"Let's be sacrificers, but not butchers, Caius.
We all stand up against the spirit of Caesar,
And in the spirit of men there is no blood.
.......But, alas,
Caesar must bleed for it!"[120]

The two kinds of images of disorder and of blood later fuse in the dream of Calphurnia and the unnatural sights seen during the night. Here dream and reality reinforce each other:

"There is one within
Besides the things that we have heard and seen
Recounts most horrid sights seen by the watch.
A lioness hath whelped in the streets,
And graves have yawn'd and yielded up their dead;
Fierce fiery warriors fight upon the clouds,
In ranks and squadrons and right form of war,
Which drizzled blood upon the Capitol;
The noise of battle hurtled in the air;
Horses did neigh, and dying men did groan,
And ghosts did shriek and squeal about the streets"[121]

The imagery combines disorder on earth and in the sky with blood in the most awe-inspiring form. To complete the picture the dream of Calphurnia contains more of blood-imagery and the way is paved for the linking of all this unnatural phenomena with blood-shedding - a thematic linking of the atmosphere and background with the action:

"She dreamt to-night she saw my statua,
Which, like a fountain with an hundred spouts,
Did run pure blood; and many lusty Romans
Came smiling and did bathe their hands in it."[122]

The blood theme thus emerging out of the links with unnatural phenomena, continues independently and finds manifestation, in Antony's speeches—first, among the conspirators followed by his soliloquy and then to the Roman public. The first speech among the conspirators has references which pave the way for the main appeal of his oration:

"Had I as many eyes as thou hast wounds,
Weeping as fast as they stream forth thy blood...."[123]

It is followed by more vivid imagery in the soliloquy:

"Woe to the hand that shed this costly blood!
Over thy wounds now do I prophesy—
Which like dumb mouths do ope their ruby lips
To beg the voice and utterance of my tongue"[124]

It shows how the movement through the imagery directly leads to a powerful movement in the plot and linking them together displays a rising curve. What Antony says in the funeral speech now becomes its cumulative movement. It was disorder which led to blood-shedding and now blood begets disorder which is let forth like a deluge. The imagery gains power by the intensity it has already achieved. No accuracy of detail is needed in this surging movement at the climatic point:

"Through this the well-beloved Brutus stabb'd,
And as he pluck'd his cursed steel away,
Mark how the blood of Caesar follow'd it,
As rushing out of doors, to be resolv'd
If Brutus so unkindly knock'd or no!"[124]

The deluge of disorder draws on the citizens' cry: "Revenge! About! Seek! Fire! Kill! Slay!"

Antony's words show how his plan of setting Ate afoot with 'havoc' as its cry has succeeded:

"Now let it work. Mischief, thou art afoot,

Take thou what course thou wilt."[126]

From the point in the play when the imagery of disorder and blood first enters the thoughts of Brutus to this, we can trace the thematic movement through the imagery.

In *Hamlet* which has a great resemblance with *Julius Caesar* in the concept of tragedy, other kinds of imagery combine with those of disorder and blood, but they can be seen as basically connected with them. The killing of elder Hamlet by Claudius does not actually spill blood but the implication is the same and the use of poison and moral perfidity (with which by her marriage with Claudius, Gertrude is also connected in Hamlet's mind) combine it with contamination which manifests mentally and all over the environment as rottenness, sickness and disease. Since order has been disrupted by usurpation and the moral order too is violated by sin and evil, there is a pervasive sense of disorder on both planes. This combines with blood and poison, moral perfidity, sickness and disease in Hamlet's mind and creates an image of overwhelming disorder. It is the sense of as well as the effect of this disorder which almost paralyses Hamlet's will by making all its claim on his mind. This constitutes the inner landscape of Hamlet's mind while the task of revenge is imposed upon him in addition to his self-imposed task of setting right "the cursed spite"—the general evil in Denmark—which includes the 'saving' of his mother from her sin.

We can thus see that it is through the imagery that we can best understand 'what happens' to Hamlet's mind because what happens in Hamlet is mostly a projection of mental phenomenon.

Treating the disorder image with its various manifestations, as basic to *Julius Caesar* and *Hamlet*, we may proceed to explore it with reference to other plays in our range. The play which chronologically and in spirit, comes nearest to these two, is *Troilus and Cressida* which presents a continuous opposition between order and disorder existing on many planes. All aberrations from order—manifested as violation of a code of conduct and values compatible with a moral order—create chaos and disintegration of values. which determine the structure and tone of the play. In the Greek and Trojan councils we hear debates on the code of behaviour which would prevent disintegration and ruin.

The play is a vast spectacle of disintegration and the most convenient single angle of viewing its changing landscape is through the mind of Troilus. His early idealism and the values cherished by him in relation to Helen and Cressida determine the entire action in his subjective world and most of the outer action in the play. His passionate argument for retaining Helen as a theme of honour and renown brings about the prolongation of the Trojan war, the death of Hector and the final ruin—a collapse of the very 'honour and renown' on which Troilus had based his argument. The other value ardently cherished by him was that of Cressida's faith which like "a baseless fabric" collapses and leaves only 'fragments' and 'greasy relics' to remind him of reality which cuts through his image of Cressida. The food imagery which is as characteristic of this play as the disease imagery in *Hamlet*, provides an expression for the disruption of that moral code in which Troilus thought faith in love to be inviolable. This faith had crumbled to bits and "the fractions of her faith, orts of her love, / The fragments, scraps, the bits, and greasy relics"[127] stand for "the heap of broken images" of all that he had cherished on the foundation of that faith.

In other words the moral order which sustained him had collapsed confronting him with a reversal of those values of which Thersites, had been a perpetual spokesman. The counterpointing was not without design. Thersites whips out the same comments on the disorder among the Greeks which was, ironically, aggravated after Ulysses' speech on order.

The problem plays which follow *Hamlet* and *Troilus and Cressida*, also partake of similar basic imagery in one way or the other. We have seen in *Hamlet* that sickness is an ultimate effect of the disruption of the order of moral values by sin and murder. In *Measure for Measure* (which we shall take first as being nearer in spirit to the preceding plays), the moral order has been so much disrupted by evil, inner and outer, that the body politic and the inner selves of persons are equally affected by it. The Duke had seen that it had been his fault to give scope to his people and vices had multiplied to the extent that the normal order of "decorum" had almost disappeared:

"For terror, not to use, in time the rod
Becomes more mock'd than fear'd: so our decrees,
Dead to infliction, to themselves are dead,
And liberty plucks justice by the nose,
The baby beats the nurse, and quite athwart
Goes all decorum."[128]

In this respect the scene with Elbow, Froth and Pompey is not without point. Even Pompey, when questioned squarely by Escalus, confesses to being a bawd but adds,

"Truly sir, in my poor opinion, they will to't then. If your worship will take order for the drabs and the knaves, you need not to fear the bawds."[129]

And the problem of curbing these knaves and drabs was so acute that even Escalus thinks that mercy is not the only solution:

"Mercy is not itself, that oft looks so;
Pardon is still the nurse of second woe."[130]

It is characteristic of the play that the Duke's more categorical statement comes after there is an exposure of inner evil—the judge is as immoral as the culprit and what appeared to be said somewhat without context in *King Lear*, a later play, had proved a serious question valid at all times. Angelo confesses to this evil within him:

".....it is I
That, lying by the violet in the sun,
Do as the carrion does, not as the flow'r,
Corrupt with virtuous season."[131]

It echoes Hamlet's remark to Polonius ("For if the sun breed maggots......") which, seems to extend beyond the immediate context. To emphasize this evil, Shakespeare makes Angelo says more clearly how far he has fallen in the whirl of "the strong and swelling evil" till he identifies himself with the devil:

"Let's write 'good angel' on the devil's horn;
'Tis not the devil's crest."[132]

The internal disorder has grown to the extent of "dispossessing all my (Angelo's) other parts / of necessary fitness."[133]

If Vienna is outwardly infected with evil, Angelo contains hell within and vice is fast driving both to a point of dissolution. As the process is fast in the case of 'drabs and knaves', it is faster in the case of Angelo, who in Isabella's words, appears "A pond as deep as hell"[134]

The Duke's description thus covers both internal and external evil which has made Vienna an Inferno. When Escalus asks him of news abroad, the Duke says:

"None, but that there is so great a fever on goodness that the dissolution of it must cure it."[135]

What he has told Claudio preparing him for death, acquires a full significance in the general context of all human life which, drained of its vitality and significance has lost its worthwhileness:

"Thou hast nor youth, nor age,
But, as it were, an after-dinner's sleep
Dreaming on both".[136]

The imagery of disorder in the body-politic which includes Angelos, Claudios and Lucios who extend beyond the scope of the play—as does the image of human life just referred—has made *Measure for Measure* extend beyond the time it was written and join in spirit poems like *Gerontion* and *The Waste Land*. The play also provides an answer to the question raised in *Gerontion*, "After such knowledge, what forgiveness?"[137] The same would be a clue to regeneration so urgently needed in "the Waste Land".

The imagery of 'a fever on goodness' which is primarily due to disorder, external or internal, can be seen to be integral to the concept of *All's Well* which deals with the power of love to redeem good which has gone astray. Partly under the influence of Parolles and partly under the impulsion of 'the old Adam' in him, Bertram discards true love and as an escape turns to Florence. He has gone on the way to moral degradation with Parolles "a very tainted fellow, and full of wickedness" till he has "sick desires" and becomes "an engine of lust." This changes him so far as to lose all his former virtue, truthfulness, and even his balance of mind. As Parolles says later to the king:

"......indeed he was mad for her, and talk'd of Satan, and of Limbo, and of Furies, and I know not what. Yet I was in that credit with them at that time that, knew of......things which would derive me ill will to speak of...."[138]

This is an account of a delirious state when sin had already bred "sick desires" and the lies which Bertram tells the king reveal a frame of mind still convulsed by guilt, the after-effect of sin:

"You boggle shrewdly; every feather starts you"[139]

The king had already called him 'inhuman', and his conversion to evil was complete.

However, as in *Measure for Measure*, virtue redeems him and the play closes with his oath to "love her (Helena) dearly, ever, ever dearly".[140]

Apart from the imagery of conversion to evil and the consequent sickness and fever, we find a rare admixture of cosmic imagery which makes *All's Well* look forward to *Antony* and *Cleopatra*. Caroline Spurgeon calls it astronomical imagery:

"Helena, in the first scene, sums up her position in an astronomical image,

"Twere all one
That I should love a bright particular star
And think to wed it, he is so above me.
In his bright radiance and collateral light
Must I be comforted, not in his sphere."[141]

Spurgeon further refers to the idea of being born under good or evil stars and of being the plaything of fortune, running through a great part of the play :

"the poorer born,
Whose baser stars do shut us up in wishes."[142]

Helena declares her father's receipts shall for her legacy

"be sanctified
By th' luckiest stars in heaven."[143]

and when repudiated by Bertram, says she will ever seek with true observance

"to eke out that
Wherein toward me very homely stars have fail'd

To equal my great fortune."[144]

Thus whereas the imagery of disorder and sickness links *All's Well* with the other problem plays already discussed, the cosmic imagery establishes a common ground with *Antony and Cleopatra* which abounds in images of Heaven and the cosmos.

Antony and Cleopatra in its earlier and later parts, is bespangled with cosmic images giving an impression of the continuous presence of another world and another plane of existence belittling the secular and temporal one. Contrary impressions about the characters and their actions don't rule out the validity of this other world and the imagery is responsible for this.

Beginning with "new heaven, new earth." and moving though "Eternity.. in our lips and eyes" and "parts... a race of heaven", it reappears in

"His face was as the heav'ns, and therein stuck
A sun and moon, which kept their course and lighted
The little O, the earth," [145]

The colossal dream-figure of Antony transcends the world as his love had done and lost it:

"His legs bestrid the ocean; his rear'd arm
Crested the world.."[146]

Of this, Spurgeon says:

"The group of images in *Antony and Cleopatra*.. consists of images of the world, the firmament, the ocean and vastness generally.. continually stimulating our imagination to see the colossal figure of Antony."[147]

Of Shakespeare's poetic imagination in this play, she says, "..it is a pure flame driving throughout, fanned by emotion, whose heat purifies, fuses and transmutes into gold all kinds of material, land it is this fierce atmospheric heat which creates the pictures, dominating and directing them."[148]

W.H.Clemen develops the idea of elevating the figures of the protagonists through the cosmic imagery :

"We are indebted to Miss Spurgeon for the listing of those images in *Antony and Cleopatra* which strike the keynote of the play—the expanse of the world and the tremendous consciousness of power on the part of the character— and which elevate the figures of these great rulers to the level of demi-gods. These images, too, generally fulfill a double function : in the first place, they are a means of expressing Antony's greatness, but at the same time they create atmosphere by summoning to our minds again and again the image of the wide ocean and of the immeasurably vast world."[149]

Conversely, the image of melting is used for the dissolution of secular power as in *Hamlet* it is used for the dissolution of the contaminated flesh—a manifestation of the effect of secular evil. Earlier in the play, this image occurs in the sense of rejection of secular power: "Let Rome in Tiber melt", and later, it comes as a consequence, more or less, of the same rejection. When Antony, after his defeat, calls servants to take away Thyreus to be whipped, a lack of promptness but actually his own decline, makes him say: "Authority melts from me".[150]

Cleopatra's following defence uses the words "discandying of this pelleted storm"[151] and the same image with the other is used by Antony for describing the desertion by his followers:

"The hearts
That spaniel'd me at heels, to whom I gave
Their wishes, do discandy, melt their sweets
On blossomig Caesar;[152]

The antithesis of discandying and blossoming is implicit in the earlier juxtaposition of 'melting' with 'the fullest man" for Caesar and the still clearer opposition in the speech of Enobarbus leaves no doubt that Shakespeare intended to use it as a mode of thematic explication:

"That he should dream,
Knowing all measures, the full Caesar will
Answer his emptiness!"[153]

And yet the image is later used in a paradoxical sense of suggesting Antony's greatness even while expressing his decline and death:

"O, see, my women,
The crown o'th' earth doth melt."[154]

Another kind of imagery which establishes a common ground between *Antony and Cleopatra*, *Troilus and Cressida* and *Hamlet* is that of food and physical appetite. The image occurs in *Julius Caesar* as well in a ritualistic sense:

"Let's carve him as a dish fit for the gods."[155]

In *Hamlet*, it occurs twice in the sense of physical appetite:

"Why, she would hang on him
As if increase of appetite had grown
By what if fed on;"[156]

and subsequently in the closet scene it occurs in the sense as in *Troilus and Cressida* which we have already noted:

"Could you on this fair mountain leave to feed,
And batten on this moor?"[158]

The Ghost had spoken almost in the same imagery:

"So lust, though to a radiant angel link'd,
Will sate itself in a celestial bed
And prey on garbage".[158]

In *Antony and Cleopatra*, in the most paradoxical of all speeches which combines blessing with rakishness, Enobarbus speaks of

"Other women cloy
The appetites they feed, but she makes hungry
Where most she satisfies;"[159]

An indictment altogether to the contrary comes from Antony which surpasses Troilus' reference to Cressida's disintegrated faith:

"I found you as a morsel cold upon
Dead Caesar's trencher. Nay, you were a fragment
Of Cneius Pompey's, besides what hotter hours,
Unregist'red in vulgar fame, you have
Luxuriously pick'd out".[160]

The imagery of disorder which appeared so conspicuously in the earlier plays under consideration, is implicit in the reversal of values in the choice made by Antony and appears in the tension it creates in Antony's mind at certain stages in the play. It appears when he wants to "break off" from the "enchanting queen" and refers to "the courser's hair" which "hath yet but life/And not a serpent's poison".[161]

The image points to coming disorder and later on, as in *Julius Caesar*, when an ill-omen is presented presaging a final defeat for Antony, the effect is of a disorder in Nature:

"Swallows have built
In Cleopatra's sails their nests. The augurers
Say they know not, they cannot tell; look grimly,
And dare not speak their knowledge. Antony
Is valiant and dejected; and by starts
His fretted fortunes give him hope and fear....."[162]

The image "fretted" is significant and establishes a correspondence between the unnatural phenomenon and Antony's fortunes.

The other instance when several images of disorder are used to bring out the agony which Antony undergoes due to Cleopatra's 'betrayal' (which is never justified) is unique as far as their thick conglomeration is concerned:

"Ah, thou spell! Avaunt!....
Vanish, or I shall give thee thy deserving
And blemish Caesar's triumph. Let him take thee
And hoist thee up to the shouting plebeians;
Follow his chariot, like the greatest spot
Of all the sex;......'Tis well th'art gone,
If it be well to live, but better't were
Thou fell'st into my fury, for one death
Might have prevented many. Eros, Ho!
The shirt of Nessus is upon me; teach me,
Alcides, thou mine ancestor, thy rage;
Let me lodge Lichas on the horns o'th' moon,
And with those hands that grasp'd the heaviest club
Subdue my worthiest self. The witch shall die."[163]

It parallels Lear's agonized outbursts and the subsequent scene with the dissolving of 'appearances' seems to restore Antony to a consciousness of what he really was and that his life had been like "black vesper's pageants."

There is no other play of Shakespeare in which there is so much counterpointing in character and action and the imagery plays a vital role in bringing it out. It is a measure of Shakespeare's supreme poetic power that he can carry the plot through all the dizzy depths and heights and make Antony's love for Cleopatra come back with a rebound at the news of her death which the audience knows to be a lie— the greatest touch of dramatic irony in the play. The suicide it leads to, is the culminating part of it. Another irony is implicit in Antony's invocation of the spirit of Hercules which the audience knows, had just left him.

Thus we see that while the imagery of disorder establishes the most meaningful common ground amongst the problem plays, the imagery of blood, food-imagery and cosmic imagery also reveal a common ground shared by most of them with reference to each kind. Certain other kinds of images such as light and darkness, the winds and the sea and of fertility significantly occur in most of them.

To conclude this comparative view of the six problem plays under discussion, it may be worthwhile emphasizing the role of the double vision in each of the points under which we have considered the similarities. When we take into account the contrary facets like reason and passion, sense and soul or 'grimness and grace' standing for evil and good, whether in the scheme of the play or in the characters and their actions, we can also see each of these facets projected by the positive or the negative vision of the dramatist. Such an analysis leads us to one important conclusion that problems exist when the two facets are not reconciled although the existence of each of these is made plausible by the art of the dramatist and on occasions of the greatest incompatibility, it is the sheer power of poetry or the power of some positive emotion reinforced by the positive vision which makes the character human and credible as in the case of Cleopatra and Helena. This opposition in points of view, when held in a balance, also creates the effect of ambivalence which is the basic quality of a problem play leading to uncertain and divided responses on the part of the audience or the reader. Often, the imagery is a very authentic index to the tension between these opposite points of view as we have seen in the last section of this chapter and the study of these plays becomes much more illuminating by the recognition of common grounds in the imagery.

REFERENCES

1. Philip Edwards, *Shakespeare and The Confines of Art* (Methuen and Co., London, 1968) p.1.
2. R.A. Foakes, Shakespeare, *The Dark Comedies to the Last plays* (Routledge and Kegan Paul, London, 1971) p. 5.
3. E.M.W. Tillyard, *Shakespeare's Problem Plays* (Chatto and Windus, London, 1950, Penguine Books, 1965) p. 10.
4. Ibid., p. 10.
5. F.L. Lucas, *Tragedy* (Collier Books, New York, 1965) quoted from *The Birth of Tragedy* by Nietzsche, p. 62.
6. Jonathan Dollimore, *Radical Tragedy* (The Harwester Press, Brighton, 1984) p. 8.
7. Frederick S. Boas, *Shakespeare and his Predecessors* (John Murray, London, 1896) pp. 288-89.
8. Ernest Schanzer, *The Problem Plays of Shakespeare* (Routledge and Kegan Paul, London, 1963) p. 6.
9. *All's Well that Ends Well*, Act II, Sc III, 11 32-33.
10. Ibid., Act I, Sc I, *ll.* 169-70.
11. Ibid., *11*. 212-13.
12. Ibid., Act I, Sc III, *ll.* 182-97.
13. Ibid., Act II, Sc III, *l.* 102.
14. Ibid., Act III, Sc II, *ll.* 107-17.
15. Ibid., Act V, Sc III, *l.* 308.
16. Ibid., Act V, Sc III, *ll.* 32-33.
17. Philip Edwards, *Shakespeare and the Confines of Art*, p. 109.
18. Ibid., pp. 109-10.

18 (a) *Othello*, Act III, Sc III *1*. 450.

18 (b) *Hamlet*, Act I Sc V, 1 27 and Act V, Sc II, *l.* 372.

18 (c) *King Lear*, Act III, Sc VI, *ll.* 76-77.

19. John Lawlor, *The Tragic Sense in Shakespeare* (Chatto and Windus, London, 1960) p. 64.
20. Kenneth Muir, *Shakespeare's Sources* Vol I (London, 1957) p. 105.

20 (a) John Lawlor, *The Tragic Sense in Shakespeare*, p. 65.

21. Larry S. Champion, *The Evolution of Shakespearean Comedy*, (Princeton University Press, 1974) p. 128.
22. *Measure for Measure* Act I, Sc I, *ll.* 28-32.
23. Ibid., Act II, Sc II, *ll.* 162-81.

24. Ibid., Act II, Sc IV, *l.* 15-17.
25. Ibid., Act V, Sc I, *l.* 472-75.
26. Hamlet, Act I, Sc II, *l.* 75.
27. Ibid., *l.* 85.
28. Ibid., *ll.* 43-44.
29. Ibid., *l.* 57.
30. Ibid., Act III, Sc IV, *ll.* 66-67.
31. *Antony and Cleopatra*, Act III, Sc XIII, *ll.* 116-18.
32. *Hamlet*, Act III, Sc I, *ll.* 141-46.
33. Ibid., Act II, Sc II, *ll.* 246-47.
34. Ibid., *ll.* 293-307.
35. Ibid., Act III, Sc IV, *ll.* 63-77.
36. Ibid., Act III, Sc II, *ll.* 354-63.
37. Ibid., Act III, Sc I, *ll.* 46-48.
38. Ibid., *ll.* 49-53.
39. Ibid., Act V, Sc II, *l.* 349-50.
40. Ibid., *l.* 373.
41. John Lawlor, *The Tragic Sense in Shakespeare*, p. 44.
42. Mark Van Doren, *Shakespeare* (George Allen and Unwin London, 1941) p. 201.
43. Anne Barton, *Introduction to Troilus and Cressida* 'The Riverside Shakespeare' (Houghton Mifflin Company, Boston, 1974) pp. 445-46.
44. E.M.W. Tillyard, *Shakespeare's Problem Plays*, p. 79.
45. Ibid., p. 79.
46. *Troilus and Cressida*. Act II, Sc II, *l.* 52.
47. Ibid., *ll.* 81-83.
48. Ibid., *ll.* 200-03.
49. Ibid., Act III, Sc II, 11 82-85.
50. Ibid., Act V, Sc II, 11 153-54.
51. Ibid., 1 156.
52. *Antony and Cleopatra*, Act I, Sc II, *ll.* 106-7.
53. Ibid., *ll.* 121-22.
54. Ibid., *ll.* 141.
55. Ibid., Act V, Sc II, *ll.* 237-39.
56. Ibid., Act IV, Sc XIV, *ll.* 2-12.
57. Ibid., Act IV Sc XV, *ll.* 54-58.
58. Ibid., Act V, Sc II, *ll.* 236-37.

59. *Measure for Measure*, Act I, Sc III, *ll.* 53-54.
60. Ibid, Act II, Sc II, *l.* 18
61. Ibid., *ll.* 29-30.
62. Ibid., *ll.* 59-64.
63. Ibid., *ll.* 72-79.
64. Ibid., *ll.* 137-42
65. Ibid., *ll.* 143-44.
66. Ibid., *l.* 146.
67. Ibid., *ll.* 161-8.
68. Ibid., *ll.* 180-1.
69. Ibid, Act II, Sc IV, *ll.* 7-15.
70. Aeschylus, *Agamemnon*, tran. E.D.A. Morshead, 'Seven Greek Plays' (Random House, New York 1950) p. 55.
71. *Hamlet*, Act III, Sc I, *ll.* 64-67.
72. Ibid., Act II, Sc II, *ll.* 251-3.
73. C.S. Lewis, *The Problem of Hamlet.*
74. *Hamlet*, Act III Sc I, *ll.* 121-5
75. Sophocles, *Oedipus at Colonus*, trans, E.F. Walting (Penguin Classics 1947) pp. 108-9.
76. F.R. Hardie, *Aristotle's Ethical Theory* (London, 1968) p. 73 and F.W. Russel, *Encyclopaedia of Religion and Ethics*, Vol. VI, p. 513-15.
77. Eugene O'Neill, *The Great God Brown*, Act II, Sc III.
78. Ibid., *The Geeman Correth*, Act I.
79. *Hamlet*, Act III, Sc I, *ll.* 62-63.
80. Ibid., Act V, Sc II, *ll.* 211-17.
81. John Keats, *Ode to a Nightingale* Stanza V.
82. *Measure for Measure*, Act III, Sc I, *ll.* 5-40.
83. Ibid., *ll.* 42-43.
84. Ibid., *ll.* 78-82.
85. *Antony and Cleopatra*, Act IV, Sc XIV, *ll.* 90-92.
86. *Measure for Measure*, Act III, Sc I *ll.* 84-86.
87. Ibid., Act III, Sc I *ll.* 114-16.
88. Ibid., *ll.* 119-33.
89. Ibid., *ll.* 134-37.
90. Ibid., *ll.* 170-2.
91. Ibid., *ll.* 105-7.
92. *Antony and Cleopatra*, Act V, Sc II, *ll.* 351-53

93. Ibid., Act I, Sc II, *ll.* 138-40.
94. Ibid., Act I, Sc V, *ll.* 25-29.
95. Ibid., Act II, Sc II, *ll.* 232-6.
96. Ibid., Act IV, Sc XIV, *ll.* 51-52.
97. Ibid., Act IV, Sc XIV, *ll.* 99-101.
98. Ibid., Act IV, Sc XV, *ll.* 78-82.
99. Ibid., Act V, Sc II, *l.* 6.
100. Ibid., *ll.* 37-40.
101. *Measure for Measure*, Act III, Sc I, *ll.* 14-16.
102. *Antony and Cleopatra*. Act V, Sc II, *ll.* 306-7.
103. *Richard* II, Act V, Sc I, *ll.* 57-59.
104. *Antony and Cleopatra*, Act V, Sc II, *ll.* 292-93.
105. G. Wilson Knight, *The Imperial Theme* (Methuen, London, 1931) p. 342.
106. *Antony and Cleopatra*, Act V, Sc II, *ll.* 343-45.
107. *Measure for Measure*, Act IV, Sc III, *ll.* 155-56.
108. Ibid., Act III, Sc II, *ll.* 254-57.
109. Ibid., 11 226-27.
110. Mary Lascelles, *Measure for Measure* (The Alpire Press, London, 1953) p. 41.
111. William Rosen, *Shakespeare and the Craft of Tragedy*, (Cambridge, Mass. 1960) (Page nos. are from the collection of critical essays by Clifford Leech) p. 201.
112. Ibid., p. 203.
113. Ibid., p. 211.
114. *Julius Caesar*, Act I, Sc II, *ll.* 39-41.
115. Ibid., Act I, Sc III, *ll.* 10-28.
116. Ibid., Act I, Sc III, *ll.* 72-78.
117. W.H. Clemen, *The Development of Shakespeare's Imagery*, (Methuen, London, 1951) p. 99.
118. *Julius Caesar*, Act II, Sc I, *ll.* 61-69.
119. Ibid., *ll.* 27-34.
120. Ibid., *ll.* 166-171.
121. Ibid., Act II, Sc II, *ll.*, 14-24.
122. Ibid., *ll.* 76-79.
123. Ibid., Act III, Sc I, *ll.*, 200-01
124. Ibid., *ll.*, 259-62.
125. Ibid., Act III, Sc II, *ll.*, 176-80.

126. Ibid., *l.* 261-62.
127. *Troilus and Cressida*, Act v, Sc II, *ll.* 155-56.
128. *Measure for Measure* Act I, Sc III, *ll.* 26-31.
129. Ibid., Act II, Sc I, *ll.* 230-32.
130. Ibid.. *ll* 280-81.
131. Ibid., Act II, Sc II, *ll.* 165-67.
132. Ibid., Act II, Sc IV, *ll.* 16-17.
133. Ibid., 11. 22-23.
134. Ibid., Act III, Sc I, *l.* 93.
135. Ibid., Act III, Sc II, *ll.* 216-18.
136. Ibid., Act III, Sc II *ll.* 32-34.
137. T.S. Eliot, *Gerontion*, *l.* 34.
138. *All's Well*, Act V, Sc III, *l.* 255-59.
139. Ibid., *l.* 230.
140. Ibid., *l.* 310.
141. Ibid., Act I, Sc I, *ll.* 80-84.
142. Ibid., 170-71.
143. Ibid., Act I, Sc III, *ll.* 236-238.
144. Ibid., Act II, Sc V, *ll.* 72-75.
145. *Antony and Cleopatra*, Act V, Sc II, *ll.* 79-81.
146. Ibid., *ll.* 82-83.
147. Caroline F. Spurgeon, *Shakespeare's Imagery and What it tells us* (Cambridge University Press, 1961) p. 350.
148. Ibid., pp. 349-50.
149. W.H. Clemen, *The Development of Shakespeare's Imagery* (Methuen and Co., London, 1951) p. 160.
150. *Antony and Cleopatra*, Act III, Sc XIII, 1 89.
151. Ibid., *ll.* 165.
152. Ibid., Act IV, Sc XII, *ll.* 20-23.
153. Ibid., Act III, sc XIII, *ll.* 34-36.
154. Ibid., Act IV, Sc XV, *ll.* 62-63.
155. *Julius Caesar*, Act II, Sc I, *l.* 173.
156. *Hamlet*, Act I, Sc II, *ll.* 143-45.
157. Ibid., Act III Sc IV, *ll.* 66-67.
158. Ibid., Act I, Sc V, *ll.* 55-57.
159. *Antony and Cleopatra*, Act II, Sc II, *ll.* 240-42.
160. Ibid., Act III, Sc XIII, *ll.* 116-20.
161. Ibid., Act I, Sc III, *ll.* 186-88.
162. Ibid., Act IV, Sc XII, *ll.* 3-8.
163. Ibid., *ll* 30-48.

CHAPTER X

Conclusion

In our exploration of the role of the double vision in character and action in the problem plays of Shakespeare we isolated certain salient points characteristic of the six problem plays, many of which are common to them and serve as their distinguishing features in relation to other groups of plays preceding and following them. The most outstanding feature—the baffling and enigmatic quality along with the contradictions and paradoxes in the characters and in the nature of the plays themselves—which confronts any reader or spectator of these plays, must be brought out and explained in such an inquiry. This was, in fact, the object of this book and of the idea of the role of Shakespeare's double vision. In the light of our conclusions evolved during the discussion of the individual plays in the previous chapter on common characteristics, we shall make a final attempt to discuss this question.

It is in short, the problem arising out of the treatment of problems in these plays. It is not an overstatement if we say that the period 1599 to 1607 in Shakespeare's career which exceeds by two years the span which Dowden called "in the Depths", was the most creative and puzzling at the same time. He was driven by some kind of demonic energy and we are not far wrong if we say that, taking only the plays written during this period into account, no other writer in the world has written so richly, deeply and widely during the span of eight years. Six great tragedies and three plays which defy common classification—one of which shares common ground with all categories and breaks all barriers, is an unparalleled creative outcome. *The Merry Wives of Windsor*—the sole exception—is also not a pure comedy. All of them are plays of questioning, doubt and disillusionment. Even the other tragedies not in our scope—*Othello*, *King Lear* and *Macbeth*—

barely escape being caught up in the welter of problems they raise only because those problems are perfectly assimilated into the form and the tragedies sweep ahead without being retarded by them.

This leaves no doubt that the plays which share the rich creativity with the tragedies have not suffered in terms of form or clarity due to any deficiency of creative power. Then it remains a moot question whether deviation from conventional forms is due to the excess of some element in Shakespeare's creative vision, or due to the conscious notion of a specific design which he gave to the plays with full awareness of what he was doing, or due to some crisis in his personal life which got unconsciously projected in the plays written during this period, or finally, due to the intractable matter in terms of plot which he was shaping into a play in each case. There is a fifth possibility that these plays in the course of their essemplastic shaping, "due to the overgrowth of some complexion" deviated from the normal design, became lop-sided and unwieldy and the dramatist (instead of rehandling or revising) let them remain as such and wound them up as best as he could.

In order to come to a conclusion about these possibilities which would take us as near the heart of the matter as possible, let us consider two characteristic features of Shakespeare's art—those which are true of Shakespeare's dramatic mode generally but are seen to appear at this part of his career in a more complex and intriguing form. In any approach to Shakespeare's plays, they must be kept in mind, above all others—that he transmuted everything he touched and that he also transvalued all valuations. J.M. Robertson has effectively argued about Shakespeare's power of transmuting the material he borrowed—the characters and their actions underwent a sea-change during his handling and by their exposure to his artistic vision. As we have seen, Janus-like, he gave contrary aspects to many of them and often, in some characters and situations, there were two or more layers of significances. One underlay the other; reality underlay appearance, but under this 'reality' there was yet another which made the first look like an illusion. This was due to one important tendency—perhaps the most important quality of Shakespeare as an artist—of transvaluing his previous valuations. This quality is mostly implicit in the situation and Shakespeare uses it in comedy and tragedy alike. It is responsible for the effects which intrigue and mystify us. In *A Midsummer Night's Dream*, the spirits like Oberon and Titania on the one hand and the 'mechanicals' like Bottom on the other, provide us a 'valuation' of the emotions of the lovers and their fickleness. But the Titania-Bottom episode is a transvaluation which includes the spiritual world as well, in the indictment first spoken only of human lovers : "Lord, what fools these mortals be!"[1] In *As You Like It*, the life of the Duke Senior in the Forest of Arden belies the appearance of joy in court life but the remarks of Jaques who had been 'all day to avoid him'[2] and his preference to stay in the forest provide another interpretation to this joy in Arden and to the verdict of the Duke when he said "I would not change it"[3] but subsequently does so. The position of Jaques himself is transvalued by Touchstone who befooled him into thinking that he was 'deep contemplative'.

These tendencies are implicit in several plays written before *Julius Caesar* but they become more pronounced in plays written after it. Even the judgement of Brutus in assessing the danger to the liberty of Rome is transvalued by time and circumstances.

This process of revaluation or a contrary valuation is seen to develop in *Hamlet* when Hamlet's own valuation of sin and evil in Denmark is shown to lead to fallacious reasoning and to its culmination in two acts—rejection of Ophelia because she was a potential sinner like his mother and sparing of Claudius because he wanted to damn his soul—followed by the killing of Polonius which was a mistaken act in the design to damn Claudius. The transvaluation is implicit in his being wrong in these moral valuations which becomes more glaring in the irony that the king was not praying when he spared him on that ground.

In *Troilus and Cressida* this process reaches a pitch. Troilus has judged Helen to be 'a theme of honour and renown' as against Hector's idea that it was "mad idolatry" to keep her. He had similarly valued Cressida in her faith. The contrary valuation comes with the ruin to Troy (the death of

Hector in the scope of the play) and with the scene in Calchas' tent, the transvaluation of Troilus' own position comes first in the ironical silence which Ulysses maintains, only speaking the words,

"May worthy Troilus be half-attach'd
With that which here his passion doth express?"[4]

Next it comes with a shattering iconoclasm in Thersites' words,

"....that same young Troyan ass that loves the whore there might send that Greekish whoremasterly villain with the sleeve back to the dissembling luxurious drab..."[5]

The implicit transvaluation can be best put in the words of R.A. Foakes:

"This is not a sudden transformation in her Cressida; from the beginning her language has been 'wanton', and Troilus has made her wanton in act. What she becomes is a reflection upon him as much as upon her and reveals the distance between his 'honour' and 'love'....his love is on one level mere lechery; he had made Cressida his mistress.....As for her, she follows the fashion of Helen...."[6]

In *Measure for Measure* Isabella's 'virtuous' rebuke to Claudio is implicitly pitted against the idea of sacrifice for saving the life of her brother and even though Shakespeare was not aware of it, Antigone's example to sacrifice her life to ensure her brother's burial might serve as a fair contrast. The words,

"I'll pray a thousand prayers for thy death,
No word to save thee."[7]

appear to be so callous that an implicit contrary valuation of Isabella's judgement of her brother seems to be present. The fact of its presence is proved by its being recognized as a point of controversy. This transvaluation makes the whole scene one of the greatest artistic triumphs of Shakespeare presenting the moral problem with an ambivalence which makes both attitudes justifiable. If it had been a situation in a Greek tragedy, the chorus would have said: (as in *Antigone*) "There is something to be said,.....for his point of view, / And for yours as well; there is much to be said on both sides."

In *All's Well*, there are two distinct selves of Helena—the woman who relentlessly pursues the object of her love and the divine instrument who works the miracle of the King's cure. The former self is valued by the latter and this is further put to a transvaluation when she emerges as a contriver on the secular plane. Finally, her role emerges as a synthesis in which she combines the function of a redeeming agent (as she saves Bertram from the evil into which he had drifted), and her initial self—the secular pursuer of her rightful husband whom she "doubly won".

This complex juxtaposition and synthesizing of her two selves creates an effect like that of shot-silk when Helena appears to be one or the other according as we change our angle of vision.

By now it is abundantly clear that it is the double vision of the dramatist which, in all these plays, creates the effect of a different plane of existence and opens up to our view those facets of the character which otherwise had been a sealed world for us. The negative picture is reviewed in a sudden positive light and the positive one is eclipsed by a sudden darkening by the negative vision. The positive idealism and patriotism of Brutus is eclipsed by the negative light of his fallacious reasonings which cleverly exploited by Antony make him appear in a changed light—from a sacrificer to a butcher. Hamlet who thinks himself to be a moral agent reveals his incapacity to sustain this role in the light of the negative vision and turns out to be only one more instrument of evil. Only at the end, the positive vision partly brings him to a vindication of his original mission. The mystery which shrouds him is that of a figure whose exterior prevents anyone from probing beneath his skin. He wears the mask of Dionysus which completely conceals his Apollonian face. The mask tortures and consumes his real self and his self, failing to come to any activity, speculates on getting a release into death or into meaningful action both of which he cannot achieve. As has been already pointed out, Hamlet remains under the shadow of the negative vision almost till the end (with momentary flashes of the positive vision) because he cannot strip his Dionysian mask.

In *Measure for Measure*, Isabella, in both her major confrontations—with Angelo and Claudio—represents the Apollonian element in the play. She is coldly chaste and regards virtue more precious than life. Even when she argues emotionally, it is of mercy and grace. It is the positive vision which illuminates her in every word or gesture in her encounter with Angelo, whereas Angelo is presented uniformly in the light of the negative vision. Her influence paradoxically converts Angelo into a beast—the Dionysian element in him possesses him and eclipses the Apollonian, the saintly and rational. Towards the end when she forgives him there is a greater emphasis on her Apollonian balance unshaken by desire for revenge. Incidentally, a parallel which has not struck anyone who has dealt with this aspect of Isablella, may be mentioned. In the *Oresteia*, it is Apollo who argues for the acquittal of Orestes and for his forgiveness by the Furies. Thus overcoming the instinct of revenge and extending forgiveness are Apollonian traits.

In *All's Well*, it is a more complex juxtaposition of opposites—a hard schemer with a divine agent—that is presented in Helena and appears irreconcilable. But the sheer power of love activates the positive vision of the dramatist and it projects upon the character which appeared to be created in the light of the negative vision and transforms it. It goes beyond it and transforms Bertram through her. Without taking this role of the double vision into account, it would be impossible to view Helena and all that happens in the play in a natural light and the two aspects of her nature symbolizing the two aspects of the play, would fall asunder. It is this failure to see how Shakespeare's vision integrates the two aspects which accounts for turning this point into the problematic aspect of the play and tracing it to an imaginative failure on the part of the dramatist. It is therefore surprising that critics like Tillyard complain of a weakness in Shakespeare's art where his strongest point lies—his power of synthesizing opposites by his double vision. Instead of superimposing the one contrary aspect on the other, it fuses the two into an organic unity—the miracle which was again performed on a grander scale in the case of Cleopatra.

We have kept *Antony and Cleopatra* for a separate consideration because both the process of transvaluation and the fusion of opposites by the double vision reach a point of the greatest subtlety in this play. Philip Edwards calls it "a positive demonstration of 'contrary valuations'." [8] All readers and critics of the play find it difficult to arrive at a final interpretation of the play due to this. Derek Traversi remarks of this:

"Sooner or later, he finds himself faced by two possible readings of the play, whose only difficulty is that they seem to be mutually exclusive.. but to give each its due, to see them less as contradictory than as complementary aspects of a unified artistic creation which neither taken in isolation, can exhaust, is as difficult as it proves, in the long run, necessary for a proper understanding of the play." [9]

These two aspects—the romantic and the secular, of ecstasies of love and its frailties, or in the Nietzschean phrase, the Dionysian and the Apollonian—are both integral to the play and they determine the play's rising and falling curves. In the more usual symbolism they are termed Egypt and Rome, the spiritual and the secular. It would be more accurate to term the former as physical-spiritual because by his power of transmuting his subject-matter, Shakespeare has created the impression that the passionate love of 'the strumpet's fool' and 'the serpent of the Nile' (which looks like one of myth) was also spiritual. At the same time, the Egypt-Rome polarity also serves one important purpose from the technical point of view. While the positive vision of the dramatist is mostly associated with Egypt and the negative vision with Rome, we find that the one transvalues the other.

So we have four approahces to the understanding of Shakespeare's treatment of his theme and subject-matter in *Antony and Cleopatra*. Shakespeare has so transmuted the two characters and their passions as to imbue theme with a spiritual quality. They are expressions of the Dionysian element in human nature as opposed to the Apollonian in Caesar. The positive and the negative vision are mutually complementary in determining the total picture in the play. And finally, there is a constant transvaluation of these characters and their experience.

How has Shakespeare transmuted the characters of Antony and Cleopatra and their passions in the play? They were characters of history and even Plutarch presented them as no better than what Shaw calls, "the soldier broken down by debauchery, and the typical wanton in whose arms such men perish." [10] The clue lies in his poetry and the positive vision which highlights the moments of exaltation in the play which probably never existed in history. Since it was Shakespeare's own concept, he has projected it in his vision and he had a command of poetic power adequate to the task.

The one clue to the effectiveness with which this power has been expressed is the evocation of sublimity which, in a flash, glances "from heaven to earth, from earth to heaven" and lifts our own minds to those heights. It is the power of the highest art to exalt us and overwhelm as Longinus said, with the effect of a thunderbolt. There is what Arnold would call "the magic of poetry". Thus when Antony speaks of a "new heaven, new earth" or when Cleopatra says, "Eternity was in our lips and eyes", or when Enobarbus says that "Age cannot wither her," or when she says before dying, "I am fire and air", followed by Charmian's remark "O Eastern star!" to give stray instances—we are swept not merely by the language but by what Blackmur calls the gesture of which the language is a medium and which communicates the incommunicable by virtue of its power which has created the gesture.

"When the language of words most succeeds it *becomes* gesture in its words." [11]

So says Blackmur, and adds, "which is a gesture that must overwhelm us." [12]

Our imagination is compelled by these sublime gestures and in spite of our knowledge to the contrary, we are converted to the belief that there is something divine about this love and even the characters transcend time and space.

If on second thoughts, this disparity between the secular reality (which Shakespeare has focused by the negative vision) and the concept to which the dramatist has converted us by his positive vision, seems to involve us in contradictory feelings, the positive image still remains impressed upon our minds and we either take the contradictions as a part of the scheme of the play and stop at that or try to resolve them.

We have already dealt with the Dionysian and Apollonian antithesis in the play. Here we may emphasize that it is Shakespeare's greater elaboration of the Dionysian element in Antony—almost an enlargement to the nature of the primitive, passionate, self-annihilating wine-god—over the Apollonian element in Caesar—which is presented with that zest which accounts for the aggrandizement. The element is also incorporated in the character of Cleopatra as 'the femme fatale', who possesses what Northrop Frye calls "a colossal exuberance of powers".[13] The same critic calls Cleopatra's world "a Dionysian world". She illustrates Nietzsche's statement "the sense of tragedy increases and decreases with sensuality".[14] in her subsequent capacity for tragic experience. There is no doubt that the belittling of the secular element points forward to the last plays.

As regards our third approach we have referred to the role of the two visions at every point of evolution. In general, in relation to all the plays under consideration, the positive and the negative visions correspond to a revelation of the possibilities of good and evil in human nature. But sometimes the good and evil may be inherent in the same character, situation or action. It is here that the two visions bring out the one or the other. This is done in turn by the positive or the negative vision as the dramatist intends to display the facet of good or evil. The effect may also be ambivalent revealing good or evil according as we change the angle of vision. The two visions are interconnected and the one may be interpenetrated with the other. Sometimes, for moments during the course of the play, the characters rise above the limit of their temporal existence and there is a resolution through integration. This can be best seen in flashes towards the end of *Hamlet* and during the earlier and later part, particularly at the end, of *Antony and Cleopatra* which is the most fascinating play of the double vision ever written.

The two visions, as it finally appears in moments which we have called those of resolution through integration, are complementary. This notion, which has been called that of 'complementarity', has been set forth by G.R. Hibbard with a reference to an idea of Robert Oppenheimer:

"This sort of vision finds a parallel in the ideas of some modern physicists, such as Nils Bohr and J. Robert Oppenheimer.. Oppenheimer, sets out the notion of 'complementarity', an application to difficult problems in physics of the double vision we all have of the world we live in..Shakespeare had this sense of complementarity and his art was built on it.. the art and the vision modified each other by reciprocal action." [15]

This view, as we have sought to apply it in our analysis of separate operations of each of the two visions and, at certain points in the plays, with an effect of complementarity, would help to solve the problems of contradictions and paradoxes which we so often enounter in the problem plays and which the critics have attributed to the failure of the dramatist's imagination or his lack of sustained interest in the theme or characters.

This brings us to the five kinds of difficulties in the interpretation of the problem plays which we enumerated in the beginning of this chapter, and we find that the fourth and fifth of them postulating 'intractable matter' and 'lop-sided and unweildy growth' respectively become untenable. The theory of a failure of the dramatist's imagination or his lack of interest which was put forth to account for the incongruities, can also be dismissed.

The conjecture that the disillusioned and sometimes pessimistic attitude in the plays written between 1600 and 1608 (till *Timon of Athens*) is due to some crisis in Shakespeare's private life, has found acceptance among the critics from time to time. Since the three problem plays—two of them comedies and the third with some semblance of a comedy in the earlier part—were written during this period, the problems posed in these plays were supposed to be due to the infiltration of an autobiographical element. In this connection Tillyard says:

"Many readers have found in the problem plays a spirit of gloom, disillusion, and morbidity that exceeds dramatic propriety and demands some extrinsic explanation in Shakespeare's private life at the time. Others on the contrary think that such readers have unconsciously begun from Shakespeare's supposed biography and have insisted on reading that biography into this group of plays. Between these two extremes there may be many intermediate positions... such personal explanations (are) superfluous, or at least too uncertain to be worth anything. I agree here with Sisson on the mythical sorrows of Shakespeare and with R.W. Chambers in his prefatory remarks on *Measure for Measure* concerning the early years of James I and the small need Shakespeare had to be unhappy just then, or with this sentence of W.W. Lawrence:

"Critics have been too much inclined to emphasize one or more possible explanations of the problem comedies—personal misfortune or bereavement, disappointment in friendhsip or in love, the degeneration of the age,... haste and carelessness." [16]

This comment by itself makes a cogent case against treating any emphasis on disillusionment and disgust as arising from biographical reasons. Even so, the comment to this effect by Dover Wilson found general acceptance for a long time. Speaking about *Measure for Measure* he said:

"At the time when he wrote *Measure* for *Measure*, Shakespeare "quite obviously believed in nothing; he was cynical as Iago, as disillusioned as Macbeth, though he still retained, unlike the first, his sensitiveness, and unlike the second, his hatred of curelty, hypocrisy, and ingratitude."[17]

The reason was that Shakespeare possessed that unique quality—negative capability—to such an extent that his vision of evil and of the Waste Land is as vivid as that of Paradise. To this he added Purgatory in which we see his tragic heroes moving and gave a three-fold vision of the movement of the human soul in the manner of Dante's *Divine Comedy*. The problem plays present the picture of Inferno at a greater length and with such vividness of detail that one gets the mistaken view and overlooks the fact that redemption and grace are also implicit in several of these plays.

The clue to an understanding of the problem plays should now lie in one of our two remaining hypotheses—excess of some element in Shakespeare's creative vision or a conscious design to give expression to the particular kind of vision which was occupying him at this time.

In the light of what we have seen during the discussion of all the problem plays included in the scheme of this book, we find that we can arrive at the truth if we combine both these postulates and state that the plays written during this period (except *Antony and Cleopatra*) display an intellectual verve in combination with Shakespeare's creative imagination. His intellectual power, at times, reached a pitch which taxed his creative imagination and like a rider on a horse who never lost control, it went further than warranted by the design of the play. But it became a conscious design too, because his creative imagination retained control and ultimately rounded off the play giving it an essemplastic form.

The case can be more plausibly put by taking Euripides, the Greek dramatist, as a parallel, and adopting the last criterion of transvaluaton (which we reserved for discussion at this stage) as a common quality.

In relation to the three Greek tragic dramatists, whereas Shakespeare is nearest to Aeschylus in the matter of tragic form and resembles Sophocles in treatment of character, he has the greatest kinship with Euripides in his use of double vision and transvaluation of experience. It also leads to a portrayal of contradictions and anomalies in human nature. Like Euripides, particularly in the problem plays, he evinces an overplus of intellect and critical faculty with the concomitants of scepticism, analysis and revaluation of experience. We have already referred to Anne Barton's comparison of *Troilus and Cressida* with *Orestes* and the possible influence of Euripides in translation. Part of it is worth repeating here:

"More speculative, but tantalizing is the possible influence of Euripides. In play after play Euripides took up the matter of Troy. Elizabethans knew many of these plays in translations.. If Shakespeare ever encountered the *Orestes*, he would have found there an attitude towards the myth strikingly like his own. For Euripides too the Trojan war was an expense of spirit in a waste of shame.. Everywhere, Euripides measures the epic grandeur of the story against the unlovely reality of these events and people when seen up close. Like Shakespeare's, his play is brilliant and savage.. It is mixed in form, a combination of tragedy, comedy, and satire..."[18]

The last sentence is almost a definition of the problem play common to both Euripides and Shakespeare. Excepting the Roman plays in our group, all the rest are covered by it.

This critical and intellectual element is manifested in both dramatists in another way—a transvaluation of the earlier valuation in the play and also in the treatment of convention, myth, or history.

As already pointed out in the opening chapter of this book, although the problem play as a dramatic form originates with Sophocles' *Antigone*, it is in the plays of Euripides, that the sceptical, questioning spirit is first found and in plays like *Ion*, *Helen* and *the Bacchae* the entire fabric of anthropomorphic belief is challenged. Baffling moral problems are posed and the quality of the iconoclast—the typical quality of the problem-playwright is first encountered. Disillusionment and disgust such as we find in *Hamlet* and *Troilus and Cressida* are found in *Ion* and partly in *Helen* and *the Bacchae*. Realism also becomes the keynote.

Ion is a straight attack on religious belief and the conclusion is that, if the gods do evil, they are not gods. It is a drama of disillusionment. Ion is the son of Creusa by Apollo who had conveyed him to Delphi. Later Apollo wanted to foist Ion as a son on Xuthus, Creusa's husband, so that he could be his successor to the throne. Creusa tells Ion how she was ravished by Apollo and without knowing that he was her son, he says:

"I must remonstrate with Apollo.. He ravishes girls by force, then abandons them ? He begets children by stealth, then leaves them to die? Apollo, no! Since you possess power, pursue goodness! Why, if a man is bad, it is the gods who punish him. How can it be right for you to make laws for men, and appear as lawbreakers yourselves?.. You put pleasure first and wisdom after—and it is sin!"[19]

It poses a pertinent question for the holders of power and authority, apart from demolishing the belief that gods do not err. The plan of Apollo is almost miscarried due to

Creusa's jealously that Xuthus should have a son who is not hers and it is only with the failure of the plot which the old slave is to carry out and the disclosure by the Delphian priestess that Creusa discovers that Ion is her son. Even so, Xuthus must not know this fact, and so Athene has to appear as deus ex machina and command Creusa:

"Now, tell no one that Ion is your true son; so that Xuthus may enjoy his delusion, and you may enjoy the happiness, that you know to be yours." [20]

This theme of make-believe and disillusion is so typical of the twentieth century that T.S.Eliot borrowed it to write *The Confidential Clerk* in the same vein.

Troilus' make-believe and his final disillusionment resembles this and Hamlet's disgust and questioning are very much like Ion's, only that they apply to a more secular plane of being.

Similarly, *Helen* ends in the feeling that Aphrodite, the goddess of love, "traffics in lust and falsehood, crooked intrigue and secret drugs" as her "instruments of death". [21]

The following conversation demolishes the romantic halo around the battle of Troy:

Theoclymenus: Then Priam and his people perished for nothing.

Helen: And I was involved in their disaster—for nothing." [22]

It is very much the same feeling we get after reading *Troilus and Cressida*.

As already seen from the above examples, the way Euripides criticized established myths and beliefs was by a transvaluation which put the person or object in a hard, realistic light. The veil of illusory appearance is stripped away. We see the person of Apollo (who was anthropomorphic) or that of Helen in a new light. In Shakespeare, we see Cressida and Troilus almost from a Shavian angle although the subsequent view of Raina and Sergius may not exactly resemble theirs. But Shaw flouts as Euripides does, one view which existed unchallenged. In Shakespeare, transvaluation is of this kind but sometimes it is a more complex process of debunking. One image after another of the same person is "broken" as can be seen in *Antony and Cleopatra*,

Hamlet and to some extent, in *Measure for Measure* and *All's Well.* It will be worthwhile to illustrate it to get an insight into this intricate process.

The secret lies in Shakespeare's use of his double vision. In *Antony and Cleopatra,* Cleopatra is, at the very opening of the play, presented in a negative light. The word 'strumpet' is used for her. The subsequent reference to 'new heaven, new earth' elevates Antony's concept of love, but does not appreciably alter Cleopatra's estimate. The reference by Cleopatra to "eternity", "bliss" and "a race of heaven" again adds to their image, but the original view of Cleopatra remains valid due to the intervening remarks of Enobarbus about her sighs and tears being as powerful as storms and tempests and her feigning of death (a strain which reappears in her false report of death from the monument). Her behaviour during the interval Antony is away, with the imagery of serpents and fishing and her violent outbursts with the messenger further establish the original image. But in the middle of Act II, when Cleopatra's estimate is at a low ebb and Antony's marriage with Octavia makes a break almost certain, a different image supersedes and an altogether new facet is revealed in the description of Cleopatra on the Cydnus and the 'Age cannot wither her..' speech of Enobarbus. Poetry was never more effectively used to alter an image and to transvalue a character. We never doubt that it is Cleopatra's real image and it dominates the imagination standing out like a snow-capped peak. We feel the positive vision operating like a flash of lightning.

Then with battle of Actium and Cleopatra's implied betrayal of Antony's cause, the negative vision swiftly prepares for another transvaluation and after the betrayal in the final battle, her positive image is wiped away and she becomes what she was at first: the "foul Egyptian", the "grave charm", "monster-like" and "the witch" whom Antony swears to destroy. It is the crumbled image of her former self which is seen dissolving like black vesper's pageants in the subsequent scene. But this is followed by another feat of transvaluation to which the entire fifth Act is devoted—

Shakespeare's imagination was so seriously engaged that he not only restored the positive image but validated, with all the poetic magic he was capable of, the finally transvalued form. The positive vision has again come to the fore and suffuses the whole Act not excepting the scene with Seleucus.

The same process of transvaluation can be seen in the case of Antony. His portrayal follows a uniformly downward curve after the first speeches till his death (with the exception of Caesar's speech recalling his past but without an appreciable change in his image) but there is a steep rise in stature with Cleopatra's evocation of his dream-image in cosmic imagery which remains permanently impressed on our minds. This transvaluation makes us forget the negative image which had remained before us till his death.

In *Hamlet* we find a negative image (with the sole exception of a faint flash in Ophelia's speech of what Hamlet was before the beginning of the play), almost throughout the play, till in the very last scene, the positive vision brings about a transvaluation. It is an altogether new facet of Hamlet which is revealed—a calm, positive, reconciled Hamlet who has given up the attitude of negation and rejection which was the basis of his identity from the first view we had of him in the play. It was such a being who sat brooding, dressed in black, in the court of Claudius, who faced the ghost, entered Ophelia's closet, and subsequently tore his passion to tatters in the nunnery scene, and the closet scene; who in short, rejected life and rejected death too. That such a man affirms and accepts is no less than a miracle; only a conversion could do it. It is also a transvaluation taking account of the new man in him. The old valuation is forgotten and it is the new man who completes his belated task.

In *Measure for Measure*, Isabella is transvalued more astutely than any other character elsewhere. In the confrontation with Angelo, she wins by arguments which establish her as a spiritual superior but in the subsequent meeting with Claudio we get a different picture. She counters Claudio's entreaty by a fierce outburst not only vindicating virtue but condemning his vice which is not lust but love of life. Love of chastity is pitted against love of life and the rarest kind of ambiguity in response of the reader or the spectator emerges. By all standards, Isabella is morally right but is she so in a human sense? There is the suggestion of a transvaluation not of her character but of her values. That there is a moral ambivalence here is undeniable, however right Isabella was.

In *All's Well*, Helena's initial self with purely secular intentions, becomes a divine instrument with 'great power, great transcendence'; then she is transvalued and pursues Bertram as a pilgrim with her original end in attaining which she doesn't scruple even if it comes to a bed-trick.

We find this process in *Troilus and Cressida* when Cressida is so valued by Troilus that he is 'giddy' with love and 'like a strange soul' waits upon 'the Stygian banks for waftage' to her. In all his earlier evocations of love for Cressida there is hardly any concrete image. When he is disillusioned by her transformation in Calchas' tent, the bitterness of his disillusionment is expressed in the most concrete imagery including that of food. Implicitly, it is not so much Cressida's person or character which is transvalued as Troilus' love which lacked concreteness and is now contrasted with Cressida's perfidity in more tangible imagery.

Thus it is a transvaluation of values in *Troilus and Cressida* and *Measure for Measure* which is a basic feature of these two most characteristic of the problem plays.

We referred to *Antigone* as the archetypal problem play in the beginning of our work and it is fitting to end it by assessing how far Shakespeare contributed to the form. We have noted the advance which Euripides, the younger contemporary of Sophocles, made in adding the sceptical, questioning temper to this dramatic mode. Shakepeare either invented his own form, or presumably got it from the translation or adaptation of any of Euripides' plays; he did not borrow it directly as he did not pattern *Othello* after *Oedipus Tyrannus* or *King Lear* after *Oedipus at Colonus*,plays so closely like those of Sophocles. Similarly, *Measure for Measure*, so neatly balancing the cause of justice and mercy was not directly written under the influence of *Antigone* which as neatly balances the cause of love and duty. Even so, the conflict of wills and the moral dilemma are as acute and would have continued unresolved were it not for the religious strain to back up Isabella's argument and Angelo's moral fall to weaken his. Creating this inequality in the weight of the arguments, Shakespeare made his plays lose something of the balance which makes for a moral dilemma and made his implied preference clear as he did in *Troilus and Cressida* and *Antony and Cleopatra*. He was interested in the more intriguing quality of the problem play—the ambivalence or ambiguity inherent in the same character and situation which would make it appear different from different angles or create a different response at successive moments. Thus varying responses which Schanzer calls "uncertain and divided' would be created in the minds of the spectators or the readers. Each of the plays discussed in this book breaks new ground in presenting moral dilemmas embodied in characters and situations rather than in the theme as in *Antigone*. Shakespeare's double vision projects these characters and situations providing a three—dimensional view of the negative and the positive side and sometimes at the far side,—emerging as the result of their interaction, the final image of truth.

This two-fold view puts the problem plays of Shakespeare in a special category: a play of trial and reckoning of values, quick with intensity and energy released by thought and speculation which, for the time-being, appear to be adopted as an end in themselves.

REFERENCES

1. *A Midsummer Night's Dream.* Act III *l.* 115.
2. *As You Like It.* Act II, Sc V, *ll.* 28-29.
3. Ibid., Act II, Sc I, *l.* 17.
4. *Troilus and Cressida,* Act V, Sc II, *ll.* 159-60.
5. Ibid., Act V, Sc IV *ll.* 6-10.

6. R.A. Foakes, *Shakespeare, The Dark Comedies to the Last Plays* (Routledge and Kegan Paul, London, 1971) p. 54.
7. *Measure for Measure*, Act III, Sc I, *ll.* 147-48.
8. Philip Edwards, *Shakespeare and The Confines of Art* (Methuen and Co, London, 1968) p. 121.
9. Derek Traversi, *Shakespeare and The Roman Plays* (Hollis and Carter, London, 1963) p. 79.
10. Philip Edwards, *Shakespeare and the Confines of Art*, p. 121.
11. R.P.Blackmur, *Language as Gesture*, from 'A little Treasury of American Prose' (Scribner, New York, 1940) p. 616.
12. Ibid., p. 638.
13. Northrop Frye, *Fools of Time* (University of Toronto Press, 1967) p.70.
14. Ibid., p.70.
15. G.R. Hibbard, *The Year's Contribution to Shakespeare Study* (Shakespeare Survey Vol. 22 Edited by Kenneth Muir, 1969, Cambridge University Press) p. 147.
16. E.M.W. Tillyard, *Shakespeare's Problem Plays*, (Chattoand Windus, London, 1950) pp. 10-11.
17. John Dover Wilson, *The Essential Shakespeare* (Cambridge University Press, 1935) p. 11.
18. Anne Barton, Introduction to *Troilus and Cressida* in 'The Riverside Shakespeare' (Houghton Mifflin Company, Boston, 1974) p. 445.
19. Euripides, *Ion* trans. Philip Vellacott, (Penguin Classics, 1954) p. 55.
20. Ibid., p. 87.
21. Euripides, *Helen*, trans, Philip Vellacott (Penguin Classics 1954) p. 170.
22. Ibid., p. 174.

[illegible]

8. [illegible] Atlantic [illegible] the University of [illegible]
[illegible]

[illegible] p. 20.

[illegible]

[illegible] Cambridge [illegible]

[illegible] the University [illegible]

[illegible]

Bibliography

(A) TEXTS

The Arden Edition of the Works of Shakespeare (Routledge, 1988) (All plays under reference).

The Complete Works of William Shakespeare Ed. by Peter Alexander (Collins, London, 1979).

The Riverside Shakespeare (Houghton Mifflin Company, Boston, 1974).

The Signet Classic Shakespeare (The New American Library, 1963) Editions of *Measure for Measure* and *Troilus and Cressida*.

Nine Plays of Eugene O'Neill (Modern Library, Random House, New York, 1950).

(B) GENERAL

Abrams, M.H. *The Mirror and the Lamp*, (Oxford University Press, London, 1971).

Aeschylus, *The Oresteia* tran. by Philip Vellacot (Penguin Classics, 1947).

Aristotle, *Poetics*, trans. Ingram Bywater (Oxford University Press, London, 1920).

Aylen, Leo, *Greek Tragedy and Modern World* (Methuen and Co., London, 1964).

Berry George (Ed.), *A Little Treasury of American Prose* (Scribner, New York, 1944).

Boas Frederick S., *Shakespeare and His Predecessors* (John Murray Ltd., London, 1896).

Bradbrook, M.C., *The Growth and Structure of Elizabethan Comedy* (Cambridge, 1955).

Bradley, A.C., *Oxford Lectures on Poetry* (Macmillan, London, 1955 ed.).

Bradley, A.C., *Shakespearean Tragedy* (Macmillan and Co, London, 1904).

Calarco, Joseph N., *Tragic Being, Appollo and Dionysus in Western Drama* (The University of Minnesota Press, 1968).

Champion, Larry, *Evolution of Shakespeare—an Comedy* (Princeton University Press, 1978).

Charlton, H.B., *Shakespearean Tragedy* (Macmillan, London, 1950).

Charlton, H.B., *Shakespearean Comedy* (Methuen and Co., London, 1938).

Clark, B.H., *European Theories of Drama* (D. Appleton and Co., London, 1938).

Clemen, W.H., *The Development of Shakespeare's Imagery* (Methuen and Co., London, 1951).

Dollimore, Jonathan, *Radical Tragedy* (The Havester Press, Sussex, U.K., 1984).

Dowden, Edward, *Shakespeare: His Mind and Art* (Macmillan and Co., London, 1875).

Edwards, Philip, *Shakespeare and the Confines of Art* (Methuen and Co., London, 1968).

The Selected Poems of T.S. Eliot (Faber and Faber, London, 1935).

Euripides, *The Bacchae and Other Plays* trans. Philip Vellacott (Penguin Classics, 1954).

Foakes, R.A., *Shakespeare, The Dark Comedies to The Last Plays* (Routledge and Kegan Paul, London, 1971).

Frye, Northrop, *Fools of Time*, Studies in Shakespearean Tragedy (University of Toronto Press, 1967).

Frye, R.M., *Shakespeare and Christian Doctrine* (Princeton University Press, 1963).

Gassner, John, *Masters of the Drama* (Dover Publications, New York, 1940).

Geckle, George L., *Measure for Measure* (Ed.) (Twentieth Century Interpretations, Prentice-Hall, 1970).

Harbage, Alfred (ed.), *Shakespeare: The Tragedies*, (Twentieth Century Views, Prentice-Hall, New York, 1964).

Kerr, Walter, *Tragedy and Comedy* (The Bodley Head, London, 1967).

Kitto, H.D.F., *Form and Meaning in Drama* (University Paperbacks, Methuen and Co., London, 1960).

Knight, G. Wilson, *The Wheel of Fire* (Methuen and Co., London, 1930).

Knights, L.C., *Some Shakespearean Themes* (Chatto and Windus, London, 1960).

Kott, Jan, *Shakespeare Our Contemporary* (Methuen and Co., London, 1965).

Lawrence W.W., *Shakespeare's Problem Comedies* (Frederick Ungar Publishing Co., New York, 1931).

Leech, Clifford (Ed.), *Shakespeare, The Tragedies* (The University of Chicago Press, 1965).

Lerner, Laurence (Ed.), *Shakespeare's Tragedies* (Penguin Books, 1963).

Lawlor, John, *The Tragic Sense in Shakespeare* (Chatto and Windus, London, 1960).

Lucas, F.L., *Tragedy* (Collier Books, New York, 1965).

Mc-Collom, William G., *Tragedy* (The Macmillan Company, New York, 1957).

Muir, Kenneth (Ed.), *Shakespeare Survey, Vol. 22* (Cambridge, University Press, 1969).

Nevo, Ruth, *Tragic Form in Shakespeare* (Princeton University Press, 1972).

Nicoll, Allardyce, *World Drama*, George G. Harrap and Co., London, 1949.

Nicoll, Allardyce, *British Drama* (George G. Harrap and Co., London, 1949).

Ralli, Augustus, *A History of Shakespearean Criticism* (2 vols., 1932).

Ridler, Anne, *Shakespeare Criticism* (1919-35) (Oxford University Press, 1936).

Ripley, John, *Julius Caesar on Stage in England and America 1599-1973* (Cambridge University Press, 1980).

Rose, Mark, *Shakespearean Design* (Harvard University Press, 1972).

Scott, Wilber (ed.), *Five Approaches of Literary Criticism* (Collier Books, Macmillan, New York, 1962).

Schanzer, Earnest, *The Problem Plays of Shakespeare* (Routledge and Kegan Paul, London, 1963).

Sophocles, *The Theban Plays* tran. E.F. Watling (Penguin Classics, 1950).

Spurgeon, Caroline, *Shakespeare's Imagery and What It Tells us.* (Cambridge University Press, 1935).

Steiner, George, *The Death of Tragedy* (Faber and Faber, London, 1963).

Tillyard E.M.W., *Shakespeare's Problem Plays* (Chatto and Windus, London, 1950).

Tillyard, E.M.W., *Shakespeare's History Plays* (Penguin Books, 1962).

Index